ROLLS OF ROLLS-ROYCE

Lord Montagu of Beaulieu

ROLLS *of*
ROLLS-ROYCE

A Biography
of the Hon. C. S. Rolls

Research by Michael Sedgwick

South Brunswick
New York: A. S. Barnes and Co.

Library of Congress Catalogue Card Number: **67-12837**

A. S. Barnes and Co., Inc.
Cranbury, New Jersey

6589
Printed in the United States of America

Contents

List of Illustrations

Facing page 74

The Llangattock Stud: A photograph of the garage at the
Hendre taken about 1905

Advanced Service Methods, or how C. S. Rolls and Co.
coped with hauling in the wrecks in 1903

The 26·4-litre Dufaux racer at the Brighton Speed Trials,
1905

Wearing the Green. Rolls at the wheel of his 1905
Gordon Bennett Wolseley

GORDON BENNETT ELIMINATING TRIALS, 1905

Charles Rolls prepares to leave Castletown Control in the
96-h.p. Wolseley

The Wolseley at full speed

Rolls on his way to winning the 1906 T.T. with the
20-h.p. Rolls-Royce

Rolls, Platford and Northey try out their 1906 Rolls-Royces
in the Isle of Man

Rolls with the Rolls-Royce with which he won the 1906 T.T.

Rolls with the 'Light Twenty' at the Empire City Track,
New York, 1906

WELBECK PARK SPEED TRIALS, 1900

The Racing Cars prepared to start

Dispatching the cars on Flying Start

Stripping the cars for speed

AUTOMOBILE CLUB 1000 MILES' TRIAL, 1900

Facing the gale out of Edinburgh

On the road out of Edinburgh

Arrival Home. At Whitehall, 6.45 p.m., May 12th

Charles Rolls puts the demonstration 'Silver Ghost' through
its paces at Cannes, 1909

Following page 154

The Aero Club's first official ascent at Stamford Bridge
in 1901

Ascent of the *Mercury* at Monmouth, 26 December 1908

Acknowledgements

An elusive personality such as Charles Stewart Rolls is far less comprehensively documented than an obscure make of car, and I have therefore been more than ever dependent on personal sources, and on the unending patience of people who have been subjected for nearly a twelvemonth to lengthy *questionnaires*. Without them this book could never have been written.

Tracking down such sources is one thing, their collation and interpretation quite another. Once again the industry, perception and erudition of my Curator, Michael Sedgwick, has made what initially appeared a formidable task seem easy. I am confident that his work will be recognized by historians the world over as a remarkable achievement: it helped me attain my ambition to write the first definitive biography of a man whose name will for ever be associated with the pioneering days of mechanized transport on land and in the air alike.

I must also acknowledge my debt of gratitude to Colonel John Harding-Rolls, whose co-operation has opened many doors to me. In Monmouth, Mr Percy Harris, Councillor Keith Kissack, Mr Philip Mathew, Mrs N. S. Price and Mr George Ward went to a great deal of trouble to fill in invaluable details of the Llangattock family's background and Charles Rolls's early years; while Mr W. H. Baker, County Archivist of Monmouthshire, allowed us full access to the Rolls Archives now in his care. Mr W. P. Bourne, Headmaster of the Glamorganshire County Council's school now in occupation of the Hendre, is to be thanked for allowing Michael Sedgwick to visit the house and acquire some invaluable 'atmosphere'.

On the car side, our gratitude is due to Mr Michael H. Evans of Rolls-Royce Ltd., who not only helped to put the story of Charles Stewart Rolls and Frederick Henry Royce in its true perspective, but kindly consented to read the chapters dealing with his own company and C. S. Rolls and Co. Equally invaluable were the contributions of Miss Florence Caswell, C. S. R.'s former private secretary, and Mr T. O. Smith, his former mechanic, who both gave us unstintingly of their great knowledge and understanding of my subject. Their patience was unlimited, while they remained sympathetic even in the face of those endless and tiresome 'elephant's child' questions that one has to ask in the quest for the truth. Mr Harry Fleck was most helpful in matters relating to the early days of C. S. Rolls and Co. Captain Rex Tulloh-Hatchett very kindly lent us the script of a broadcast he made on C. S. Rolls some years ago: Mrs Norman Dakers, C. S. R.'s god-daughter, gave us the benefit of her childhood memories of him: while that great historian and motoring artist Peter Helck spent hours in tracking down and transcribing elusive material on 'Rolls's activities during his American tour of 1906–7. Mr Marvin W. McFarland of the Library of Congress, the recognized authority on the Wright brothers, went to much trouble tracing Charles Rolls's relations with those pioneers of aviation.

Few of Rolls's contemporaries are still alive, and we are therefore profoundly grateful to the survivors for all the help they have given, and for the generous spirit in which it was offered. The late Lord Brabazon of Tara recorded his memories on tape shortly before his death, while his widow, Hilda, Lady Brabazon, and his sister Lady Lambart, contributed some fascinating first-hand information, chiefly on ballooning and the earliest days of flying. Sir Thomas Sopwith, C.B.E., who motored and ballooned extensively with Rolls, allowed us to draw liberally on his memories, as did Mr Oswald Short, who was closely associated with my subject as the sole survivor of the famous triumvirate who made and serviced his aeroplanes and balloons. Those *doyens* of motoring journalism, Messrs. W. F. Bradley and St. John C. Nixon, answered floods of questions with their characteristic energy and patience, as did Mr Henry Knox, whose understanding and knowledge of pre-1914 motoring is unparalleled, and whose memory is prodigious. Time and time again we owe it to him that we have been able to place some aspect of the story in its true perspective. Mr E. Keith-Davies, who was associated with Charles Rolls in the last months of his life, accorded Michael Sedgwick a long and illuminating interview for which I would also like to express my gratitude.

x

Contemporary authorities have also furnished invaluable help. On the cycling side, Mr Derek Roberts of the Southern Veteran Cycle Club conducted a one-man intelligence campaign lasting several months. Mr John Blake, Librarian of the Royal Aero Club, once again proved a more than competent guide through the intricacies of the aeronautical part of the story (still largely *terra incognita* to a mere motoring historian), and also read the relevant chapters for me; while Mr Charles Gibbs-Smith kindly gave us access to and permission to use, his unpublished account of Rolls's final accident at Bournemouth. Mr Anthony Bird, already the author of an admirable book on Rolls-Royce cars, and one of the most erudite of automobile historians, not only allowed us to pick his brains, but also (at a time when he was very busy) read the entire manuscript and made numerous helpful suggestions. Mr H. E. Radford, Borough Librarian of Bournemouth, opened that town's archives to us, and these gave us a comprehensive picture in perspective of the Centenary Celebrations at which Rolls met his death.

As ever, contemporary sources afforded us a background from which to work, and our especial thanks under this head are due to Mr Harold Drayton, the owner of the Shelley-Rolls collection of press-cutting books. These vital historical documents were entrusted to our care for several months; since they represent a complete record of the reports of Charles Rolls's doings, both private and professional, from 1899 to 1910, the reader may imagine just how much toil was saved by Mr Drayton's generosity. The motoring and aeronautical press was also consulted at length, and the following furnished much invaluable material on Rolls and his times: the *Aero*, *The Autocar*, *The Automotor Journal*, the *Car Illustrated*, *Cycling*, *Flight*, *Motor Car Journal*, *Motoring Illustrated*, *Motor Sport*, *Motor Transport*, the *Motor*, and the *Veteran and Vintage Magazine*. Existing books on Rolls and allied subjects have also been consulted, notably Morriss's *Two Brave Brothers*, Meynell's *Rolls: Man of Speed*, Massac Buist's *Rolls-Royce Memories*, Nockolds's *The Magic of a Name*, Bird's and Hallows's *The Rolls-Royce Motor Car*, and Volume One of Morton's monumental *History of Rolls-Royce Motor Cars*.

One of the most heartening aspects of authorship is the vast number of letters one receives from people offering help, advice or information. Space does not permit of my mentioning them all by name, but we must single out the following who have contributed signally to the present book.

John Adams, D.F.C., M.B.E., Frank Armond, Kenneth Ball (Autobooks Ltd), McA. Bexon, C.B.E., Cecil Bianchi, William Boddy (Editor, *Motor Sport*), John Bolster, John Braybon (Southern Television Ltd.), Colonel Rixon Bucknall, S. T. Capener, Mrs Henry Compton, Continental Gummi-Werke A.G., A. L. Cranch, F.R.P.S., Dr D. A. Dale, Bernard Davies, L. F. Dixon, Dr Walter H. Dollfus, Phil Drackett (the Royal Automobile Club), Cyril Durlacher, D. E. A. Evans (The Star Register), Dennis C. Field, A.M.I.E.E. (Research Historian, The Veteran Car Club), E. H. Gale (The Stanley Club London Ltd.), Mrs P. Gantle, G. N. Georgano, Dr R. H. Glauert (Trinity College, Cambridge), Ross S. Giles (*Wolverhampton Express and Star*), Walter Gray, George W. Green, Flight Lieutenant P. L. Heaver, P. F. Hediger, J. F. Hedley, R. V. Herring (General Accident, Fire and Life Assurance Corporation Ltd.), Harry Hill, Miss A. Horner, the Misses Johnson, E. F. Jones (Society of Motor Manufacturers and Traders Ltd.), R. Le Grain-Eiffel (Automobile Club de France), Dr Alfred S. Lewerenz (Horseless Carriage Club of America), Ronald Lightowler (London Vegetarian Society), Lady Mander, Keith Marvin, E. V. Matthewman (the *Daily Mail*), W. J. Mills, Millard W. Newman, T. R. Nicholson, Harold Nockolds, W. A. A. Pearson (Church of England Enquiry Centre), W. B. Phipps, Mrs Alice Pollock, Pontypool Conservative and Unionist Association, Colonel R. L. Preston, C.B.E., John H. Price, T. Richardson (Royal Society for the Prevention of Cruelty to Animals), Wilfred Risdon (National Anti-Vivisection Society Ltd.), the Royal Geographical Society, Geoffrey Rudd (The Vegetarian Society), David Saunders (National Army Museum), Dr F. Schildberger (Daimler-Benz A.G.), David Scott-Moncrieff, Capt. N. Seaton-Stedham, R. S. Searle (Parsons Chain Co. Ltd.), W. F. Sedgwick Ltd., Lady Segrave, the Borough of Southwark, R. A. Storey (National Register of Archives), H. A. Tarrant (Old Etonian Association), C. F. Thatcher (Metropolitan Borough of Fulham), W. White (*Health for All*), Mark Wild, Julian Wilson, Alfred Woolf, R. J. Wyatt (Vintage Austin Register), Mrs R. R. Young (City of Norwich Museum).

Liberal use has also been made of the Montagu Motor Museum Library, while again I have to thank Mrs Kathleen Gregory for her labours in deciphering and typing an often heavily amended manuscript.

MONTAGU

Beaulieu
February 1966

Introduction

For . . . the nation remains only the mournful consolation that he died a martyr to knowledge, and that his memory and example will be an incentive to continued effort in an art that crowned him with victory and claimed him as her sacrifice.
Daily Mail, July 1910

It was July 1910, and the fashionable south coast resort of Bournemouth was celebrating its centenary.

Though King Edward VII had been dead for two months, the Bournemouth Fortnight was in many ways the quintessence of Edwardianism. National mourning had not curbed the carnival processions, the parades, the *bals masqués*, and the *cafés chantants* with which the town sought to combine an anniversary with a public-relations drive, while the importation of the redoubtable M. Spagnol from Nice to direct the festivities could be interpreted as an urge to elevate the occasion from mere urban saturnalia into something altogether more sophisticated. The spirit of the times manifested itself in other ways: fresh from the impact of that *Entente Cordiale* so dear to the late Monarch's heart, the municipality had invited French mayors as well as English ones, and two of them had accepted. The cultural atmosphere, however, was wholly English, and backing Dan Godfrey, who had founded Bournemouth's own orchestra, there were such guest conductors as Sir Edward Elgar, Mr Edward German, and Sir Charles Villiers Stanford, whose works are now museum-pieces of the imperialist era. On the vocal side, the star attraction was Dame Clara Butt, indelibly associated in the minds of Britons with her rendering of *Land of Hope and Glory*. There was a 'Young England Day', highlighted by a march-past of two thousand boys from the cadets and other para-military organizations, while the tone of the decorated floats themselves reflected the carefree aura of the late reign rather than the soberer years that were to follow. A prize-winning entry was a comic street-car inscribed '1810—no Sunday trams: 1910—still no Sunday trams'—a tilt

1

at sabbatarianism that would never have been countenanced a decade earlier.

If the tone of these festivities was retrospective, it was surely because in the secure Britain of 1910 the barometer was set fair with little prospect of change. Sarajevo and Ypres were a long way ahead. Nevertheless, Edwardian acceptance of the internal-combustion engine was reflected in a motor battle of flowers, supported in the main by private owners—trade domination of this type of event was to come in the inter-War era. More important still, Bournemouth had stolen a march on its rival resorts by devoting the second week of the celebrations to a Flying Display.

Not that she was first in the field, for Blackpool had staged such a contest the previous October. But the unpredictable English climate had played a shoddy trick on the Lancashire town, and the last three days of the meeting had passed with but one flight—by Hubert Latham. More important, the Bournemouth meeting represented a concerted endeavour by the whole municipality, and further the venue was easily accessible from fashionable London.

Hampshire was also well versed in the affairs of the motorcar. Until he took his seat in the House of Lords in 1905, my father, John Scott-Montagu, had been a Member of Parliament for the New Forest, in which capacity he had firmly championed the motorists' cause, while in 1910 the village of Beaulieu was making a bid to become one of the cradles of British aviation. W. E. McArdle and Armstrong Drexel had opened an aerodrome on the heath to the west of my home, and the latter, indeed, had entered a Blériot monoplane for the Bournemouth Week. What is more, his partner had created a sensation in the local press by flying the aeroplane over for him.

Aviation had sprung into prominence in two brief years since the Wrights had come to France. Some of the great names of motor-racing had taken avidly to the new sport, notably the British-born Farman brothers in France, who were to achieve great distinction in this field until their adopted country's aircraft industry was nationalized into an anonymous sea of initials in 1936. In Britain J. T. C. Moore-Brabazon had driven his last motor-race (for Austin) in 1908, and in 1909

2

had become the first Briton to make a flight in a British-built aeroplane on British soil. But undoubtedly the man who signalized, above all, the nation's endeavours in this new element was the Hon. Charles Stewart Rolls—son of a peer, Old Etonian, and a pioneer of practical motoring, as opposed to being photographed behind the wheel of a horseless carriage for the delectation of readers of the glossier weeklies. Rolls was one of the three founders of the Royal Aero Club: he had been the first Englishman to fly with Wilbur Wright, and the first aviator of any nationality to complete a double crossing of the English Channel.

At the age of thirty-two, he had captured the fancy of the British public, and rated as a national hero. Though neither he nor his compatriots were as yet aware of it, his name was to become the symbol of all that is best in British craftsmanship through his already well-established partnership with Frederick Henry Royce. In 1910, admittedly, the Rolls-Royce 'Silver Ghost' had carved a niche for itself in the world of fine cars, but others were still mentioned in the same breath without that undercurrent of implied sacrilege that still accompanies any criticism of the hallowed *marque*.

Rolls was accepted as both a skilled and careful pilot. Yet it was he who crashed fatally at Bournemouth just after noon on 12 July 1910; and with his passing even the most hardened cynics, who had flayed him as a dilettante and as an irresponsible 'scorcher' in his motoring days, lapsed into the deepest of mourning. Though flying was resumed on the morning after his death, all the sparkle went out of the programme, and the underlying British respect for grief expressed itself in strictures against the town for not cancelling the rest of the celebrations. 'It was unfortunate,' observed the *Daily Chronicle*, 'that the carnival, which has lasted already for more than a week, could not have been stopped for one afternoon when death had stepped into the centre of this laughing frivolity.'

Yet today Charles Stewart Rolls, among all the pioneers of land and air transport, is all but forgotten. Because he did not see his first love, the motor-car, attain universal acceptance, his contribution to its teething years is glossed over. His work for Rolls-Royce, though certainly less important, is likewise overshadowed by the efforts of his partners. Claude Goodman Johnson lived on until 1926, and Frederick Henry Royce until 1933, both dying in harness, and both leaving their mark on the image of the Rolls-Royce as it remains to this day. Ballooning, a field in which Rolls excelled, became a dead horse within his lifetime, as he himself was fully aware; while by a curious irony of fate he has been deprived of much of the credit that is rightly his for his dedicated experiments with heavier-than-air craft.

In October 1908, when Rolls made his first flight with Wilbur Wright from the military manœuvring grounds at Auvours, no aviator had flown on British soil, let alone in a craft of British origin. The attitude of the British public to these primitive 'stick-and-string' devices could be likened only to their grandchildren's opinions half a century later on the subject of flying saucers. Certainly the august directorate of Rolls-Royce Ltd., at Derby, paid no heed to these lunatic innovators, and were loud in their denunciations when their colleague Charles Rolls used the facilities of their London Service Depot at Lillie Hall to manufacture unsanctioned bits and pieces for Colonel Capper's military airship *Nulli Secundus*. It was not until war came in 1914 that Royce was to be converted to aviation, and it was the very force of this conversion that was to sweep away memories of Rolls's pioneering efforts. The 'Eagles' and 'Falcons' of World War I gave way to the 'Kestrels' that powered the Hawker biplanes of the early 1930s, and it was Royce the convert (and not his associates) who made the critical decision to proceed with the development of the R-type Schneider Trophy engine, and thus pave the way for the 'Merlins' used to such dramatic effect in World War II. Rolls had been ahead of his times, and had paid the penalty— not only with his life, but with a great deal of his reputation.

History has conspired against him. In an age of technical revolution, it is the visionary who holds the stage; but once that revolution has been channelled into systematic progress along well-defined lines, the limelight becomes the preserve of the dedicated engineer or executive, the man who will not allow his attention to be distracted by an outward urge that may cut across established thinking. And Charles Rolls was too meteoric. The bare facts of his career tend to confirm this. As an undergraduate at Cambridge he was a keen cyclist, and propagandist of bicycling: as a very young man he discovered the motor-car, and in the last years of Queen Victoria's reign he missed no opportunity of using his Peugeot or Panhard for any journey, however long. Once the automobile had become the recognized plaything of the well-to-do, he turned his special gift of salesmanship to the motor trade. As early as 1901, his outward urge pointed him to the sky, towards the only medium then practicable—the balloon; but no man who wastes his time on dead ends can be classed as a pioneer, and though aeronautics engaged his attention for eight years, they never supplanted the motor-car. Yet once the aeroplane had become a viable proposition, not even his successful partnership with Royce and Johnson could hold him.

It has been argued that Rolls's divorce from the motor-car became but a question of time from the advent of the 40–50-h.p. Rolls-Royce at the London Motor Show in 1906. This is to my mind an unfair judgment, but it would be true to say that the 'Silver Ghost' formed a bridge between revolution and evolution. No longer were there any unknown worlds to conquer; Rolls's sales and engineering sense told him that the steady development of a single model was the right course for his company to pursue, but his thirst for adventure could no longer be sated by long, fast runs in cars of proven reliability. After all, he had sampled Continental touring in the days when ignition burners could blow out, fires had to be lighted under dead engines to thaw out complex cooling systems, and major portions of a vehicle's anatomy were apt to detach themselves at the most inopportune moments. Nor did a similar resource have to be brought to the sale of the finished product; a glib tongue, ready to explain away any malfunction, was not needed, when the odds against such a malfunction were long indeed.

Rolls died before aviation had passed beyond its first and most experimental stage. Thus it is easy to assert that he would have abandoned it within a few years, and utterly impossible to refute such an assertion out of hand. Apart from his Channel flight in the summer of 1910, he left no concrete memorial of the long months of experimentation at Eastchurch and Shellness, any more than it is possible to ascribe one single aspect of the whole Rolls-Royce *mystique* to him rather than to his confrères at Conduit Street and Derby. Thus he has become a mere name, a statue in the centre of his home town of Monmouth. Purists term their cars 'Royces', regarding this as a truer indication of their origin than the more alphabetically correct 'Rolls'.

To a biographer, Charles Stewart Rolls has proved his own worst enemy. The achievements are documented, but they shed precious little light on the man; this is not hard to comprehend once one realizes that even in his teens his whole personality was absorbed into whatever activity he was pursuing at the time. He had no small-talk: he was, to quote the *Car Illustrated*, 'remote and distant, when tedious twaddle was the order of the day', and conversation was apt to pass him by unless the subject was of direct professional interest. Though generally a lucid writer in an era in which prolixity was accounted a virtue, the correspondence he has left behind is singularly unhelpful as a guide to character-analysis, though most enlightening to a student of the embryonic years of motoring. Seldom is a personal note allowed to creep in; even references to family dogs at the Hendre are embedded in a mass of technical data, as Lord Llangattock is guided through the whys and wherefores of Panhard or Rolls-Royce.

Thus Rolls has never been viewed in perspective. He died at the zenith of Edwardian jingoism, and against this back-cloth he is seen as the personification of Young England— the aristocrat who turned his back on a life of leisure in the Welsh Marches to explore the unknown; and flying at all in 1910 was, if anything, more perilous than any solo flight across the Timor Sea in the early 1930s. Rolls himself was wont to liken an aeroplane to 'a ship with a big hole in the bottom. You have to keep the pumps going all the time, or you sink at once.' He was the first British aviator to pay for his temerity with his life, and the irony of his fate is that no early pilot was as innocent of rashness as Rolls.

Subsequent decades, however, have seen the emergence of the Age of Technology, the triumph of professional over amateur. Even in motor-racing, the larger-than-life, swashbuckling private owner has given way to the dedicated professional with his almost mathematical precision. And Rolls, however professional his approach, was an amateur first and foremost. He could sell a car as well, if not better, than any of his competitors, but his adventurous mind would seldom pause to consider such essential concomitants as after-sales service. He had a technical training backed by a wealth of experience, and thus his opinion of what Royce could, and should make was worthy of careful consideration. His particular abilities were invaluable to a board of directors, but the difficulty was to ensure his presence in the boardroom on the appointed day. Royce, say the historians, made cars: Johnson sold them: and Ernest Claremont kept the uncompromising ideals of his colleagues within bounds which the shareholders would accept. But what was Rolls's contribution, to the motor-car, to the industry, or to flying? Did he merely give his name to the Best Car in the World, and was he no more than a symbol of Britain's aspirations in the air?

Any study of a personality as elusive as Rolls must needs be also a study of his times, and it is against this backdrop that he must be judged.

CHAPTER ONE

Background to Adventure

I am afraid I have no very interesting adventures to relate: we have travelled a great deal, but we have escaped all thrilling adventures. I think I am rather glad of it: hazardous pleasures are upsetting to the nerves.
Lady Llangattock, quoted in *Madame*, October 1896

To a Victorian lady, an unadventurous life needed no apologia —and certainly Georgiana, wife of the first Lord Llangattock, would have been the last person to suggest that one was indicated.

Her husband, Henry Allen Rolls, was the archetype of the late-Victorian magnate. *The Car Illustrated,* in its 'Cars and Country Houses' series, summarized him as 'one of the cylinders of Monmouthshire', and the description is not inept. Throughout his long life—he was born in 1837 and died in 1912—he dedicated himself to his county, serving two terms as Mayor of Monmouth, sitting on the local Bench, holding Masonic office not only as Master of his local Lodge, but also as Provincial Grand Master for the Eastern Division of South Wales. A former Captain in the Royal Gloucestershire Hussars, he became Honorary Colonel of the 1st Monmouth Volunteer Regiment. A staunch and lifelong Tory, he was Chairman of the district's Conservative Association, and sat as M.P. for the constituency from 1880 to 1885, as well as being an enthusiastic supporter of the Primrose League. He was raised to the peerage in 1892, and, by the time he had reached the age of sixty, was the feudal landlord of six thousand acres centring on the Hendre, the family home near Monmouth. Related to Lord St. Vincent, the famous admiral of the Napoleonic Wars, he was a grandson of the ninth Earl of Northesk. His wife was a daughter of Sir Charles Maclean, a Scottish baronet—which, incidentally, gives the lie to those occasional allusions to his son Charles's 'Welsh' temperament. Rolls may have been born and brought up in the Welsh Marches, but Monmouth is a peculiarly English community in a predominantly Welsh county, and he had little, if any, Welsh blood.

As might have been expected, the Llangattocks were the Lord and Lady Bountiful of their neighbourhood. Henry Rolls, as he then was, commemorated Queen Victoria's Golden Jubilee in 1887 by presenting Monmouth with a £10,000 Public Hall, which stands to this day in Agincourt Square, fronted by a statue in memory of his third son, Charles, erected in 1912. To celebrate the coming of age of his heir, John Maclean Rolls, he built a gymnasium in St. John Street, and both occasions were celebrated on a grand scale, John's twenty-first birthday party including two ox roasts, a civic procession through the streets, an organ recital, and a tea party for all the town's school children, whose contribution to the festivities had been a rendering of 'Many Happy Returns of the Day' for the young Mr Rolls as he accompanied the dignitaries of Monmouth into Agincourt Square. Both occasions were also marked by 'Rustic Sports', an activity which has a splendidly period ring about it. The family bounty extended to the distribution of pheasants among the poorer citizens at Christmas-tide, a benevolence which ceased when it was discovered that while the cart from the Hendre was off-loading game on one side of the street, the denizens of the farther side were helping themselves in advance! As might be expected, the Llangattocks invariably preceded other parishioners into church.

Lord Llangattock was an enthusiastic breeder of horseflesh, though this interest waned somewhat in later years; he also served for seven years as Master of the Monmouthshire Hounds. Evidently (and singularly), he seems to have had some misgivings on the subject of blood sports, and at the beginning of the present century he lent active support both to the National Anti-Vivisection Society and to a now forgotten body with the resounding title of The Church of England Society for the Promotion of Kindness to Animals. Charles, his third son, also concerned himself for a while with the latter, though whether this was due to a deep-rooted sympathy for animals is not known: as a dedicated champion of the automobile, he may well have seen in the C.E.S.P.K.A., a heaven-sent medium for persuading the hippophile English that the

9

new locomotion need have no adverse effect on the well-being of the horse.

Press reports of the period dwell at some length on the family's interest in music. Certain it is that both Lady Llangattock and her eldest son were competent performers on the organ, and the instrument installed at the Hendre has survived even the mansion's conversion into a school. But in the 1890s some degree of musical proficiency was a *sine qua non* in upper, and even middle-class society, even if its best manifestation was a passable rendering of Tosti's *Goodbye* or *Pale Hands I Loved Beside The Shalimar* at a soirée. Charles, however, retained an affection for music throughout his life, being particularly addicted to Wagner. Miss A. Horner, who knew him well, recalls him as a regular visitor to concerts at the Queen's Hall around 1908.

Lady Llangattock was an avid if not always discriminating collector of *objets d'art*, who interested herself latterly in Nelsoniana. South Lodge, their London house in Kensington, was hung with Gobelin and Beauvais tapestries, the latter being a representation of Diogenes speaking. Paintings by Romney, Reynolds, Gainsborough, Hobbema, Cuyp and Angelica Kauffman rubbed shoulders with 'the identical fly-flapper with which the Dey of Algiers struck the French Ambassador, and thus gave France her greatest African possession'. There was an Eastern Room, and a French Room, and two Meissen chandeliers and a clock 'presented to the Earls Court Bazaar for soldiers and sailors by the German Emperor'—and won, it was noted, by Lady Llangattock in a raffle.

This secure life should have been an ideal background for the Llangattocks and their four children, but the family life was underscored by a peculiar parsimony that manifested itself not only in money matters, but in terms of personal relationships. For a mansion, the Hendre is notable for the small, almost poky landings; while the main staircase, so often the redeeming feature of the most atrocious specimens of Victorian Gothic, is narrow, and unworthy of such a house. Generous their support for charities may have been, but the Llangattocks pursued a peculiarly disjointed form of home life. None of the three sons married, so that in the early 1900s five people were living five separate existences in the same building. This was especially the case at South Lodge, where Charles maintained his own austere, almost cheerless apartments. When Lord Llangattock added a library wing to the house, he had this arranged with a door leading out into the garden, so that he could come in and out unobserved and undisturbed by his family. He and his wife maintained cordial relations with their children, and shared a deep pride in Charles's achievements—but they knew little of each other's lives, and apparently cared less. Charles in later life never told his mother where he was going, or what he proposed to do.

The Hendre was equally formidable. Those who stayed there recall Lady Llangattock as 'very formal' even in a formal age, though 'Charlie's' younger friends were generally left very much to themselves, and were able to dance and amuse themselves in peace.

Charles was born on 27 August, 1877, seven years after his eldest brother John. It is characteristic of the family disinterest that virtually nothing has been preserved of his earliest years, bar legend. However, from the beginning he displayed a markedly mechanical turn of mind that was not inherited from either parent. Lord Llangattock, it is true, followed his son's subsequent activities with keen interest, but it is clear from Charles's surviving letters to his father (mainly dealing with proposed purchases of Panhards and Rolls-Royces) that his comprehension of the internal-combustion engine never ran very deep. That he did not drive need occasion no surprise; he was nearly sixty when Charles bought his first Peugeot, and though octogenarian motorists did exist in the pioneering years, and furnished excellent copy for the infant motoring press, they were the exception rather than the rule, since the crudities of the early automobile were hard on frail and aged limbs. Lord Llangattock was no more 'a keen motorist' than were many others who rated this description in the early 1900s—this despite the comment of *The Motor Car Journal* in October 1900, that he was the exemplar of a 'motoring peer'. I recently met an old lady whose picture, as a bride, appeared in *The Car Illustrated* in 1904: according to the accompanying caption, she was 'devoted to motoring', which summary amused her not a little. In fact, she had not held a driving licence until the 1920s, and all her active motoring memories were of Continental tours in the subsequent decade. Perhaps the most diverting aspect of Lord Llangattock's motoring career—and a typical commentary on the feudal scene in 1903—was his 'grading out' of a hill on the road running past the gates of the Hendre so that his car could climb it at all!

Charles, however, was more practical even at the age of nine. Morriss, in *Two Brave Brothers*, records a visit he paid to a Monmouth shopkeeper; on this occasion he borrowed the price of an electric bell which he rigged up between his bedroom and the stables. There was also an unauthorized escapade with the estate steam roller on one of the drives leading to the Hendre, though it is not clear which was the more heinous of Charles's two offences on this occasion—the smearing of his best suit with assorted coaldust and lubricant, or the operation of such a vehicle, in full view of 'an influential house-party', on the Sabbath. Rolls himself, in later life, claimed that his first practical experience of locomotion was gained with a superannuated bathchair, 'which could it have spoken, would, I am sure, have expressed great indignation at the indecorous part which it was compelled to play in its old age'. This device was hauled to the top of a long and twisting drive, and then had to convey its youthful pilot as far down as possible without a spill. If he 'baled out' too soon, he might well be run over by his carriage, but when he hung on too long, there was the risk of being thrown out on a corner. And there were victims other than the experimenter. 'One happy day', Rolls reminisced, 'my bag included a curate, a butcher's boy, and a dog-cart.' When this entertainment palled, there were bicycles belonging to estate workers on which to exercise his ingenuity, and on one occasion, certainly, Lord Llangattock had to pay for a new machine after Charles had reduced its predecessor to a heap of irreconcilable spare parts.

As the third son—the second brother, Henry, was un-balanced, and was entrusted to the care of a doctor and his wife after a breakdown in 1908—Charles was naturally spared the responsibilities of feudalism in Monmouth. After he reached manhood, his visits to the Hendre became less frequent and he is not remembered as a regular attendant at the Parish Church. He neither hunted nor shot, and even in his earlier years was already showing signs of that aloofness which was to mark him down; though people who knew the family did not regard him as nearly as shy as his brother John. It is perhaps significant that he apparently never referred to his childhood, apart of course from adventures with bathchair or steam roller.

His official education began at Mortimer Vicarage School, Berkshire. This type of institution is now defunct, but was a regular feature of Victorian days, since it furnished more individual attention than was offered by the larger preparatory schools, and enabled learned but impecunious parish priests to augment their stipends. Further, these establishments seem to have been more humane than their more pretentious competitors, and one seldom finds them associated with charges of organized sadism. Only a single end-of-term report, dated 1890, has been preserved, and this indicates that the thirteen-year-old Charles was not academically minded. A bottom place in Latin is not, perhaps, surprising, but Mathematics failed to appeal, either, for he could manage no better than seventh place in a class of eight. Even the 'outside' subjects, which can often redeem an unpromising scholar's record, were of little help, for his Bible History was rated 'remarkably poor', and his geography master was disinclined to venture beyond a monosyllabic 'bad'. He was not keen enough on his music to practise regularly, and the school was unenthusiastic about his cricket.

Nor did his first months at Eton, where he entered the Rev. H. Daman's House in May 1891, show much promise. Admittedly Charles did not stay long—he left at the end of the Easter Half, 1894—and thus was unable to make much of an impression, but it is hard to conceive of such a natural 'solitary's' doing so in any case. It is interesting to note, however, that he joined the College Volunteers in 1893, especially in view of the fact that in those days this ancestor of the Combined Cadet Force was truly voluntary, and not subject to the thinly

13

veiled conscription that was to obtain in the inter-War years. It is touching to read, in August 1905, of the Old Etonians, Charles included, who presented Dr Warre, their Headmaster, with a car: but the vehicle in question was a 15-h.p. three-cylinder Rolls-Royce, and the suppliers were, of course, C. S. Rolls and Company.

Academically he drifted along. His efforts, or lack of them, evoked in 1892 the comment: 'Rolls, I regret to say, is still forgetful and irregular, sometimes even to vanishing point! And moreover, at times, his thoughts are far away in dreamland or vacancy, instead of being with his work.' But listless though he might be in the form-room, he was certainly not apathetic outside it, and late that year we find him writing to Lord Llangattock urging him to install a small electric plant at the Hendre, and appealing to paternal frugality by adding that such an innovation would cost no more in either insurance or domestic staff. (He subsequently confessed that in his absence the machine took all the energies of the gardener and his minions to start.) Rather naïvely he observes: 'It would make a magnificent Christmas present.' Evidently he feels that some apologia is required for his depressing academic record in class, for he closes his letter with the words: 'I am doing my best at work, etc.'

Thus electricity came to the Hendre, and Charles supervised the first complete electric installation in a private house in the county. In March 1893, he is already recommending the replacement of this original engine with a new $3\frac{1}{2}$-h.p. Tangye set, which could be bought by instalments; though, as he is quick to remind his father, an outright cash purchase will save £9. The following November he was once more advocating modernization. In an interview with *The Motor*, he recalled that while shopping for a gas engine, he summoned representatives from firms all over the country to demonstrate their wares; it was a source of considerable amusement to him that they all booked into the same hotel in Monmouth, and spent their leisure hours squabbling among themselves!

By Michaelmas, 1893, even his Classics report was satisfactory, and correspondence between his father and Mr Daman reveals that the Army had been considered as a career, but rejected. Charles, incidentally, does not seem irrevocably to have discarded the idea of the Queen's Commission, for he was on the verge of volunteering for the Boer War in February 1900, and expressing his concern on the difficulties of operating a motor-tricycle in a country where petrol was hard to come by. I have also been told by a friend that he capitalized the allowance he would have received from his father as an Army subaltern, and that this sum furnished him with funds sufficient to launch C. S. Rolls and Co. in 1902. In 1894, Mr Daman commented that his pupil now aimed to make electricity his profession. 'He has very considerable ability, as well as interest, in what I may now call his chosen career.'

Nevertheless, a certain amount of coaching was needed before he could pass on to Cambridge, and the services of Mr Herbert Pigg were enlisted. Mr Pigg had already coached Charles, and reported on his academic prowess in somewhat disparaging terms during the transition period between Mortimer Vicarage School and Eton, but now he was altogether happier, writing in November 1894, to reassure an anxious father 'that there is no doubt that he will be able to enter upon a University career'.

During his school holidays, Charles had accompanied his parents on their travels. Lord Llangattock was a keen yachtsman, undertaking long cruises in the S.Y. *Santa Maria*: these extended beyond the familiar stamping grounds of the Mediterranean to the Crimean battlefields of Sebastopol and Alma, and as far north at St. Petersburg (Leningrad). On this latter trip the family visited Moscow, but Charles's impressions of the Russian capital have not survived. Indeed, his nautical interests, as might be expected, centred round the engine-room, where he took his share of the watches.

Interestingly enough, Rolls was not destined to take any active part in marine motoring. Motor-boat racing came to the fore in 1903 with the first race for the Harmsworth International Cup, and during its heyday the sport was to furnish car manufacturers with an admirable testing-ground for new power units. Such motoring personalities as S. F. Edge and J. E. Hutton supported it energetically, as did my father who won the Cup twice, in 1905 and 1906. But C. S. Rolls and Co., the firm Charles had founded in 1902, never went beyond announcing their sponsorship of a single racing boat, and there is no evidence that this ever got off the drawing board, or even on to it! Rolls's subsequent appearances on the *Santa Maria* were infrequent, and took place only where the ship's itinerary dovetailed into his—for instance during Lord Llangattock's winter cruise in 1909, when the yacht put into Monte Carlo just as Charles's tour of the French flying-grounds had brought him southwards towards Pau.

But if his family's voyages failed to make a yachtsman of Charles, they at least took him to Paris in 1894, where he saw some of the earliest motor-cars. As yet, however, the young freshman of Trinity was still content with his bicycle.

Rolls's career as an active cyclist spanned only his time at Cambridge, and in his last year his Peugeot was already occupying more of his leisure hours. In any case, in the middle 'nineties the bicycle was on its way out as fashionable transport and recreation, for in August 1897 *Cycling* was telling its readers, on the advice of 'an authority on society matters', that this particular 'craze' was at an end in London. But a few years earlier, thanks to the replacement of the vertiginous 'Ordinary' by the Safety Bicycle, and to John Boyd Dunlop's re-invention of the pneumatic tyre, cycling clubs were all the rage, and there was even one reserved for vegetarians. The sport had long rated a Half-Blue at the two major Universities, and the first Inter-Varsity meeting had been staged as far back as 1874.

Much has been made of Rolls's performances as a competition cyclist at Cambridge, and there is no doubt about his Half-Blue. But he never held an amateur's riding licence, and he was never Captain, or even Secretary, of the University Bicycling Club, as has often been stated. Only once is he recorded as a competitor at an Inter-Varsity Meeting—at Wood Green on 26 June, 1896, and on this occasion he finished sixth and last. Admittedly, he was doing a good deal of bicycle racing around this time, as on 13 June he took part in four events during an 'internal' event at Cambridge, and a week later was in his University's team in a match against London at Herne Hill, taking third place in the Four-mile race. *The Sportsman* listed him as a competitor in a fifty-mile challenge race run by the

C.U.B.C. in May 1897, but he did not figure in the results. According to H. W. Bartleet, he frequently steered a pacing triplet, but by 1898 finals and the lure of the motor-car were taking a heavy toll of his time and he is mentioned only as a judge.

But even if his record is less spectacular than is generally believed, the fact that he cycled seriously lent prestige to a sport of which *Cycling* sadly observed in May 1897: 'It is a plain, bald fact that there are very, very few racing men of what is generally known as good social position.' This sounds ominously like the wail that went up in motor-racing circles in 1904, when the so-called amateurs like Rolls and Edge began to give place to works employees of the stamp of Gabriel or Théry. Even as a very young man, Rolls had become a contributor to the press on specialized subjects, 1896 seeing a long piece on bicycling technique from his pen in *Our Boys' News*. On mounting he has the following to say:

> You will at first find it necessary to hop two or three times or more till proficient, when one hop should be sufficient. A series of hops when mounting is anything but graceful, and should be avoided as soon as possible.

Already the mechanical perfectionist was coming to the fore, and in this long catalogue of 'do's' and 'dont's' we can see the genesis of the driver, who seldom, if ever, used the clutch when changing gear, and disliked seeing anyone else do so.

At Cambridge, Charles was in his element. At last his studies had a direct bearing on his future career, and on his passion for things mechanical. 'I go three times per week to the engineering workshops under Prof. Ewing, which is very interesting', he told his father. Charles had also taken to using a typewriter, and was even embarking on a course of dancing lessons. He was disappointed to find that Cambridge's gymnasium facilities were confined to a school-of-arms where fencing and boxing were taught, and that this building contained no vertical bars.

He had already had his first brush with the law in May 1895, while still living in Herbert Pigg's house. The offence was riding a bicycle without lights, and though he pleaded that he was only riding because there was no room in the cab he had chartered for both himself and his luggage, and that he was following closely behind the same cab, which had two rear lamps, it was all to no avail. He was duly mulcted of two and sixpence, plus two shillings costs.

Charles Rolls graduated as a B.A. in 1898, but in the meantime he had had an encounter that was to speed up the tempo of his mechanical interests. In February 1896, he spent a weekend with Sir David Salomons at his Kentish home, Broomhill. Sir David was already the owner of a Peugeot motor carriage, and had organized the first exhibition of motors in Britain at Tunbridge Wells in 1895. Further, he had just been elected President of that forerunner of all British automobile clubs, the Self-Propelled Traffic Association. In a letter to his father upon his return to Cambridge, Charles admitted that Sir David had persuaded him to read for a Tripos instead of merely for the 'Engineering Special', but his main news was unconnected with his academic career. 'On Sunday last', he wrote, 'I had a ride in Sir D. S.'s autocar, which was delightful, and we attained a speed of about 20 at one time. I intend going in for one of these some time, and have been saving up for a considerable time for the purpose.'

He had embarked upon the path that was to lead to his meeting with Frederick Henry Royce, to victory in the Tourist Trophy, to triumph over the Channel, and to the final reckoning at Bournemouth.

Two Wheels to Four

The chief trouble in those days was generally loose nuts: split-pins were rarely troubled about. Consequently, anyone walking behind a car with a basket would pick up a varied assortment of nuts, bolts, chains and lubricators, bits of the engine, belts, etc.

C. S. Rolls, *Some Roadside Experiences*, 1903

When Charles Rolls went to stay with Sir David Salomons at Broomhill in February 1896, motoring in Britain was still virtually non-existent. While such pioneers as the Hon. Evelyn Ellis, T. R. B. Elliot, and Salomons himself had imported cars from the Continent, F. W. Lanchester, Herbert Austin, Fred Bremer, and John Henry Knight were experimenting with their own designs, and F. R. Simms had paved the way to the exploitation of Gottlieb Daimler's patents, any real progress was stifled by restrictive Acts of Parliament dating back to 1865. Even if, as has since been proved, the 'Man with the Red Flag' was a legal fiction after 1878, the police paid little heed to this, and in any case there was not, and never has been any dispute about the speed limits in force: 4 m.p.h. in the country, and 2 m.p.h. in towns. Further, police witnesses had no experience of speed-judging, and thus little evidence to support their cases. A good lawyer could often make mincemeat of such prosecutions, and in September, 1899—long after 'Emancipation'—Rolls was able to secure an acquittal on a charge of 'driving furiously' in Palace Gate, Kensington, by calling an expert witness in the person of Professor C. Vernon Boys, who testified that the electric carriage Rolls was trying for Alfred Harmsworth was incapable of more than 5 m.p.h. Often, however, a discreet approach to one's local Chief Constable was a better means of distracting the attentions of over-zealous Dogberries than fighting a case in Court. This was true even after 1897, when barrister members of the newly formed Automobile Club of Great Britain and Ireland, such as T. W. Staplee Firth, were always willing to put up a spirited defence for the champions of the new locomotion.

19

Granted, the hysterical hostility of certain Members of Parliament was as yet to be aroused. The menace was so insignificant that it had not attracted the notice of such doughty opponents as Mr Cathcart Wason, who sat for the car-less constituency of Orkney and Shetland, and was later to refer, in 1903, to motors as 'those slaughtering, stinking engines of iniquity'. But in that year Parliament was asked not only to sanction a road race in the British Isles, but also to pass through a Bill for the regulation of motor-cars sponsored by a motoring M.P.—my father, then the Hon. John Scott-Montagu. Worse still, the 'slaughtering engines' had come to stay, and even enjoyed Royal patronage.

Not so in 1896, though the automobile already had its own specialist press, for *The Autocar* first appeared in November 1895, and the *Automotor Journal* followed shortly afterwards. None the less, a horseless carriage was an odd acquisition for a nineteen-year-old undergraduate, even at Cambridge, always more technically-minded than Oxford. In 1932, we read of the late R. J. B. Seaman's being given an all-night *exeat* to run in his M.G. after an overhaul, a concession that I cannot imagine being given by the Dean of any Oxford college, even in my own time in 1948.

But nineteenth-century Cambridge was surprisingly tolerant. It had to be. The strange ways of primitive machinery were mastered only by trial and error, for there were no instruction manuals; the first of these to gain widespread currency were in fact sponsored by keen private owners such as R. J. Mecredy and Archibald Ford. Thus breakdowns on the road were frequent, and return to College in the small hours of the morning the inevitable result. Rolls quickly realized that the best way out of a gating was to enlist the support of dons by giving them rides in his car; at the same time he could extract a good laugh from their caps and gowns flapping from the *tonneau*. Some of them were not amused, or even very interested: Professor Ewing, Rolls's engineering lecturer, summed up his baptism by Peugeot with the terse comment: 'There was a dense fog, and we could not see the lights of the car.'

It has been asserted that Rolls owned a motor-car in France as early as 1894, and that 1896 only marks the stage at which

he deemed it advisable to ship it across the Channel. In a
letter published in *The Autocar* in November 1916, J. D. Roots
claimed that Charles had been a passenger on several of the
early trial runs by his experimental car in 1895. Yet the letter
Rolls wrote to his father in February 1896 firmly gives the
lie to this, and it is clear that, even after he had made up his
mind to take the plunge, his studies caused him to delay still
further. On 24 September he was writing to Lord Llangattock
in tones which make it apparent that he had yet to join the
ranks of the car owners. It is also evident that his father had
been subjecting him to something of an inquisition, for he
observes:

> The reason you did not see any in Town was that the new
> Act does not come into force till 3 months after date of
> passing thereof, i.e. Nov. 14, consequently they cannot run
> without special leave.

In the meanwhile, Charles was carefully surveying the
market, and he waxes enthusiastic about the Panhard, which
has recently undergone considerable improvement. He adduces
a reason for his preference which would clearly appeal to his
father. 'They are built', he says, 'on English lines', a curious
statement to make at a time when the native industry consisted
of a handful of unknown 'one-offs', until one realizes that he is
referring solely to the bodywork. As ever, finance had to be
considered, but in 1896 the motor-car had not progressed
beyond the alliance of crude machinery to hippomobile *carros-
serie*, and a new Panhard complete cost only £240, while
£100 could be saved by buying second-hand. Evidently
Charles already saw the motor trade as a gold brick: 'the friend
of a man I know' had made quite a profit out of buying and
reselling vehicles of 'an inferior make'. He was in a position
to put up half the purchase price, if Lord Llangattock could
manage the rest. It is to Lord Llangattock's credit that neither
then nor on any subsequent occasion did he fail to come
forward with the necessary funds: the mantle of a 'motoring
peer' might fit but clumsily on his shoulders, but this was no
reason to thwart the rising generation.

Charles was still in no great hurry. The Motor Car Club's 'Emancipation Run' to celebrate the repeal of the Locomotives on Highways Act was several weeks ahead, and in the meantime he had accepted an invitation from T. R. B. Elliot, the Scottish pioneer, to visit him at Kelso and inspect his autocar.

One month later he was back at Cambridge after a shopping trip to Paris. He apologizes for the delay in writing, but the selection of a vehicle has taken time, and after his impassioned eulogies of the Panhard, it must have come as a surprise to Lord Llangattock when his son chose the rival *marque* of Peugeot—maybe under the tutelage of Sir David Salomons. The new purchase—a rear-engined 'twin' variously credited with $3\frac{1}{4}$ and $3\frac{3}{4}$ h.p.—was described in glowing terms worthy of the 'classified smalls' of today, Charles being especially proud of the canopy he had added. It had only left the factory at the end of August, and had been put up for sale as a result of the original owner's death. It even came complete with a *written* guarantee—a brave gesture on the part of *Les Fils de Peugeot Frères*, but one that seems to have been warranted by the sterling service the vehicle gave during the next three years. Charles had been rather optimistic, it transpired, in his forecast of the discounts available on the second-hand market, but he had not done badly to pick up a machine with works mileage only, list price £270, for only £225, and Lord Llangattock duly put up £140, his share of the deal. Evidently some incentive was demanded, though, as Charles rounds off his ecstatic catalogue of the Peugeot's virtues with a postscript: 'You may be pleased to hear that I passed alright in my exam, and took a 2nd class in it, which is satisfactory.'

Disillusion all too often follows one's first car, be it a Daimler-engined Peugeot or a Singer Le Mans rescued from a bombed-lot vendor. In Charles's case it did not, but there were other problems to face. This 'very powerful and almost dangerous machine' had to be transported to Cambridge; and the new regulations had not come into force, not that this trifling point was going to deter him from making the journey under his own steam. No sooner had he off-loaded the car at Victoria Station than he was waylaid in the yard by a constable, and summoned 'for not having a Red Flag'. (The Metropolitan

Police, unlike later historians, did not concern themselves with the niceties of the Law.) After some discussion, however, Robert agreed to look the other way—as he often does, with a really unusual vehicle—and Rolls settled down to the long grind across Hertfordshire and Cambridgeshire, religiously observing the speed limit in town, and taking it in turns with his crew to carry a lantern in front. There was some light relief, when a policeman on his beat was given a lift. Curiosity overcame official vigilance on this occasion, and the motorists were invited to 'just let 'er go as you please down this 'ere 'ill, for there ain't no one on the beat for another mile an' an 'alf'.

So they laboured on through the night for eleven and a half hours, at an average speed of 5 m.p.h., which suggests either that Rolls had observed speed limits only in towns, or that his advance negotiations with Chief Constables had been singularly successful. Once he went to sleep at the steering bar—hardly a hazard at such dizzy speeds. As they passed through villages, anxious night-shirted figures rushed to their bedroom windows, to see what manner of monster was making such a curious din. An alarming thirst for water was assuaged by clandestine raids on ponds in private gardens, while maintenance of the pump turned out to be an uncomfortable proceeding:

> You had to ascertain if the pump was working by stretching your hand under a pipe in a box behind, and as it was usually boiling hot, the passenger got tired of being burnt, and got into a habit of saying 'yes' whenever he was asked if the water was circulating.

All of which, as his later writings show, appealed to Rolls's broad, 'banana-skin' sense of humour. The curiosity of the ignorant made traffic driving hazardous in the extreme, especially with constant-speed engines and negligible brakes. The frantic reactions of horse and donkey generally led to a stampede. Charles has preserved a delectable word-picture of a butcher's cart bolting in the middle of a delivery round, 'scattering various spare parts of animals about the road'.

Once the motor-car was firmly established, Charles Rolls

would summarize these early days with a flippancy which suggests that he never took motoring seriously. But from the beginning he was prominent, even if his claim to be *primus inter pares* is open to dispute. It is impossible to assert with complete confidence that any of the pioneers was the first to motor in all weathers, and to use the primitive horseless carriage as a means for getting from A to B, rather as a healthful and hazardous open-air pastime to be indulged in only within reach of an efficient and comprehensive railway network, much in the same way as the aeronauts of 1904–8 'went ballooning with a Bradshaw'. In the 1890s such enthusiasts as Henry Sturmey and Montague Grahame-White embarked upon marathon drives just as ambitious as any of Rolls's exploits, though it is doubtful whether any of them selected as their baptism of fire a night drive of fifty-four miles, followed shortly by a mid-winter run from London to Monmouth, a journey which still has its excitements in bad weather. It is amusing to note that during the preparation of this book, our trip to Monmouth coincided with a blizzard sweeping the West Country, and that the crossing of the Forest of Dean, in a 1964 saloon equipped with all modern conveniences, occupied two hours.

Further, Rolls's social position gave him an influence disproportionate to his age. The 'yeoman service' which he rendered in getting signatures for the repeal of the 'Red Flag Act' may have been exaggerated, and almost certainly was, but by his very enthusiasm he persuaded others that there was something to the new locomotion. Throughout his life Rolls was to charm people into accepting his ideas. And not only was he the son of a peer, but he was a complete 'independent' in an era when the infant industry was being swept by a wave of patent-gobbling commercialism as typified by H. J. Lawson and his creatures. In 1896, the Lawsonians might already be suspect, and the affairs of the Great Horseless Carriage Company and E. J. Pennington, the subject of near-actionable strictures in the press, but until the formation of the Automobile Club in June 1897, Lawson's Motor Car Club, with its pseudo-nautical uniforms, represented the spirit of active motordom in this country far more than did Salomons's quiet and learned Self-Propelled Traffic Association, of which Rolls was already a member. His early letters to *The Autocar* were signed 'C. S. Rolls, member, S.P.T.A.', and in 1897 he attended both the Paris–Dieppe Race and the French Heavy Vehicle Trials as one of the Association's official delegates, quite a distinction for a nineteen-year-old, and an indication of the esteem in which he was already held. He can also claim responsibility for the first appearance of the motor-car at a society wedding, in April 1898, when his sister Eleanor was married to Sir John Shelley. 'An elegant motor victoria' (almost certainly the Peugeot) transported the guests, though not the happy pair, to ceremony and reception alike. 'Of course', commented *The Autocar* in a snobbish passage, 'the autocar has been requisitioned more than once at a wedding, but we believe in each case the bride or bridegroom was indirectly interested financially in the carriage of the future.' Nowadays, the wheel has come full circle, and happy is the bride who rides to church in a Veteran or Vintage vehicle. Rolls would have been pleased, I feel sure, to know that the first outing of his particular 'baby'—the only surviving three-cylinder Rolls-Royce—after restoration in March 1963, was to take the daughter of C. W. Morton, the *marque's* biographer, to her wedding.

Already Rolls was a dedicated propagandist for the horseless carriage. He was never active in the affairs of the Motor Car Club—though as we shall see, his failure to make the pilgrimage to Brighton on the first Emancipation Run was the result of an accident: but he supported the S.P.T.A., and was one of the first recruits to the new Automobile Club of Great Britain and Ireland, formed by F. R. Simms as a consequence of general dissatisfaction with the M.C.C.'s commercial aura. He served on the Club's Committee from November 1897, only resigning in 1909 when his interest in flying finally took precedence over matters of land transportation. He was elected to membership of the Automobile Club de France in August 1897, while in Paris on S.P.T.A. business.

If anything was needed to set the seal on Rolls's popularity in the confused climate of 1897, it was the unwanted attention of the Lawsonians, and the British Motor Syndicate, a Lawson company, soon showed that it was not above instituting legal proceedings against a minor. In fact, as St. John Nixon has pointed out, Rolls's extreme youth may well have prompted their pursuit of him, as Mr Nixon cannot recall any other case involving a private individual. In January, the Syndicate obtained an injunction restraining Charles from using a Peugeot motor carriage in infringement of their master patents. They were magnanimous enough not to exercise their right to confiscate or destroy the offending vehicle, as they told the public through the medium of their two-colour advertisements in *The Autocar* (the *Automotor Journal* declined to accept their advertising). To them, the Rolls affair was a test case, and the young man was let off with £15 damages and permission for the continued use of his car.

Rolls clearly did not regard £15 a high price to pay for his amusement, but the gloating tone of the Syndicate's publicity goaded him into publishing a *riposte*, in which he pointed out that he had played the game according to the rules laid down by the Lawsonians, and had even endeavoured to buy a car from them. The delivery of vehicles was never that organization's strong suit, and they prevaricated. After choosing a Peugeot, Rolls again wrote to the Syndicate asking them for the name of the *marque's* accredited representative in Britain, but this they either could not or would not tell him, any more than they were willing, at this stage, even to hint at possible proceedings. Having stated his case, Rolls concluded by setting the record straight on something that had never been mentioned in the offending advertisements, namely that the payment of £15 was not in the form of damages, but was the agreed price of a licence to use his Peugeot. He also reminded readers that both sides had undertaken to pay their own expenses.

The Syndicate replied through its solicitors that 'it was not our clients' wish to be oppressive to Mr Rolls, because he was not endeavouring to injure the plaintiffs', and the weekly two-colour exposé of his heinous conduct continued, though a little of their force was lost by careless use of the words 'on Friday last' a good six months after the action. However, subsequent wrangles with the British Motor Cycle and Carriage Company (who were unwise enough to use the forbidden

Charles Rolls at the age of eight.
Photo by courtesy of Monmouth Museum

The Hon. C. S. Rolls.

Family Group. Lady
Llangattock and her
children. At back John (later
second Lord Llangattock)
and Eleanor (Lady
Shelley-Rolls). At front
Charles and Henry.

Loeffler. Hon C.S. Rolls, Trin. F.A.K. Stuart (½ Blue) Cai. L.F.Kenny, corp. J.R.Garrood.

Quad at Cambridge. The Hon. C. S. Rolls at front. *Photo by courtesy of Mr H. L. Newton Edwards.*

The tricyclist. Charles Rolls's affection for the little De Dions was short-lived, but he is seen here on one in 1897. *Photo by courtesy of Mrs Rosamund Sarginson.*

△ A Bollée made for two. Charles Rolls with Louis Paul, his passenger, in 1897. He appears to be enjoying the car on this occasion though later memories were less affectionate. *Photo by courtesy of Monmouth Museum.*

▽ Cambridge, 1896. The Hon. C. S. Rolls and Sir Digby Legard on a racing tandem. *Photo by courtesy of Mrs Rosamund Sarginson.*

Weather protection, 1896. Charles Rolls poses proudly with his first car, the 3½-h.p. Peugeot. *Photo by courtesy of Monmouth Museum.*

Young Man With His First Sports Car. The 1896 8-h.p. Paris—Marseilles Panhard had four cylinders and was a great step forward from the little Peugeot. *Photo by courtesy of Monmouth Museum.*

Ready for a Spin, 1897. A spruced-up Rolls with a spruced-up Panhard at the Hendre. *Photo by courtesy of Monmouth Museum.*

The First of Three. Rolls at South Lodge with the 1901 Paris—Berlin-type Mors. *Photo from the Montague Grahame-White Collection by courtesy of the Montagu Motor Museum.*

Night start: an evocative picture of Rolls with his mechanic Claud Crompton ready to set out on the Paris—Berlin race, June 1901. The car is a Mors. *Photo by courtesy of* THE AUTOCAR.

Spacious Days. The A.C.G.B.I. members pose outside the Hendre in October, 1900. The second car from the right is a Renault, driven by Frank Hedges Butler and his daughter Vera. *Photo by courtesy of Monmouth Museum.*

◁
Lunch with the Llangattocks. Some of the A.C.G.B.I. tourists at the Hendre, October, 1960. *Photo by courtesy of Monmouth Museum.*

The Practical Motorist. Rolls and a friend all ready for an outing in a stylish Panhard, *circa* 1902. *Photo by courtesy of Captain N. Seaton-Steadham.*

Royal Command Performance. Rolls with H.R.H. the Duchess of York (later Queen Mary) and Lady Llangattock at the Hendre, October 1900. The car is a Panhard. *Photo by courtesy of Monmouth Museum.*

◁
Thousand Miles' Trial, 1900. Rolls with the Panhard at St. Albans. In the light of previous experience, his mechanic's look at dejection is understandable even though the only mudguard is on his side of the car. *Photo from the Montague Grahame-White Collection by courtesy of the Montagu Motor Museum.*

Mixed Bag at Portmarnock, 1904. Left to right, Rolls on the 1903 Gordon Bennett Mors, Algernon Lee Guiness on the Weir-Darracq and Macdonald on the six-cylinder Napier L48. *Photo by courtesy of* THE AUTOCAR.

Irish Fortnight, July 1903. A friendly match in Phoenix Park between Rolls on the Paris—Vienna Mors and J. E. Hutton on a Mercédés Sixty. *Photo by courtesy of* THE AUTOCAR.

adjective of nationality in their title), and Roots and Venables, makers of carriages with crude-oil engines, overshadowed the tiff with Rolls, and the matter was allowed to die a natural death. The whole incident suggests a degree of *naïveté* in his make-up, since Lawson's bluff was very easily called.

In these years of experimentation, *marque* loyalty as such was not understood, if only because series production was confined to one firm, Benz, with whose solid confections Rolls had no truck—indeed, the adventures of his ballooning partner, Frank Hedges Butler, with the early products of Mannheim were a constant source of mirth to him. Make identity was not always clearly defined, and this went a long way beyond the complex nomenclature of the Benz and its imitations and derivatives. As late as December 1897, *The Autocar* was referring to Rolls's famous Paris–Marseilles–Paris Panhard as a 'Daimler', and the names of body styles could be confused with those of their makers. Thus the 'Iveagh' which Gretton drove in the A.C.G.B.I.'s Richmond Trials in 1899 was in fact a M.M.C.—whatever may have been the true origins of this enigmatic breed! But even after allowance has been made for this confusion, there was already quite a diversity of machines on the market, the motor vehicles on display at St. Stephen's Hall in London in May 1897, including Arnold, Hewetson, Cambier, Lutzmann, Opperman, Duncan *et* Suberbie, Hildebrand *und* Wolfmüller, and Pennington. Admittedly the Hewetson was a Benz named after its original importer, and the Arnold an English copy of the Benz, but in addition to these breeds there were also the well-established Daimler, Panhard, Peugeot, and Bollée, which were not shown.

Up to the end of 1897, Rolls did most of his motoring on the Peugeot, so much so that the *Automotor Journal*, reporting upon its appearance at that year's Agricultural Hall Show at Islington, remarked that it 'needed renovation'. But when the Motor Car Club celebrated its second Motor Car Day with a modest jaunt from the Hotel Metropole to Sheen House, Richmond, Rolls turned up on the 2·4-litre, four-cylinder Panhard with which Mayade had won the Paris–Marseilles–Paris Race at an average speed of 14·5 m.p.h. in 1896. He had paid £1,200 for this rapid machine, if contemporary reports are to be believed. Already retired racing cars were fetching astronomical prices, and three years later Panhard were selling off their 'works' 24-h.p. racers at £3,000 apiece. In 1898 Charles Rolls is seen driving a new 6-h.p. Panhard, while in the same year a De Dion tricycle was added to the stud at South Lodge. Though he rode this in the Richmond Trials of 1899, it is perhaps significant that he never shared the enthusiasm of other pioneers such as Charles Jarrott, S. F. Edge, and St. John Nixon for these machines, a fact that would appear to give the lie to some of the charges levelled against him as a 'scorcher' for scorching's sake. Such allegations were prompted by his remarkable performance on the 12-h.p. Panhard in the Thousand Miles' Trial of 1900, but had he been as speed-crazy as is often suggested, he would surely have fallen heavily for the little De Dion. This single-geared machine, devoid of suspension and almost equally innocent of brakes, was light enough to wear the primitive pneumatic tyres of the period with relative impunity, and in the later 'nineties was about the fastest thing on wheels. On the Dunkirk–Ostend stage of Paris–Ostend in September 1899, Levegh's Mors and Girardot's Panhard, both out-and-out racing cars, averaged 38 m.p.h.; in the tourist class, my father's 12-h.p. Daimler put up a creditable 30·3 m.p.h.; but Baras, the fastest of the tricyclists, recorded a formidable 39·7 m.p.h. Rolls, however, always preferred bigger cars for his personal use.

He tried all manner of makes. In 1897 we find him road-testing a Duryea with a view to the design's possible manufacture under licence in Britain—nothing came of this project, and when Duryeas were eventually produced in Coventry some years later, the sponsor was Henry Sturmey, and not Rolls. He also tried his luck with that lethal weapon, the Bollée tricar, taking one over, after a brief demonstration by Charles McRobie Turrell, for a night run to Cambridge, on which characteristically, 'no supplies were taken on board except sandwiches and buns'. Though at the time he professed himself delighted at the absence of side-slip on muddy roads, his later evaluation of the Bollée is probably nearer his true sentiments. A backfire, he found, could land the operator in hospital for a couple of days, while if the engine started, the handle would administer a smart clip to the cranker's nose. Its exhaust note was comparable 'to an old pig grunting', and its engineering was suspect. 'The car was mostly made of old tin boxes, and you got plenty of practice in soldering.' Memory clearly had not softened his views on this contraption, for he speaks of alarming tail-slides. In fairness to Monsieur Bollée, though, there is little doubt that in his published writings, especially those with a retrospective flavour, Rolls was inclined to hyperbole.

Thus the Bollée was rejected as a dead-end. So were electric cars, despite Rolls's early training. Steam, in his view, was admirable for heavy haulage, and lorries engaged his intermittent interest for some years. There survives in the Rolls family papers a memorandum of agreement with Norman Macdonald and A. D. Smith, dated 1900, to produce a five-ton steam wagon, 'by the earliest possible date and at all events in ample time to have it suitably tried and tested before the motor trials that are to take place in Liverpool in July 1901'. According to the *Commercial Motor*, this target date was not achieved, and the only further information we have of this abortive scheme is a disc wheel which the three partners patented in 1902. Among Rolls's fund of early motoring anecdotes, however, was one which concerned an attempt to ferry a Leyland steam wagon down from Rugby. This vehicle was addicted to elephantine side-slip; winding ropes round the wheels proved useless as the Leyland chewed them up at a rate of knots, but steel cable similarly applied was very nearly a success, as it took wheel-spin on a particularly steep hill to grind them into shreds. The motoring press reported his keen interest in the American Whitney steamer exhibited at the Agricultural Hall Show in 1899—possibly because of its claim to have steamed down from Liverpool. He also serviced Serpollets in the early days of C. S. Rolls and Co., and owned a Locomobile runabout for a short while in 1901, driving it in the A.C.G.B.I.'s demonstrations to County Councillors and Chief Constables in that year. But already he was telling the *Daily Express* that such vehicles, though excellent for town work, were less efficient on open roads in the country. Veteran motorists who recall the Locomobile's limitless appetite for water will endorse this comment!

In any case Rolls, though he was constantly advocating the introduction of a small, cheap, and reliable runabout to retail at around the £100 mark, was interested in selling such a vehicle rather than driving it, and it is interesting to note that he reverted to public transport for many of his longer journeys once the automobile was established. But none the less, he was a genuine progressive, as witness his view on overall speed limits:

> It should be remembered that safety depends not upon mere speed itself, but upon the controllability of a vehicle, and experiments have shown that a motor car travelling at twenty miles an hour is under better control and can be pulled up in less distance than a handsome [*sic*] cab travelling at ten miles an hour.

By 1899 he had his own workshop at South Lodge, and was in process of installing drilling and milling machines. Despite constant talk of experiments, Rolls was no designer, and Sir Thomas Sopwith, who knew him well, does not believe that he ever designed anything. At most he seems to have served as a consultant, albeit one who by his combination of knowledge and experience would be an asset to any company, as Henry Royce was to find out. In a technical sense, Rolls was not an innovator. While ever in quest of new spheres to conquer, he seldom strayed far from the conventional or the well-established for long, and flirtations with mechanical oddities like the huge Dufaux racer or the Rolls-Royce 'invisible Vee-Eight' were short-lived. He was to remain loyal to Panhard long after the Avenue d'Ivry had begun to lag behind in design, a conservative gesture that was to bring his company to the verge of disaster, while his allegiance to the well-tried Wright biplane, at a time when it was already recognized in France as an aeronautical blind alley, was to cost him his life. Thus it was throughout his career. It is true that he was quick to realize the limitations of tube ignition, and as early as April 1899, he was inveighing in print against the constant maintenance that the burners demanded. Of the Bollée, he complained, not without justification, that 'to start at ten, you got up at six', and that the ignition in full cry made a noise reminiscent of a cross-Channel steamer ready to weigh anchor. But he was voicing misgivings over Montague Napier's rejection of the old system as late as 1900.

The protagonist of advanced ideas *per se* could not bank on support from Rolls, and Montague Grahame-White recounts in his autobiography, *At the Wheel Ashore and Afloat*, his experiences when he was commissioned by Rolls and Claude Johnson to prepare a series of design studies for coachwork to be constructed for Rolls-Royce chassis by the London coach-builder Barker. Not only the conservative Johnson, but also Rolls asked Grahame-White 'if he had collaborated with Mr Heath Robinson in arriving at this preposterous drawing'. Traditionally, of course, the engineer has a healthy contempt for the stylist, and one's sympathies are certainly with Rolls when one recalls that Grahame-White was contemplating the sacrilegious step of *raking* the Rolls-Royce radiator. More truly illustrative of Rolls's cautious approach are his reactions when Lord Llangattock suggested fitting his car with electric lighting in 1908. 'It is not advisable', Charles warned, 'to rush into the adoption of these lamps everywhere without careful consideration. The first cost . . . is very high, and the fact of not being able to buy them in less than one pair at a time, and the fact that they are not made in low candlepower, makes them very expensive, and counteracts the supposed advantages.' During his lifetime, acetylene was good enough for the family Rolls-Royces at the Hendre.

His youth, the circumstances of his birth, and his absorption in the newest follies of the upper class had already stigmatized Rolls as the personification of the Motor Age, and we are thus vouchsafed few glimpses of the man, as opposed to the image. His letters to his father reflect his elation at the new Loco-motives on Highways Act. 'What a relief it will be', he writes (12 November, 1896), 'to run about everywhere free after so many years of absurd, unnecessary, and prejudiced restriction', and as yet the modest 12 m.p.h. allowed under the new laws was regarded as a relief. However, all was not serene; though generally he held aloof from the constant bickerings of the Lawsonian Era after his lawsuit over the Peugeot, he became involved in May 1897 in a well-publicized dispute with Frank Wellington, another pioneer motorist who later published a weekly 'register' of used cars. Wellington had lately accomplished a 300-mile run on a Peugeot, averaging a suspicious 12 m.p.h. and 25 m.p.g. on 'oil' (by which, of course, 'petrol' is meant). When the *Automotor Journal* hinted that this was Rolls's car, Rolls wrote a letter in confirmation, evidently feeling that some of the credit for the exploit was due to him. Whereupon the truth emerged: he had hired the car to Wellington for £5 a week, and Wellington felt that this was not cricket.

He was not, however, invariably ungenerous to fellow-motorists, and Mr Fred Frentzel of the Automobile Association Ltd. (a firm of motor agents quite unconnected with the A.A., which was not founded until 1905) was to discover this when he ran out of petrol at night in Kensington. By a happy chance his car expired almost at the gates of South Lodge, and he was delighted to encounter a gate-keeper who was under orders from Charles Rolls to assist any autocarist in distress.

In the nineteenth century, the objective of manufacturer and owner alike was simple: to make cars work, by hook or by crook. Thus every drive was a contest—not against other vehicles, but against mechanical ignorance, unreliable components, and the weather. It is more than mere chance that Charles Rolls entitled his contribution to the Badminton Book of Motors *Caprices of the Petrol Motor*. It had them aplenty. As far as Britain was concerned, serious competitive motoring was out of the question. Town-to-town events were impossible in the face of the 12 m.p.h. speed limit, there were no circuits, and thus the devotees of the horseless carriage had but two outlets for corporate exuberance. The first of these were the A.C.G.B.I.'s social runs, which might take the form of quite lengthy tours spread over several days. For instance, the Easter Outing in 1898 started from London on a Thursday, visiting Winchester on Friday, Chichester on Saturday, Worthing on Sunday, and Tunbridge Wells on Monday, the cars returning London-wards on the Tuesday. Such a programme was eminently feasible in those days of leisure and empty roads.

The alternative to a tour was a gymkhana-type event on the lines of modern-style Club driving tests, generally run on the handicap basis, and with separate classes for 'gentlemen' and 'professionals'. 'Starting from cold' was a natural in those days of tube ignition, while the bending and obstacle races are with us to this day. That scourge of present-day drivers of big Vintage cars, the garaging test, was also on the agenda, albeit known as the 'coach-house handicap'. But the Coat and Waistcoat Race is a period piece which I would commend to those clubs who find weekend congestion, 'black areas', and the generally jaundiced views of Whitehall hard to stomach.

At the end of the first lap, the driver dismounted, took off his coat, hung it on a numbered peg; at the end of second lap, took off waistcoat, hung it up on same peg: at the end of third lap, put on coat and waistcoat, fully buttoned both, and finished at end of fourth lap.

It is only fair to state that this game was reserved for tricyclists!

In the early years, Charles Rolls entered for both types of event, though I cannot imagine he would have relished the garden parties often attendant upon the gymkhanas, with their tea-cups and small talk. This is borne out by the fact that though these social junketings were held well into the twentieth century, the name of the Hon. C. S. Rolls, if it appeared at all, figured only among the list of judges or stewards. High jinks for coat and waistcoat were the smallest of small beer to a man who had sampled Paris–Vienna and Paris–Madrid.

His failure to take part in the Emancipation Run of 1896 was ascribed by the *Automotor Journal* to 'inadvertence', and by Rolls himself in a letter to his father to 'a slight hitch in the mechanism', but in fact the Peugeot broke its back axle *en route* from Cambridge, and overturned, administering a good shaking to the somnolent passengers. A friendly innkeeper put them up for the night in the 'state bedroom', a euphemism for a cupboard-like chamber in which it was hard to find the window, and they continued the journey by train—a fate less humiliating, in Charles's view, than being rescued by a horse. He boasted that this had only happened on one occasion, when his car was marooned by floods. Such a failure was not to his liking, and he determined to celebrate Christmas by driving down from South Lodge to the Hendre in the now repaired Peugeot.

To moderns, to embark on such an adventure in winter with primitive brakes which overheated at the least provocation appears sheer lunacy. There were no chains to cope with ice; no appreciable weather protection apart from one's own clothes, and the *tonneau* of an open car is a very cold place indeed; while such pneumatic tyres as were available were treadless and thus incapable of any degree of grip. Anti-freeze was unknown, and one thawed out one's cooling system by lighting fires under the car. To make matters even trickier, Rolls had elected to make an overnight stop at his aunt's house at Purton, near Swindon; and instead of the easy grades of what is now A40, between Oxford and Cheltenham, he had to face the hillier route through Cirencester, and, worst of all, the steep 1-in-6 descent of Birdlip Hill. In those days the easier road past the 'Air Balloon' Inn did not exist.

Rolls and his crew set off from London at 6.45 a.m., and ran straight into frosty conditions. They lost their way, and did not reach Purton, eighty-one miles from the start, till 8.30 p.m. Understandably enough, petrol was not available in this small Wiltshire village, and it was 2.30 p.m. the following day before they were on their way once more. Birdlip all but proved their Waterloo. The side-brake expired on the steepest part of the hill, while the foot-brake linkage bent under the constant pressure, and the pedal went flat to the floor, leaving the Peugeot careering downhill towards a light which appeared to be a vehicle in the road, but was fortunately a lantern in a cottage window. They narrowly missed heaps of stones by the wayside, but reached the foot of the hill in safety.

Nor were their troubles at an end. Contemporary reports suggest that they reached Ross at 9 p.m. that night, entering Monmouth at midnight, but Rolls himself subsequently admitted that after the Birdlip episode he deemed it wiser to spend the night at Gloucester. Next morning, when they came to start up, the clutch pedal jammed down, and he had the humiliation of being run over by his own car. He was unhurt, but his companion was so thunderstruck that he made no attempt to arrest the Peugeot's wild career, and it rammed a dog-cart, which Rolls had to repair before going on his way. The engine seized on a long hill, a gale sprang up which extinguished the candle-lamps as fast as the crew could light them, and finally their supply of matches was soaked and they had to drive without lights. Yet when they reached Monmouth, they found people who had been waiting as long as forty-eight hours for a sight of the car.

'Everything used to go wrong', he remarked, almost nostalgically, 'except for the tyres, which were solid, and even these used to come off sometimes, and catch in the tyre brakes.'

But the local press in both Cirencester and Monmouth was most impressed, and a reporter from the latter town who had a ride in the car commented on the Peugeot's 'marvellous capabilities in the matter of speed regulation, both in ascending and descending hills, and also in steering'.

The following year he repeated the journey, but this time in the big four-cylinder Panhard, carrying three passengers and their baggage. Understandably, he had a much easier trip, though he tempted providence by carrying eight people and luggage equivalent to an extra two between Purton and Cirencester, and was rewarded by trouble with a pump bearing. But this was almost the sum total of their tribulations. At Maidenhead, the sprag failed to bite, and doubled up, losing him twenty-five minutes, and on Birdlip 'one of the brakes fired'. But a frost-coated crew dismounted from the Panhard at the Hendre at 7.57 p.m. on the second day, having averaged 11 m.p.h. on running time.

With Final Schools on the horizon at Cambridge, Charles decided to give the A.C.G.B.I.'s Easter Tour a miss in 1898, though he accompanied the tourists as far as Esher on his De Dion tricycle. Nor did he take any active part in the Whitsun event, though as its destination was Cambridge he was at the finish to welcome his fellow-enthusiasts. But he was very much in evidence once more on the Autumn run, driving a new 6-h.p. Panhard, and taking the Chair at the first night's dinner at Maidstone. The same Panhard was entered for the Motor Car Club's Third Motor Car Day.

His first appearance in competition in England in 1899 was at a gymkhana held at the Crystal Palace in the Spring. The Panhard's chains were slack after a run from Paris, and one of them came off. *The Autocar* opined that he would have done better had his car been equipped with tiller steering, but it is not surprising to hear that the Panhard was off colour when one realizes that it had just averaged 22 m.p.h. between Paris and Havre. By this time Charles Rolls was planning a season of real racing in France, and he made only a token appearance in the Club's Whitsun Tour, returning early in the proceedings to London.

The A.C.G.B.I., however, were seeking to vary the diet somewhat, and in June they staged an ambitious exhibition—cum-driving test at Richmond. This ran for the inside of a week, and attracted quite an impressive field, including Léon Théry (as yet unknown) on a Decauville. Rolls entered both his Panhard and the De Dion tricycle.

Among the odder features of this meeting was a series of contests between motor tricycles and a well-known trotting horse, Gold Ring. This was not entirely a unique idea, for that year horses were to compete against motor vehicles in the Paris–Trouville Race. On the first day Rolls was pitted against the horse, but, in the words of a contemporary report, 'the hay motor was evidently flurried by the contiguity of the purring, spitting, motor', and declined to co-operate. On the second day, however, the hay-motor had its revenge, beating a Barrière tricycle, though the latter was admitted to be off form. The rider, being a professional, was not named. Thereafter S. F. Edge took up the cudgels on behalf of tricycling, but could only manage a dead-heat in his first race, losing 'by a neck' in the return match.

Once again, the Panhard started inauspiciously by breaking a chain on the first day, putting Rolls out of the Driving Backwards Race, but there ensued a ding-dong battle against Campbell Muir—later, like Rolls, to drive Wolseleys for Herbert Austin—which ended with honours even. A Lanchester was successfully defeated in the Forward Driving event; this, it is clear, was in the section reserved for amateurs, since first place in the 'professional' category went to Théry on the Decauville. One of the third day's items declared itself openly as a 'gentlemen's driving competition', and this Rolls won from Buttemer on a Benz. He also distinguished himself in the obstacle events, winning on two occasions, while he was runner-up to Jarrott in the tricycle section. He retired in the two-mile tricycle handicap. In the accompanying road trials, the Panhard won a Silver Cup for the best private entry, and also distinguished itself by using less water than any other liquid-cooled car, its consumption of four pints comparing favourably with the 6 gallons 6 pints consumed by an International-Benz.

Further trials were run in conjunction with the Agricultural Hall Show at Islington in July. These included an 'evening sports', in which competitors had to dismantle and reassemble their tricycles, and ride them round the arena to prove that they had done it properly, while for the less mechanically-minded there was a demonstration of tent-pegging by a Volunteer Cycle Corps. Rolls, however, won a Gold Medal for a more practical series of runs between London and Baldock during the Show. On the first day he did 144 miles in 8 hrs. 21 mins., and on the second he did the double trip of 72 miles in 3 hrs. 23 min. Private owners exhibited at these early shows as well as the Trade, and in October Rolls again won an award of £11 18s. at a small exhibition held at Dover.

Both the A.C.G.B.I. and the Motor Car Club staged runs to Brighton in November 1899, but the latter was rather a fiasco, since one of the official press cars broke down, prompting the *Daily Graphic* to observe that 'the promoters of this affair could scarcely have done more in the way of mismanagement'.

The A.C.G.B.I.'s Run was a much happier affair, even if Ernest Owers retired with a broken crankshaft, and Charles Cordingley's Daimler shed a tyre as a consequence of what *La Locomotion Automobile* charmingly termed 'un demi-tour sur les rails du tramway à Brixton'. Edge drove his Panhard with Napier engine—the shape of things to come—Rolls a remembrance of things past in the form of the now elderly Peugeot, while Claude Johnson, the Club's Secretary, was a passenger in the so-called Parisian Daimler driven by G. Foster Pedley, later to work for my father on the editorial side of *The Car Illustrated*. Johnson, though a superb organizer, was never a competition motorist, and it has always surprised me that he served as Arthur Callan's mechanic on the Wolseley in the 1902 Gordon Bennett Cup Race. Perhaps it was as well for his peace of mind that this particular entry did not get very far!

The Automobile Club might have come out on top against Lawson's Motor Car Club, but its finances were by no means happy, and the Richmond Show had resulted in a deficit of £1,600. Something more dramatic had to be done, something that would sell the automobile to Britain. Racing was out of the question, but a long-distance rally, taking in all the major centres of population, would kill several birds with one stone, since exhibitions could be staged *en route*. Such displays were to be held at Bristol, Birmingham, Manchester, Edinburgh, Newcastle-on-Tyne, Leeds, and Sheffield. In addition to normal road-work, there would be punishing test hills—Taddington, Dunmail Raise, Birkhill, and Shap, though the latter was almost too gruelling for the cars of the period, and attempts on it were to be optional, as was the speed trial on the Duke of Portland's estate at Welbeck. In November 1899, a meeting to discuss this project was held at the Club and Rolls was among those present. Along with his colleagues, he pledged himself to find two new members—most important, if the deficit left over from Richmond was to be made up.

Though he served on the Draft Rules Committee for the Thousand Miles' Trial of 1900, he did not play a major part in its organization, which was the work of Claude Johnson. But he was fully aware of the vital importance of this nation-wide demonstration of the automobile, and was determined to compete, whatever the cost. In January 1900 he refused to accept a further loan from Lord Llangattock, unless he could pay 5 per cent interest, but by 14 April his finances had been seriously strained by his preparations for the Trial. A special body and a set of wheels were being rushed through for his new 12-h.p. Panhard. All manner of advance arrangements were in train: a stockpile of spare parts, supplies of fuel at every appointed stopping-place, rooms to be booked for himself and his crew, 'making the business cost me far more than ever I anticipated, tho' I laid aside a good sum for it, and for this reason I'm afraid it may be necessary for me to ask your assistance again (tho' I hope not). I ought not really to have gone in for this 1,000 mi., but it is a sort of duty, and people would have been so surprised if I had not.'

Already Rolls was being pursued by the daemon that was to drive him to the day of his death.

CHAPTER THREE

Selling the Automobile to Britain

The initiatory stage successfully accomplished, the motorist has with him a companion more human if possible than the most intelligent of horses. His engine will gasp feebly for more air, will scream for oil, or languish even to the point of death should the petrol supply become inadvertently restricted.

C. S. Rolls, 1902

The Thousand Miles' Trial of April–May 1900, marked the turning point of the automobile's fortunes in Great Britain. It formed the spearhead of an attack which Rolls and the other pioneers of motoring were launching on the unthinking conservatism of Britain. In subsequent years the initial onslaught was followed up by a campaign that went far beyond the mild social tours and gymkhanas of the nineteenth century. Rolls and his friends toured the country lecturing to bodies which ranged from relatively learned engineering societies to the Ladies' Automobile Club, founded in 1902, with which my father's first wife, Lady Cecil Scott-Montagu, was closely associated. Demonstrations of the new locomotion were arranged for all classes of officialdom; while British motorists were venturing in increasing numbers on to the Continent, not only familiarizing themselves with technical developments in France, Germany and Belgium, but also following closely the town-to-town races that were still in their heyday, for the disaster of Paris–Madrid was not to take place till 1903. That the British were learning their lesson was to be forcibly brought home to France in 1902, when S. F. Edge won the Third Gordon Bennett Cup Race on a Napier; a victory that nobody could have foreseen in 1900.

Charles Rolls was not the only motorist who conceived it his duty to support the Thousand Miles' Trial irrespective of expense, even though this expense could be formidable: his tyre bill alone for the 12-h.p. Panhard was in the region of £80. But it is interesting to note that as early as 1900 he recognized the value of racing. In an interview published in the *Motor Car Journal* on the eve of the Trial, he said:

Racing made the industry in France, and one of the most hopeful signs of the present time is that English makers are turning their attention to the subject. The result should be seen in a higher class of car, for the maker who can produce a vehicle to stand the strain of a great race is best able to build one for ordinary touring or pleasure.

And as racing was still out of the question in the last year of the nineteenth century in Britain, a long-distance rally was clearly the next best thing. Nor was Rolls as yet contemplating an entry into either trade or industry. Though he considered the Panhard the best *marque* available, he still had no clear loyalty to any breed. In 1901 he bought a Mors and a Locomobile, and as late as 1902 he was canvassing the directors of the Daimler Motoren–Gesellschaft with a view to driving one of their cars in the 1903 Gordon Bennett Cup Race. His main concern at this stage was to convince the public that the motorcar—any motor-car, irrespective of nationality or specification —could successfully withstand a punishing schedule under official observation.

As seen from hindsight, the Thousand Miles' Trial was unremarkable, even by the standards of the day. It might even be argued that the ability to average the legal maximum speed of 12 m.p.h. over a circuitous route in the British Isles was no great achievement in comparison with Charron's victorious average speed of nearly 30 m.p.h. over 328 miles in the previous year's Paris–Bordeaux Race. But this had happened in France; the situation in Britain was very different. Garages were virtually non-existent; indeed, the opening of the Imperial Motor Works at Lyndhurst, on the Southampton–Bournemouth road, as late as March 1902, was regarded as something of a major motoring event, which attracted quite a few celebrities, among them Charles Rolls—this in spite of the fact that his own firm of C. S. Rolls and Co. was still in the teething stage. Petrol was hard to find, and tourists had to rely on chemists' shops, and on the generosity of A.C.G.B.I. members who maintained supplies at their country houses. As to the industry, this consisted at the time of the Trial of Daimler, the always shaky Motor Manufacturing Company, and a handful of firms putting together variations on a tricycle theme by De Dion-Bouton, or a horseless carriage theme by Benz. In the former category were Enfield and Ariel, both of whom undertook car and motorcycle manufacture on a substantial scale later; the latter included Star of Wolverhampton, and Marshall (later Belsize) of Manchester. The New Orleans, supposedly British, was at best a Belgian Vivinus built under licence at Twickenham by Burford and Van Toll, but in all probability was one hundred per cent Belgian at this stage. Of the big names of subsequent years, Lanchester, Napier and Wolseley were competing in the Trial, but their entries were frankly prototypes. Thus the A.C.G.B.I. might lament Rolls's choice of a Panhard for the 1899 French racing season, and in the Trial itself, and praise my father for using a Coventry-built Daimler, but as far as serious racing was concerned, the facts were inescapable: John Scott-Montagu had been running a touring car in the Tourist category, and anyone who aimed to pit his ability directly against men of the calibre of Charron, Girardot, or Levegh had to do his shopping on the other side of the Channel.

Rolls may have played no part in the Trial's organization, but nevertheless he fully appreciated not only the herculean task that confronted Claude Johnson, but also the event's great importance. In a paper he read to the A.C.G.B.I. in April 1900, he outlined some of the problems facing the organizers. Few motorists, he opined, had yet driven one hundred miles in a single day, and this accounted for the different opinions held on the sort of schedule that should be maintained. Some people were pressing for a two-hour lunch break, to give them time for coffee and liqueurs, whereas others grudged any stop at all. Rolls defended the break, not so much on grounds of human weakness, but because such stops would give the public an opportunity to examine the cars. They and their potentialities must be clearly demonstrated to the British people, and thus the Trial should be a test of machinery, and not merely one of human endurance. He also warned against 'scorching'.

Whilst admitting that the route included several deserted stretches of road on which bursts of speed could do no harm, he considered that the optional sprint at Welbeck should be sufficient for those who put performance first. Mechanical reliability was not the only element on trial: the image of safety had also to be sold. As Rolls put it:

> People now take no notice whatever of a bicycle going along at 20 miles an hour; they have got used to it, and it no longer shocks them; but when they see a heavy motor vehicle driven by a man in a mask, with a weird-looking shining black jacket, and overall appearance of being in armour plate, travelling at 30 miles an hour, raising a cloud of dust, and propelled by a force which they do not understand, and leaving behind it a smell, which, sweeter than *eau de Cologne* to the motorists, is to them abominable, they naturally say we are 'madmen in motors', and that such practices must end in the death of thousands of people.

If the description of a motorist's attire appears to be portrayed too dramatically, we have only to turn to a contemporary description of a cold-weather drive, and find that on this occasion one of the crew wore a warm knickerbocker suit, a Cardigan jacket, and waterproof hunting apron, a heavy, double-breasted ulster, a waterproof cape, and a cap with ear flaps pulled down, the whole swathed with half a driving rug. The combined effect of all this apparel must have suggested something from Regent's Park Zoo.

The Trial itself is history—the first of 65-odd vehicles to essay the course left Hyde Park Corner at 7 a.m. on 23 April, 1900, and 35 of these returned to London having travelled the whole way under their own power. A dozen only maintained the legal average speed of 12 m.p.h. throughout, though no one made the obvious comment that in order to do so they must all have broken the law. Rolls, certainly, was unable to practise what he preached for long. *Bicycling News*, reporting on the first stage of the run from London to the lunch stop at Calcot Park, a few miles west of Reading, observed that he 'had positively adhered to his determination not to race, for he was a long way behind the leaders, notwithstanding the fact that his car could probably have easily beaten the crowd', and praised him for enduring the dust-clouds raised by other competitors. But beyond Calcot it was a different story, though the same paper had to admit that Rolls was 'the safest, though speediest scorcher of them all'. Between Marlborough and Bristol quite a race developed between his Panhard and Kennard's Napier, driven by S. F. Edge—it was noted that neither crew stopped for tea on this stretch. At Birmingham, the *Yorkshire Post* was commenting that Rolls 'still forges to the front, no matter in what order the cars start'. His progress from Darlington through Yorkshire on the southward leg was almost indecently rapid, and at Bradford, where school children turned out to cheer the cars, any thought of a speed limit had manifestly been forgotten. The *Yorkshire Gazette* sniffed: 'Those who motor with the Hon. Charles have merely to say their prayers and hold tight.' Between Otley and Guiseley he raced an express train for a short distance, while his performance on the observed hills was what might be expected of one of the most powerful vehicles in the Trial.

On Taddington the Panhard was off form, for it was beaten by A. J. Wilson's Ariel tricycle; though in the eyes of the *Automotor Journal* Wilson was somewhat of a superman whose 'skill in pedalling is a factor in this case which an ordinary flabby mortal in like conditions would have to allow for'. His speed was 18·9 m.p.h. to the Panhard's 17·7 m.p.h. By contrast the Brown-Whitney steamer which had engaged Rolls's attention at the last Agricultural Hall Show staggered to the top at a speed of 4·56 m.p.h. On Dunmail Raise Rolls tied with Edward Iliffe's Enfield Quad for first place with a speed of 17·6 m.p.h., while his speed up Shap was 27·5 m.p.h., according to some accounts the best ascent, though others credited an Empress tricycle with a better performance. This speed seems almost incredible by the standards of 1900, and in fact represents Rolls's time over the total observed section of seven and a half miles: over the stiffest part of the climb he recorded a still creditable 17·71 m.p.h. His average of 16 m.p.h. over the 354 yards of Birkhill was a demonstration of the Panhard's superiority over such relatively rapid cars as

Edge's Napier (11·5 m.p.h.) and my father's 12-h.p. Coventry-Daimler (10·4 m.p.h.). The International-Benz averaged 4·1 m.p.h., which must have tried the patience of driver and spectators alike, but this is not so laughable when one considers that it was a case of one and a half litres and 3½ b.h.p. against four litres and twelve nominal b.h.p. No wonder contemporary reports described Rolls as the 'giant of the Trial'.

Needless to say, he was one of those who opted to run at Welbeck, and his time of 1 min. 25·2 sec. (37·63 m.p.h.) was more than 10 m.p.h. faster than his closest rival, the Napier. My father managed 26·08 m.p.h.—slow by contrast, but an alarming thought when one contemplates his car, which is still in existence and on display in my Museum at Beaulieu; while Edwin Cheel's Ariel tricycle, with pedal-assistance from the rider and the fourteen-year-old St. John Nixon (lent by the Kennard-Edge *équipe* for the occasion) in the trailer, turned in 29·45 m.p.h. Car design was catching up with the tricycles.

Not that even Rolls was immune from troubles. It is true that he suffered no major *contretemps*. His car did not 'disintegrate' (the fate of the Orient Express between Carlisle and Edinburgh); it did not become uncomfortably involved with the tramway system, like the Simms Motor Wheel and Mrs Edward Kennard's De Dion: it did not develop a dipsomaniacal craving for water, like Mann's Marshall, which had to be replenished every five miles, and only crept into Bristol sixteen hours after leaving London: and it never had to be rebuilt by the roadside, a misfortune which overtook Sidney Straker's Daimler. This machine, incidentally, was fitted with a new cylinder head, piston, connecting-rod, and carburettor, a feat which makes the present-day performances of works pit-crews in International Rallies appear trivial!

But Rolls had his share of headaches. Just before the start he discovered that his fourth speed gear had never been hardened, and was only able to start at all through the kindness of T. B. Browne, who lent him the required 'bits' off a smaller Panhard. As it was, he had to work all night on the car, which was ready a mere half hour before it was due to leave Hyde Park Corner. Fortunately South Lodge was only a few minutes' run from the start. The Panhard caught fire near Dunmail

Raise, and its bonnet had to be repainted at a wheelwright's shop *en route* for Carlisle, a contingency for which the owner was prepared, since he informed reporters that he invariably carried a pot of paint in his tool-kit. More alarming in his eyes was the Lancashire clog found embedded in one of those expensive tyres. It may have been on this occasion that a short-sighted old lady, seeing Rolls lying under the car, asked: 'Is that poor thing lying crushed under the wheels?'

More serious was the incident on the Cat and Fiddle Pass on the way into Manchester. Rolls took a corner too fast, decanting Poole, his mechanic, and some baggage. The damage done was slight, but Rolls was furious, and told the young man in no uncertain terms that if he fell out again, he would not stop to pick him up. It was probably this spill, rather than any actual fast driving, that aroused the animosity of the press against Charles, who for the next few years was frequently subjected to scathing comment. In September 1902 he and his ballooning partner Vera Butler were involved in a well-publicized collision with a horse and trap returning from Barnet Fair. This was hardly a grave accident, and there were no major injuries, but it did not prevent one commentator from observing that:

> The Hon. Charles Rolls, who was thrown from his motor car the other day, and at the same time overturned a dog cart, injured one man's back and ankles, and gave another concussion of the brain, described the accident as 'alarming, but not serious'. One wonders what the Hon. Charles would call a serious accident.

Other reports referred to him as a 'young Kaiser' (already Wilhelm II was thoroughly unpopular in Britain), and re-minded readers of the 'speeds, manifestly greater than that allowed by County Council regulations', attained in the Thousand Miles' Trial. In fact, up to 1903 Rolls had only two motoring convictions to his discredit, one for failing to display a red flag in front of his Peugeot in 1896, and the other for doing 30 m.p.h. at Ifield, in West Sussex, a county not noted for a sympathetic attitude towards motorists.

However, Rolls was awarded the Gold Medal in the Thous-
and Miles' Trial for the best performance irrespective of class,
and he is shown in an unusually generous mood when he asked
the A.C.G.B.I. for permission to have replicas of this medal
made for his passenger and mechanic. He also collected sub-
scriptions for a presentation to Claude Johnson, to mark the
brilliance of his staff-work in the Trial; while in the weeks
following the event, the Panhard and other machines earned
£30 for Lady Georgiana Curzon's Mafeking Fund by giving
rides to visitors at a fête at the Crystal Palace. Henry Edmunds,
whom we shall meet again in this story, bought £10-worth
of tickets, and spent them all on rides with Rolls. Some people,
however, were less favourably impressed, and one writer
dismissed the Panhard airily. 'It is certainly not', he wrote, 'a
vehicle of any interest to the average buyer of motors. Its cost
is prohibitive, and in addition to this it would need a millionaire
to pay the fines which the general use of such a car would
involve.'

Though there was talk of a 1,200-mile Trial in 1901, Rolls
and others successfully opposed this in favour of a more modest
event, which took the form of a Trial based on Glasgow,
probably because this city had been omitted from the itinerary
in 1900. In this contest, held in September, speed was certainly
Rolls's undoing. The 16-h.p. Panhard led on the first two days,
but on the return run from Ayr a piston broke, and he was out
of the Trial, though the engine was repaired by Argyll's in
time for him to drive back to London. *The Autocar's* representative commented waspishly: 'We were passed by Mr Rolls,
driving at an unnecessarily furious rate.'

Meanwhile the sedate tours and gymkhanas continued,
though the latter provoked some complaints from the *Motor
Car Journal*, on the understandable grounds that they invariably
attracted the same, familiar list of entries. At Mr and Mrs De
Stern's garden party at Twickenham in 1900, Rolls won a
'gentlemen's contest' from Mark Mayhew. A contemporary
report tells us, with obvious relief that 'thanks to pneumatic
tyres the lawn was practically undisturbed' by all these antics!
That same season he collected four places at Ranelagh, one
of them in that hardy perennial, the Coat and Waistcoat Race,

in spite of being thrown by his De Dion tricycle in the course of the afternoon's sport; while he repeated his success at the A.C.G.B.I.'s Sheen House Gymkhana.

He also made periodic appearances in the A.C.G.B.I.'s Tours. There was an uncomfortable moment in the Whitsun Run of 1900, when a bee entangled itself in his goggles, and availed itself of the only redress in its power. His passenger, Dr Hutchinson of Cambridge, administered appropriate treatment on the spot. In October 1900, the Club accepted an invitation from Lord Llangattock to visit the Hendre, and the tourists were duly photographed at luncheon there, as well as being treated by their host to a personally conducted tour of Raglan Castle. But trips from London to Monmouth were no longer exceptional and the only hazard deemed worthy of mention was Birdlip Hill. It would seem, though, that some of the visitors did not drive with due care and attention, for Mr William Hughes, a Monmouthshire County Councillor, hinted darkly at injuries to life and limb when replying to an invitation from the A.C.G.B.I. in 1902, and shortly afterwards the county acquired a reputation for being ill-disposed towards motorcars. In 1904 Charles Rolls even put up a vocal protest when Monmouth took the not unreasonable step of imposing a 10 m.p.h. speed limit within the town boundaries. I do not think that this hostility can have lasted long: for at a time when *The Car Illustrated* was urging residents of unsympathetic counties to show their disapproval by registering their cars elsewhere, C. S. Rolls and Co. were registering a surprising number of early Rolls-Royces with Monmouth County Council, the index letters 'AX' being worn, among others, by the first 'Silver Ghost' of all, which was never Charles Rolls's personal property.

But these tours were not without their diversions. As police persecution increased, so advance warning systems were worked out, and the Club tourists *en route* for Oxford in 1903 were greeted at Dorchester-on-Thames by a cyclist carrying a placard inscribed 'Beware—Police Trap just Ahead', until the objects of the notice confiscated the offending document and threatened its instigator with prosecution. On this occasion Rolls was present with a 10-h.p. Panhard, and claimed the only

distinction obtainable in these stolid affairs—a non-stop
certificate. One of the more engaging aspects of these jaunts
was the competitors' practice of assigning names—punning,
exotic, or plain facetious—to their steeds. This was dis-
continued after the introduction of number plates at the end
of 1903, but it is characteristic of Charles's sense of humour
that he favoured the pun, his successive Panhards being
designated 'Petrolls'. My father, being of a more classical turn
of mind, christened his Daimler 'Xantippe', while on this
occasion Claude Johnson's entry of a 14-h.p. New Orleans was
dubbed 'The Sluggard'. Those of us who are opposed to the
practice of painting funny names on the bonnets of Veteran and
Vintage cars may be disappointed to know that this habit has
an excellent historical precedent!

The surviving programmes of these tours make diverting
reading. For instance, when the A.C.G.B.I. visited Oxford on
an earlier occasion—in 1901—we are told that the price of 'a
single bedroom, with bath, boot cleaning, light, and attendance' at the Clarendon Hotel was only six shillings and sixpence, while a breakfast calculated to fortify the motorists
against the worst that recalcitrant machinery could inflict,
consisting as it did of 'ham and eggs, chop, steak, meats and
fish, tea and coffee, bread and butter, toast and preserves, with
attendance', would set them back only an additional three
shillings. One is surprised that they had energy left for the
morning session with the starting-handle after working their
way through all this! By contrast, the two shillings charged
for covered garage accommodation seems almost excessive,
and we may no longer be surprised at the anger expressed by
the Club when it arranged excursions to races in such outlandish places as Athy and Clermont-Ferrand, and discovered
just how much members were expected to pay for how little.

Still, even modest jaunts to Dunstable or Guildford, inadequate though they might be to seasoned veterans of Paris–
Berlin like Rolls, certainly carried on the good work of the
Thousand Miles' Trial. For the first few years of the century
the A.C.G.B.I. fought alone, for the A.A. was not founded until
1905. Ephemeral organizations came and went: among them
was the Motor Vehicle Users' Defence Association, founded

in March 1900 and aimed at protecting motorists from 'severe handling' in the police-courts. Its Committee was impressive enough, including as it did Edge, Rolls, his old adversary Frank Wellington, Colonel Holden of four-cylinder motorcycle fame, Claude Johnson, and Charles Cordingley, founder both of the Agricultural Hall Show and the *Motor Car Journal*, but its life was short, and I cannot trace that Charles took any part in its deliberations. Perhaps too much 'tedious twaddle' was the order of the day in M.V.U.D.A. circles. There was also the Motor Union, which set out with an admirable object—to cater for those who were not interested in the A.C.G.B.I.'s undoubted status as a London Club, and wanted merely what would now be known as 'driving membership'. Rolls sat for a while on the Executive Committee of the M.U., but his lack of active interest is perhaps explained by the comment of a pioneer motorist that 'the Automobile Association, when it came into being, did all the things that the Motor Union ought to have done, but didn't'. Shortly after Charles Rolls's death, the M.U. amalgamated with the A.A.

It was still essential for the A.C.G.B.I. to maintain the recruitment of new blood, and annual statistics were published by the *Automobile Club Journal*, from which we learn that Rolls introduced five new members during 1902. This does not seem a substantial figure beside the forty-four who joined at the instigation of Hugh Weguelin, or the thirteen contributed by my father, but Rolls, as we have seen, was not gregarious, and only conversed freely with those who shared his interests. Still, it is evidence, if any further evidence is needed, that the motor-car all but monopolized his life. He had, it is true, taken up ballooning in company with Frank Hedges Butler and Butler's daughter Vera in 1901, but though even as early as this he was forecasting a great future for heavier-than-air craft, the affairs of C. S. Rolls and Co. and the Panhard agency were to dominate his life until the meeting the Henry Royce in May 1904. At this stage, the balloon was but an adventure into the unknown: though he knew as much as anyone else about motor-cars, it was still vitally important to him to spread his own gospel.

And Rolls, though no committee man, worked hard for the A.C.G.B.I. in the first four years of the twentieth century.

In 1901 he sat on five Committees; the Club Committee, and those dealing with Races, Foreign Relations, Trials and Editing. Between 2 July and 10 August 1903 he is on record as attending no fewer than seven meetings at Club head-quarters, while in November 1903 he added to his interests membership of a committee dealing with the ever-vexed question of side-slip. As we shall see, had he followed this one more closely, he might have gained a preview of Henry Royce's work without the help of Henry Edmunds. Rolls was also among those who met to discuss a possible Bill for the Regula-tion of Motor Vehicles, two years before my father pushed such legislation through Parliament, and in 1902 we find him debating the improbable question of a Club Exhibit of historic motor vehicles. This Committee expressed concern that the Victoria and Albert Museum—surely an odd choice—had no room to house their projected display, and then vanished into limbo. By the time Edmund Dangerfield of the *Motor* launched such a scheme—in 1912—many vehicles of vital historic interest had gone without trace. Somehow one cannot see Charles Rolls devoting much time to such an idea, for he was no sentimentalist and it is hard to imagine his keeping the 1896 Peugeot or the Paris–Marseilles–Paris Panhard in honourable retirement at the Hendre in the same way as the Paris–Ostend Daimler was suffered to linger on at Beaulieu until 1919, when my father presented it to the Science Museum.

In 1904, when the affairs of C. S. Rolls and Co. must have been keeping him very busy, Charles found time to put in an appearance at 11 out of 15 meetings of the Races Committee, and 21 out of 33 Executive Committee meetings. His absence from the Committee dealing with Driving Certificates was however, conspicuous. 1904 saw an internal upheaval in the A.C.G.B.I. with an energetic dispute between the 'old guard' and the 'reform party'. Rolls took no part in this, and it is interesting to note that he was one of the relatively few committee members eligible for re-election that year who was deemed acceptable by both factions.

Though he does not in the main seem to have been an initiator during his long association with the A.C.G.B.I., he was in his element on the Races Committee, and we can see his hand in the ruling that prospective British competitors in the 1901 Gordon Bennett Cup should practise in France, and place themselves under the supervision of a member of the Committee during training, to ensure that they kept fit. This regulation was in fact academic, since no British drivers or cars competed that year. He is, however, known to have been the principal British supporter of the 1,000-kilogram weight limit imposed for the 1902 season, having witnessed the débâcle of Montague Napier's 17-litre, 50-h.p. monster in 1901. During the acrimonious interlude which followed the French threat to run a Grand Prix alongside the race for the Gordon Bennett Cup in 1905, he seconded Edge's motion that Julian Orde, who had succeeded Claude Johnson as the A.C.G.B.I.'s Secretary, should negotiate with the other national clubs with a view to bringing the A.C.F. to book. He was also a believer in some limitation of cylinder capacity in racing. While such an attitude was fashionable after the squabbles of 1905, it is surprising to find that Rolls was openly advocating such ideas in the *Car Illustrated* in September 1903; though he qualified his opinion by adding that he did not consider that time spent on the development of large racers had an adverse effect on the evolution of production touring cars. Such a qualification would, of course, be only politic for a Panhard agent, for Panhard's idea of a racing car in 1903 ran to 13·7 litres, and their regular wares were beginning to be difficult to sell in the face of intensifying competition from Mercédès. The Tourist Trophy met with his warmest support, as the first race for motor-cars 'run on rational lines'—again a judgement based on expediency, for the first two entries sent in for the 1905 event were a brace of 20-h.p. Rolls-Royces nominated by C. S. Rolls and Co., and hot on their heels came a pair of Orleans cars in which Claude Johnson, by then Rolls's business partner, had an interest.

But the Races Committee, important though its work was to British prestige and thus to the infant export trade, had to take second place to the continuing campaign for the acceptance of the motor-car at home. True, from an early date there had been sprints and hill-climbs—the short-lived English Motor Club staged a meeting at Tilburstow Hill in Kent in July 1900

—but it should be remembered that between the Locomotive on Highways Act in 1896 and the opening of the Brooklands Motor Course in 1907, only three full-scale races were held in the British Isles—the 1903 Gordon Bennett Cup on the Athy Circuit in Ireland, and the 1905 and 1906 Tourist Trophies in the Isle of Man. (The British Eliminating Trials staged in connection with the Gordon Bennett Cup in 1903, 1904, and 1905 were *not* races, as the A.C.G.B.I. was constantly stressing!) The Club's main objective was to drum up support for the motor-car in influential circles, and Rolls was presented with an unparalleled opportunity to show his mettle when Their Royal Highnesses the Duke and Duchess of York— later King George V and Queen Mary—visited the Hendre in October 1900.

Not that the Royal Family had shown themselves hostile to the motor-car. The Prince of Wales was already an enthusiastic motorist, and even Queen Victoria had had her horses paraded round the stable yard within earshot of a car to accustom them to its ways. But the Duke was not as yet a convert, while the Duchess's correspondence shows that she was certainly no devotee of the new locomotion. James Pope-Hennessy quotes in his biography a letter which she wrote from Menton in 1898, referring to an encounter with 'an odious motor-car' which 'smelt so nasty and made such a noise'. It was, however, inevitable that a sojourn with the Llangattocks would involve Charles and his Panhard, and fate played into his hands. The death of Prince Christian Victor of Schleswig-Holstein plunged the Royal Family into mourning, and thus all plans for special trains and illuminated addresses had to be cancelled overnight. John Rolls might greet the Yorks at Monmouth Station, clad in the red uniform and cockade of the High Sheriff of his county, and the pupils at the Grammar School might wave a banner inscribed *salvete principes*, but thereafter the visit must be celebrated quietly. And it was. Mourning did not, however, preclude a motor tour of Chepstow and Tintern Abbey even if ambitious mayors with loyal addresses at the ready were circumvented by brisk bursts of acceleration. It seemed likely at one point that an alarming incident might develop when the Panhard encountered a small governess cart, whose two elderly occupants were so alarmed that they endeavoured to bale out through the rear door. The horse, fortunately, did not share their concern, nor did Charles's Royal passengers. 'Her Royal Highness', reported *The Autocar*, 'showed no sense of nervousness, and seemed happiest when the speed was highest down some clear slope.' After which, it is not surprising to hear the future Queen horrifying her aunt, the Grand Duchess of Mecklenburg-Strelitz, by taking further rides in a motor-car in April 1903. Three months later the Prince and Princess of Wales, as they then were, bought a Daimler of their own.

Meanwhile the A.C.G.B.I.'s plans embraced demonstrations of the motor-car to Chief Constables and County Councillors. The Constables, naturally, came first, and in March 1902, some twenty-six of them, including Captain Sant of Surrey, a doughty anti-motorist, received their initiation at the hands of Charles Rolls, Oliver Stanton, and J. S. Critchley. The County Councillors, who came to London in June, received the full red-carpet treatment, with a luncheon at Sheen House, presided over by Lord Llangattock, who told them that they would 'go down to history as men who did not adopt the view that a new movement, because it was a new movement, should be squashed without thought of its possible importance to the country'. Careful instructions had, of course, been circulated to those members who were to act as chauffeurs: they must start off very slowly, take the earliest opportunity to demonstrate the efficacy of their brakes, keep within the legal limit, refrain from showing the car's paces unless specifically asked, tell their passengers that they must exercise the prerogative of the back-seat driver, and tell their chauffeur if they felt that they were going too fast. The route selected on this occasion ran between Hyde Park and Richmond: Rolls drove his Locomobile steamer, and my father a 24-h.p. Daimler. Lord Llangattock, as a County Councillor, was given a ride, but was assigned to Mark Mayhew rather than to his son.

In July 1903 the A.C.G.B.I. was once more calling for volunteers, this time to transport members of a Royal Commission on London traffic around the metropolis. Rolls was one of the four selected for this task. The result was predictable: a spate of bright suggestions included a proposal to extend

Pall Mall westwards across Green Park to Hyde Park Corner, but though Rolls and his colleagues trundled their influential passengers through Brentford, Ealing, Acton and Willesden, nothing came of these schemes.

Rather more fruitful were the Club's essays into exporting their interests. The Coronation of King Edward VII brought notabilities to London from all over the Empire, and the A.C.G.B.I. transported all the Colonial Premiers they could find to Clandon Park in Surrey, where they were initiated into the joys of motoring. Rolls was not present on this occasion, but he contributed a 10-h.p. Panhard to a similar party laid on for the visiting nobility from India. *The Autocar* coined a delectable headline—'Our Indian Guests Petrolize', and the *Automotor Journal* expressed their opinion that 'some of our dusky guests will return to their native land, if not with an understanding of the intricacies of motor car mechanism, at any rate having experienced the thrill of sharing in the very latest means of locomotion that Western civilization has produced'. Rolls's young motor agency in Fulham does not seem to have derived any immediate benefit therefrom, for the list of illustrious clients published in their 1905 catalogue contains no Indian names, but in the near future the Indian aristocracy was to 'petrolize' liberally, and most of them would buy Rolls-Royces.

There was also the Army to convert. The War Office, having a major conflict on its hands in South Africa, could not be expected to initiate anything, and it was therefore left to a group of Club members, under the leadership of Mark Mayhew, to suggest, in May 1901, that they should form themselves into a body to be known as the Army Motor Volunteers. This group made its official début at the August manœuvres, the four cars present being Mayhew's Napier (reputedly the legendary 50-h.p.), Rolls's 16-h.p. Panhard, a 12-h.p. Delahaye driven by Noel Kenealy of *Motoring Illustrated*, and Archibald Weir's De Dion-Bouton. Their duties seem to have been ill-defined, but in the main the vehicles were used for the transport of senior officers, Rolls having as his special charge Major-General C. W. H. Douglas, in command of a Cyclist Brigade. There were some difficulties: officers at first found it difficult to acknowledge salutes from the *tonneau* of a moving car, and Sir Redvers Buller's A.D.C. stood up throughout the crossing of Salisbury Plain, for fear of parting with his false teeth. Major-General Douglas used the cars to form a road block, and then gave his cyclists an exercise of riding in Indian file through the obstacle.

But the utility of the motor-car in war had been proven to Rolls's satisfaction, and he proudly asserted that neither water-course nor scrub had halted his Panhard. The War Office was less certain. Rolls, Mayhew and William Letts turned out in August 1902 to drive Lord Roberts and his Staff round the military establishments at Shorncliffe, but formal approval was not accorded to the new Motor Volunteer Corps until July 1903 and their uniforms did not arrive till well into 1904, forcing Rolls to attend a levee in Service Dress. Some sections of the press did not approve, and looked upon the M.V.C. as an expense-account affair, since not only did it enable motorists to pursue their favourite sport with impunity, but also earned them thirty shillings a day and a free petrol allowance. A writer in the *Critic* expressed the hope that Mayhew and his friends 'will invite me down to the annual manœuvres at the Old Ship, or other pleasant resort within reach of town that may be agreed upon. In that case I promise them to give as warlike a display with the knife and fork as the most valorous of them all.' Some army officers did not understand what it was all about, either, as at the manœuvres in 1903 cars of the M.V.C. were requisitioned, for the transport of a general's personal luggage, and one Volunteer flatly refused to do this.

But these manœuvres at Marlborough finally convinced the military. Rolls put up an epic drive on this occasion. One of the Commander-in-Chief's cars—probably a 10-h.p. Lanchester —broke down, and spare parts were urgently needed. Rolls left Marlborough for Birmingham at ten o'clock in the morning and was back at headquarters at 7.55 p.m. What is more, the offending car was running that night. No wonder Lord Roberts wrote to Mark Mayhew: 'I wish to tell you what great assistance you have afforded throughout these manœuvres. In fact it would have been quite impossible to have carried out these manœuvres without the assistance of the corps.'

Rolls took his M.V.C. duties seriously, holding the rank of Captain. He was driving Brigadier-General Crabbe in London in January 1904, and in June his official passengers included the Prince of Wales, the Archduke Frederick of Austria, and Lord Methuen, whom he drove to Farnborough. Two months later, we hear of his spending twenty-two consecutive hours at the wheel while acting as the Duke of Connaught's chauffeur in Kent. His car on this occasion was one of the first three Royce cars: on its next appearance on M.V.C. duties at Colchester, it was cited in the motoring press as a Rolls-Royce.

In August 1905 the Corps again turned out in force to transport a party of visiting French naval officers, and this time the A.C.G.B.I. also sent a contingent of drivers. A year later, the M.V.C. was reorganized as the Army Motor Reserve, every member of which was required 'to have an efficient motor car, and place this at the service of the Army Council, with himself as driver, for not less than six days in the year'. Retirement was to be compulsory at the age of sixty, but the rate of pay was unchanged at thirty shillings a day, the petrol allowance being set at $\frac{3}{4}$d. per mile, not ungenerous in those days of cheap fuel and a strong pound.

If there is little record of Charles Rolls's later service with the A.M.R., this is largely because by then the motor-car had won general, if not universal acceptance, and the use of automobiles on military manœuvres was no longer 'news'. The press concentrated its coverage on the more bizarre aspects of motoring, such as Ernest Shackleton's venture into the Antarctic in 1908 with a special four-cylinder Arrol-Johnston. But Rolls was certainly present at a King's Levee in the uniform of a Captain of the Army Motor Reserve, as late as March 1910.

There were other ways in which he could turn his knowledge and enthusiasm to good account. Some of these were tedious: on one or two occasions we find him acting as an expert witness in those periodic outbursts of technical litigation that punctuated the first decade of the motor-car's effective history. In 1903 he became one of the members of a Motor Advisory Board set up by the General Accident, Fire and Life Assurance Company. This concern had taken the lead in offering isolated motor policies as early as 1895. As the motor-car grew in popularity, it was deemed advisable to seek the advice of recognized experts. That this was necessary is shown by the increasing tendency to look upon the automobile as a safe source of compensation for misadventures with which it was only remotely connected. One insurance claim of the period arose out of an alleged collision between a car and a pony-trap: investigation of the circumstances showed that the two were never nearer to each other than thirty yards! Rolls continued to act in this capacity until 1909: among the other members of this Board were Mark Mayhew and J. E. Hutton, who held agencies for Panhard, Mercédès, and Berliet.

Not all Rolls's work for the motor movement was effectual, as witness the curious affair of the Church of England Society for the Promotion of Kindness to Animals. This was, one suspects, more a Llangattock family charity than anything else, and its meetings were sometimes held at South Lodge. For a short while, however, Charles took an active part in its trans-actions. His claim that the replacement of the horse by the motor benefited the former will stand, even if its motives were not altogether altruistic. But much of what he said at C.E.S.P.K.A. meetings was pure automobile propaganda, and it is hard to trace a connection between kindness to animals, and Rolls's plaints concerning the pollution of London's streets by the barbarous sanitary habits of the horse. I cannot credit that 'as much as four tons of microbe-laden manure' per mile were being daily removed from the city's streets in 1904. Nor could the *Bristol Mercury*, which tore Charles' effusions on the subject to pieces.

Even in the nineteenth century, he thought nothing of night driving, and before the end of Queen Victoria's reign he was turning his attention to motoring on the Continent. As yet his exploits could hardly be termed 'touring', since most of the trips recorded involve the collection of a new car from Paris. Weather did not worry him, and in the winter of 1899–1900 he seems to have made three runs. On the first of these, he was accompanied by Roger Wallace of the A.C.G.B.I. and Frank Hedges Butler, and the journey passed without incident. The next voyage was, however, fully and dramatically documented by F. W. H. Hutchinson in *The Autocar*, so much so that Rolls found it necessary to censor the copy that he pasted into his personal press-cutting book.

None the less, Hutchinson's picture of their departure from Paris reminds one forcibly of the *ensemble* of the White Knight in *Alice's Adventures through the Looking-Glass*. Their equipment included 'billycock hats in which the owners had incontinently bored holes through and attached with pieces of string, a Gladstone bag, spare inner tubes, an inflator, a little toolbag of the owner's with pet spanners and bits of things in general, and a jack, etc., all tied on with bits of string and bootlace'. Mark Mayhew, one of the other passengers, was so swathed in furs as to have lost his identity, suggesting a compound of Russian and Turk, and clasping a horn in his befurred hand. One would imagine, however, that this was superfluous, since the pots and pans, in chorus with the growl of the Panhard's chains, would give ample warning of the vehicle's approach.

The journey was inauspicious. First, they were delayed until nightfall by the 'collapse of a water joint'. To the discomfort of frozen moustaches was added the embarrassment of another stoppage. The entire cooling system froze, whereupon the crew poured petrol over the long-suffering water pump and set it alight. 'Very anxious work', comments Hutchinson, 'as the flames were at times very great.' But it had no lasting effect, and Rolls sought assistance from 'the staff of an electric light station'. The manager of this establishment proved to be a broken reed, for he merely poured boiling water all over the radiator, where it promptly froze. Unable to get the car under cover for the night, the party turned once more to arson, this time on a grand scale, since they actually lit a coal fire under the front of the vehicle. Why there were no spectacular consequences is a mystery to me, but the car survived this ordeal, and the only further alarm occurred during the thawing-out process, when Rolls suddenly discovered that the power-station's boiler was on the point of exploding, and the party withdrew to a safe distance until the manager had taken energetic action to avert this catastrophe.

Lady Shelley-Rolls was a passenger on a somewhat similar trip, but this time it was the clutch, and not the water-pump, that gave trouble. It fell to Charles's lot to walk four miles to a blacksmith's shop and borrow the necessary tools to effect a repair. One wonders if he had elected on this occasion to dispense with the paraphernalia of the White Knight, or whether the bootlaces had merely parted. Possibly the latter, as his sister has vivid memories of rushing downhill at 50 m.p.h., despite a *ralentir* sign by the roadside. Having secured the tools, Charles decided to keep them, and Lady Shelley-Rolls, as the best French speaker of the party, was detailed to walk back and make the best terms she could with the blacksmith. When the clutch again protested, they enlisted the aid of three tramps to give them a push-start. Thenceforward Rolls frequently tested his cars in France: the 24-h.p. Mors he bought in 1901 was put through its paces in snow and ice, and after Paris–Bordeaux, he took the opportunity of trying it on the Chartres–Ablis road at the same time as Edge was checking the speed of the 50-h.p. Napier. The Mors's speed of $63 \cdot 87$ m.p.h. was only 3 m.p.h. slower than the big British car, which must have helped convince Rolls that the advantages of brute force are strictly limited.

Among his contemporaries, Rolls stands out by virtue of his understanding of the motor-car and its workings. He could never have matched my father's appreciation of its social significance; he never went to such lengths in his publicity campaigns as did Edge, nor had he Claude Johnson's organizing ability. He was lacking in that courtly dignity which the Chevalier René de Knyff brought to international motoring affairs. But everyone who rode with Rolls testifies to the quickness of his reactions, and to the sensation that he was at one with his steed. 'Caprices of the Petrol Motor', the chapter he wrote for the *Badminton Book of Motors* published in 1903, is an admirable guide to the automobile as it was at the time, though some of his trips have acquired a period flavour. The ignorance of budding motorists in Charles Rolls's day is reflected in some of his injunctions, for these recruits to the new sport had to be told not to spill petrol on their clothes and then strike a match, or to turn the fuel tap on hopefully when the tank was empty. The absent-minded were adjured 'not to pedal your motorcycle for half an hour before remember-

ing the plug switch, unless the doctor recommend it'. Ostlers
are seldom encountered today, and it is doubtful whether one
would offer to fill one's petrol tank with water: while Rolls's
warnings on the occasional sadistic habits of starting handles
are alas! also academic in days when manufacturers no longer
fit them. But he recommends the addition of twenty per cent
glycerine to the cooling system in winter, where others would
have the motorist grope for the drain tap; perhaps he remembered those bonfires on the road to Le Havre! Chemical fire
extinguishers also receive a strong recommendation (C. S.
Rolls and Co. marketed an excellent line in these), but a soda-
water syphon was an adequate substitute.

But best of all is the section devoted to 'unusual noises',
which I would unreservedly recommend to those elderly
ladies who plague garage mechanics with long rigmaroles on
'that odd squeak coming from under the radiator'. 'An unusual
but regular puffing noise', keeping time with the engine, but
leaving its running unimpaired, signified the failure of an
exhaust joint, and could be ignored, as long as it did not alarm
passing horses—in those days of open cars, carbon monoxide
took care of itself! Tapping was more dangerous; at best it
presaged overheating or ignition advance too far, but a loose
flywheel or a big-end on its way out were also possibilities.
Squeaks, however, seemed to worry him more than anything
else, though their causes, as listed by Rolls, were not very
serious. A rubbing bonnet was merely a nuisance, and a loose
radiator was also suggested as a possible reason. This particular
fault, be it said, was to be the downfall of several contenders
in the 1,000 kilogram racing class: in a desperate endeavour
to eliminate weight, manufacturers deprived the wretched
cooler of all means of support, and after a few laps flexing
hoses caused the engine to boil like a kettle.

Rolls, however, was no compulsive tinkerer. 'If your motor
works well', he counselled, 'don't tinker with it, although it
may never seem fast enough. Many troubles arise from inter-
ference and undue curiosity.' And he was right: tyres gave
endless trouble, drip-feed systems were critical in their demands for lubricant, and cone clutches demanded frequent
dosages of collan oil, but already cars were capable of covering

quite big mileages without major overhaul. In January 1901 Rolls had done 4,000 miles on the 12-h.p. Panhard, Edge's Napier 9,000 miles, while my father's Paris–Ostend Daimler had no fewer than 16,000 miles to its credit.

A knowledgeable man demands a high standard from those who work with him, and Charles Rolls was no exception. There exists a remarkable document drawn up by him in 1903, when he took on Mr Frederick Choat as his personal mechanic. While he was prepared to teach Choat to drive, and did so, he expected him to be proficient in the adjustment of 'cones, chains, brakes, clutch, clutch pedal, opening of plug points, brackets for strong and weak batteries, adjustment of big-ends, and other parts'. He must be conversant with the three major makes of tyres then current—Dunlop, Continental and Michelin—and also with acetylene lighting outfits. He should be able to grind in valves, and cope with the three types of carburettor fitted to Panhard cars, while all aspects of lubrication, the starting of 'obstinate engines' and the ways of the commutator must be mastered, not to mention that bugbear of early motoring, the slipping clutch, aggravated by the Edwardian habit of never changing down if it could possibly be avoided.

Other customs which had an adverse effect on clutch linings were declutching round corners, coasting downhill with a gear engaged and the clutch pedal held down, and deliberately slipping the clutch when nearing the top of the hill so as to avoid a gear change.

It was only reasonable to expect Choat to have a good idea of those nuts and bolts 'likely to get lost in the road'; but one wonders how many garage mechanics of today would be able 'straight away to draw complete diagrams of wiring, primary, and secondary, without looking at the car'. Admittedly, there was precious little wiring before the days of a whole forest of ancillaries, but it is sobering to realize how much craftsmanship we have lost through the immediate availability of factory replacement units for everything.

Already Rolls was displaying those parsimonious traits for which he was to become famous. As yet food reform had not engaged his attention, and he had no compunction in eating the pheasants which his father sent him from time to time. But he had already learnt to side-track expensive meals by carrying a hamper in his car, and his addiction to sandwiches was a favourite form of economy. His idea of 'lunch' in the Automobile Club was to march into the dining-room, produce his packet of sandwiches, and order a glass of water, a habit which is said to have led the Club to institute the system of 'table money'. On one occasion he ran up a bill for 10d., and presented the waiter with a shilling. He duly received his change, and gave the unhappy man a penny. In those enlightened days when West End restaurants made no charge for *hors d'œuvres*, he dined off them alone. Wedding presents—for those who rated them—invariably consisted of a cigar case or a clock—price £5.

Nor was his lack of generosity confined to monetary matters. On an early run from Wales with J. T. C. Moore-Brabazon, they found themselves without matches to light their oil lamps, and were marooned by the roadside until Brabazon suggested applying a piece of cotton waste to a plug lead. Charles was delighted with this idea, which kept him amused for the rest of the journey, but it did not occur to him to give his passenger a lift home, though Brabazon lived in Cranley Gardens, only a short way from South Lodge.

But Rolls's meanness was passive rather than active. He disliked parting with money, and would go to immense lengths to avoid incurring any obligations. He was never a cadger, and those who dined with Rolls 'went Dutch'; it would not be true to say that they went fifty-fifty, for Charles preferred a bun or a sandwich to more substantial fare. There is a classic, and perhaps apocryphal story of his travelling back from France with a party of friends, who were surprised and not a little piqued to find that he had taken a third-class ticket whereas they were travelling 'first'. Unwisely, they offered to put up the difference between them, so that Charles could join the party. He accepted; but Sir Thomas Sopwith does not feel that this episode was in keeping with his character. Rolls would use people shamelessly on occasions to further his enterprises, but not to further his personal comfort.

Already, also the extraordinary loneliness of the man was

emerging. Charles had many acquaintances, and with some of them he enjoyed a moderately close relationship, but this relationship was dependent on a continuing community of interest. Sir Thomas Sopwith saw a good deal of Rolls while both of them were actively engaged in ballooning; but after 1908 Rolls turned towards heavier-than-air craft, a field which Sopwith was not to explore until some two years after Rolls's death. And though a vein of continuity ran through Charles's adult life, its direction was constantly changing, with the consequence that his friends could not keep up. Outside his own family, there were few people really close to him. No importance needs to be attached to the use of surnames rather than Christian names in his letters, for the habit of first-naming one's business associates was not practised by the Edwardians: Claude Johnson, for whom he had the highest regard, and whom he had known from the first days of the A.C.G.B.I. in 1897, was always 'Dear Johnson', though my father was 'My dear John'. But even between Johnson and Rolls the bond was one of similar professional interests—initially the propagation of the gospel of motoring, and later the promotion of the Rolls-Royce motor car—and during Charles's lifetime there is only record of one visit by Johnson to the Hendre.

Other acquaintances have testified to Rolls's 'controlled impatience' and to his inability to discuss anything that was not of direct interest to himself. To those whom ballooning left cold, flying was a closed book, and who had neither the finance nor the inclination to invest in a Rolls-Royce, he would not manifest the legendary boyish charm: though for all his lack of small-talk he was adept at turning the conversation to his own subjects—and one suspects that many persons apathetic to the motor-car ended up as owners of 'Silver Ghosts'! Unquestionably he enjoyed a happy relationship with Henry Royce, but Royce, though by no means anti-social, was as single-minded as his partner. Rolls might visit Manchester or Derby, and did so quite often in the early days of the Rolls-Royce venture, but Henry Royce seldom came south, and was hard to lure from his factory. In his early motoring years, Rolls's exploits were shared by Claud Crompton, son of Colonel R. E. Crompton, the pioneer of steam-car fame. Frank

Hedges Butler, his daughter Vera, and C. F. Pollock shared many a balloon ascent: while in the 1903–5 period J. T. C. Moore-Brabazon had taken Crompton's place as Rolls's gentleman-mechanic with the big Mors. The Brabazons remained friendly with Rolls to the end of his life, but then their careers paralleled his in many ways. Both were enthusiastic motorists: Brabazon raced a Minerva, a *marque* for which Rolls had held the agency: not only was Brabazon a skilled aeronaut, but so was his wife, the former Miss Hilda Krabbé: while the two men were rivals for the honour of making the first aeroplane flight in Britain.

With the other pioneer motorists, Rolls stood aloof. Mark Wild, who was Cecil Bianchi's mechanic in the 1905 Gordon Bennett Cup Race, Rolls's last *grande épreuve*, recalls that he lived a life independent of the rest of the Wolseley *équipe*. Bianchi's recollection that Rolls showed 'a complete lack of interest in race and car alike', is not perhaps borne out by his performance on this occasion, but it confirms his reluctance to seek out social contacts for their own sake.

By 1904, when Henry Edmunds introduced Rolls to Royce, the motor-car was firmly established, and no longer was a fight for survival required. Ballooning, though bulking ever larger in Charles's life, was still somewhat of a recreation. In the meantime he had built up for himself a reputation both as a racing driver and as a motor salesman with progressive ideas.

CHAPTER FOUR

Racing Improves the Breed

It is my humble opinion at the present time that the Auto-mobile Club should do everything in its power to prevent the high speeds of automobiles being brought before the public notice, whereas at the present time it seems to be devoting too large a part of its energies to exhibiting not only racing cars but touring cars driving at their maximum speed.
Claude Johnson, *Car Illustrated*, July 1905

Thus spake Charles Stewart Rolls's business partner in 1905. This may seem a discouraging utterance, even for a man as uninterested in racing *per se* as Johnson was. It should, however, be remembered that in 1905 international bickering had come to a head. The rush of manufacturers to jump aboard the competition bandwagon had produced an enormous field for that year's French Gordon Bennett eliminating trials, and the unsuccessful competitors were beginning to feel the cold: they had allowed the series production of touring cars to be disrupted by their abortive racing plans. The racing-car and the touring-car were, in fact, entering upon a period of trial separation, if not of divorce. Further, anything that encouraged 'scorching' in England must be avoided at all cost, for constabulary zeal was near its peak. Already the weekly motoring press was publishing maps of England marked with known speed-traps, and the Automobile Association, founded that year, was to ride to success on the strength of its determined endeavours to protect the motorist against police persecution. The appeal to 'responsibility' was to find its parallel again in 1965, when national horror at a high level of fatal road accidents, coupled with unprecedented congestion, was to vent itself against fast drivers generally, and road rallies in particular.

Johnson's pronouncement might seem, at first sight, to be connected with Rolls's withdrawal from active participation in racing. Yet both Charles's entry into the sport, and his abandon-ment of it in 1906, were entirely logical.

As we have seen, even in the nineteenth century he believed

that racing improved the breed, and he ascribed the early hegemony of Panhard and Mors to their active support of the town-to-town races. The motor-car needed selling, and it had to be sold as a tried and dependable vehicle, not just as a temperamental toy for the leisured classes, a contraption addicted to the shedding of vital portions of its anatomy at unpredictable moments. And the hammering meted out on the *caniveaux* of France, the ruts of the Arlberg Pass, and the tortuous corners of the Isle of Man circuit, all helped to expose fundamental weaknesses. Nowadays makers thrash their prototypes through Turkey, over the course of the East African Safari in Kenya, and across the Australian 'outback', but such a programme would be utterly beyond the budgets of even the biggest factories in 1900, or even 1914, and more than money would have been needed to ensure a supply of petrol in such remote spots.

By 1906, though maintenance schedules were still frightening to modern eyes (tyres had an effective life of less than 2,000 miles, and paintwork demanded lengthy and expensive refurbishing every year) we can see a trend in the direction of a type of luxury car divorced from the hairy, chain-driven monsters of a few years earlier. The six-cylinder engine was still a controversial subject, and one that could keep the correspondence columns of the motoring press more than busy, but the new generation of automobiles was there to see, and by 1914 the world's top *voitures de grand luxe*—Rolls-Royce, Daimler, and Napier in Britain, Delaunay-Belleville in France, and Locomobile and Pierce-Arrow in America—had no connection with the sport. Mercédès, of course, furnished the exception; but it was the exception that proves the rule, and throughout their career the Stuttgart firm has almost always had at least one model in their range aimed at the sporting motorist, whereas Daimler's sallies into the high-speed market have been fitful, and Delaunay-Belleville sedulously ignored the sportsman right up to their demise in 1950. Thus Rolls-Royce's logical evolution did not call for a racing programme beyond the T.T., while Charles's outside interest during what we may term 'the Rolls-Royce period'—from 1904 to 1908—was ballooning.

To Rolls, racing was a natural aspect of his 'marriage' with the motor-car. He has periodically been called a pot-hunter, whose sole interest was to win, but Lord Brabazon has testified that one of his favourite sayings was 'to win, it is necessary to finish'. And if Rolls only drove to win, why did he accept a drive in a Wolseley in the 1905 Gordon Bennett Cup Race? Even a place in the British team that year was problematic in view of the strong opposition the Wolseleys had to vanquish in the Eliminating Trials, while victory in the race itself depended on the total collapse of the formidable Brasiers, Mercédès, and F.I.A.T.s.

The answer is simple: Rolls would race if the event was sufficiently important to his project of the moment. In the early days, anything that furthered the cause of the motor-car was ample justification. As its popularity grew, lessons could be learnt by trying different cars—hence his frequent use of Mors racers, though C. S. Rolls and Co. never had any commercial interest in this *marque*. The same consideration governed his unfruitful negotiations with the Daimler Motoren Gesellschaft in 1902–3, and also his calamitous experiments with the Swiss Dufaux in 1905, though in this latter case his company contemplated an agency. C. S. Rolls and Co. supported such meetings as the Bexhill and Brighton Speed Trials, and the South Harting Hill-Climb, though Rolls himself did not always drive, and when he did, would reserve his efforts for the heavy metal. If the Wolseley episode still stands out in isolation, it should be recalled that in 1904 Rolls had not driven in a single race, and he may well have felt that a comeback was indicated, especially in view of the *Car Illustrated*'s observation during the Isle of Man trials in 1905 that 'it is so long since Mr Rolls did anything in the competitive line that there were those present who must have been unaware of the leading position he held five years ago'.

Not that Rolls was a racing man in the same sense as were Charron, Lancia, and Jenatzy; though all these three were associated, like Rolls, with makes of car bearing their names. Nor is it surprising that Rolls is not primarily remembered as a driver, since historically both his partnership with Royce, and his Channel flight in 1910, are of far greater significance, the former in terms of British industrial prestige, and the latter as a landmark in the country's strategical position. Not that Charles's competition career was unusually brief: Jarrott retired at the end of 1904, and so did Edge (apart from his drives at Brooklands); and it should be remembered that the latter entered the sport a year after Rolls. But while other drivers raced continuously throughout their active careers, his appearances were spasmodic. He was much in evidence in 1899, but competed once only in 1900, and then only in the role of mechanic. Paris–Berlin was his only effort in 1901; he was then active for two full seasons before the affairs of C. S. Rolls and Co. claimed him in 1904. He supported two major events—the Gordon Bennett Cup and the Tourist Trophy—in 1905, and crowned his career by winning the latter at his second try in 1906. This was, in fact, his sole major victory.

It is also fashionable to dismiss Rolls as unsportsmanlike. To a certain degree this charge must stand, if only on the strength of the unhappy incident on the Cat and Fiddle Pass in the Thousand Miles' Trial, and his charges of sabotage after the débâcle of the 1905 T.T. His protest at the Portmarnock Speed Trials in 1904 also has a ring of sour grapes about it. But hints of cheating could be levelled at almost anyone else. Throughout the history of motoring sport, the successful discovery of loopholes in regulations has been an accepted part of the game, and the whole story of the Gordon Bennett Cup is underscored by protests and counter-protests at infringements, real or imagined. In more recent times, weird and wonderful expedients were tried in the Monte Carlo rallies of the 1930s, including the adoption of different axle ratios for the road section and the driving tests. 'Try-ons' were frequent, and happy the man who got his vehicle safely past the scrutineers. Rolls's 'records' at Welbeck may not merit recognition in view of the downhill slope of that course, but he certainly never claimed that they were anything more than very fast runs; and to persuade a car to reach such speeds with impunity was a tribute to the machine, its driver, its mechanics, and to the tyres, even if others had gone faster on dead level roads.

But if racing was incidental to the scheme of Rolls's life, there is no doubt that he approached it with the single-mindedness which attended all his enterprises. In 1899 he accompanied Claude Johnson to France, and together they watched the *Tour de France* and the Paris–St. Malo Race. His ride with Edge in the Paris–Toulouse–Paris Race of 1900 was a reconnaissance for Napier's entry into racing the following year. Accompanied by Moore-Brabazon, he was in Ireland in March 1903, learning the Athy Circuit on a 7-h.p. Panhard. The Gordon Bennett Eliminating Trials of 1905, held over the Isle of Man course, served as extra practice laps for the T.T., while G. Foster Pedley, who accompanied him on the 20-h.p. Rolls-Royce during its preliminary trials in the Island, was required to jot down at half-minute intervals the gear in use, the speed in miles per hour, and the nature of the road, while times at all the control points and the car's fuel consumption were also recorded. Massac Buist has told of the same meticulous procedure's being applied both on the Auvergne Circuit and on the Rolls-Royce record run from Monte Carlo to London in 1906. And, according to the *Car Illustrated*, Rolls was the first of the British contingent to learn his way round the eighty tortuous miles of the 1905 Gordon Bennett course.

Rolls shares with my father the honour of being the first British driver to race on the Continent of Europe, in the Paris–Ostend race of September 1899. At the time his only racing experience had been gained on bicycles at Cambridge; by the standards of the day, he was well versed in marathon runs by car, but their duration exceeded their mileage, and it is interesting to note that in April 1900, on the eve of the Thousand Miles' Trial, he was admitting that his longest run to date had been a trip of 146 miles during the period of the 1899 Agricultural Hall Show. As we have seen, this consisted of a shuttle service between London and Baldock. His crew in the four-cylinder Panhard in this first race consisted of Claude Johnson, Robert Bird and T. W. Staplee Firth, the well-known barrister-member of the A.C.G.B.I., who was to defend Rolls on several charges of speeding. He ran in the Tourist Class, as did my father, who was driving his 3-litre, four-cylinder Daimler—the first 'four' to leave the Coventry works, and also the first car to enter the Yard of the Houses of Parliament. Even in those days, it carried a six-seater wagonette body, and the crew included Jack Stephens, the family *chauffeur* from Beaulieu, and Julian Orde, who was to take Claude Johnson's place as Secretary of the A.C.G.B.I. in 1903. Principal competition in the class came from Creux's Peugeot, as the other touring cars were more ponderous still, consisting as they did of a B.G.S. electric car, and a 9½-h.p. Delahaye bus—even in those early days the Parisian firm were truck-minded, though there is no evidence to suggest that this example had the sporting proclivities of their later, celebrated truck-derivative—the Type 135 sports car of 1936.

Rolls was delayed early on at Beauvais with mechanical trouble, thus the Daimler and Peugeot were able to forge ahead. Not so the B.G.S., which broke its axle on a hill, or the Delahaye, which fractured a spring, though it was able to continue. On the second stage, to St. Pol, Rolls led his class, but Nemesis intervened in the shape of a thoughtless carter backing into the road, and the ensuing avoidance involved the ascent of a bank and the forcible disintegration of a wheelbarrow which blocked his escape route. The resultant demise of a tyre cost him the lead, and he was beaten by Creux, who averaged 28·9 m.p.h. to Rolls's 22·7 m.p.h. My father was third. By contrast, Levegh and Girardot, who tied for first place in the racing-car category, turned in 32·5 m.p.h., while Baras's De Dion 'motorcycle' was fastest of all, his speed being 32·8 m.p.h.

My father returned to England, but Rolls's first racing season was by no means over, and within a month he was trying his luck in Paris–Boulogne. Here there was no Tourist class—only the motorcycles and *voiturettes* were accorded separate categories—and his chances of victory were thus negligible. An amusing aspect of this event was a rule stipulating that the motorcyclists must carry passengers, who must weigh not less than 8 stone 9 lb., and these were duly weighed in on a penny-in-the-slot machine at St. Germain station! Rolls finished last in his class, behind Girardot's racing Panhard, and the Mors of Levegh and Broc. Baras was again the fastest motorcyclist, but he took over an hour longer than Girardot—the heyday of the tricycles and quadricycles was nearing its end.

Charles Rolls was due back in England for the Dover

Exhibition at the end of September, but nevertheless he entered his Panhard in the tourist class of Bordeaux–Biarritz. Pouring rain wreaked more havoc among the competitors than did mechanical troubles: Boyer's Phébus *voiturette* was eliminated by water in the petrol tank, and the 'autocar *fête*' laid on at Bayonne was cancelled. Rolls's car shed chains on two occasions, while the engine also played up, so that top gear could only be engaged on down-grades. In the words of the *Motor Car Journal*:

The engine suddenly turned stupid, and it was found that the governors were acting quite too energetically, and prevented the engines [*sic*] from running properly. Rolls was not the man to sit down and weep, and promptly set to work to remedy the defect which ultimately ended in disconnecting the governor spindle, and connecting the 'cut outs' with wire to be used when necessary, and although this misfortune was not temporarily adjusted until the night, and early morning had been spent in unwearying toil, the reward was at hand, and ended next day with victory for the car.

As if these wire-and-broomstick repairs were not sufficient, Rolls was also bothered by livestock, and his 'bag' comprised five chickens, a goose, two dogs, and a sucking-pig. In addition to winning the tourist class, he was placed fifth in general classification, behind the Mors of Levegh and Antony, both of which owned to 16 h.p. as against the Panhard's 8, Bertin's De Dion tricycle, and Petit's 15-h.p. Peugeot. He also beat such 'racing cars' as Koechlin's Peugeot, Broc's Mors, and Schneider's Rochet-Schneider. As the last-mentioned firm's nineteenth-century products had a distinctly Benz flavour about them, one suspects that the designation *voiture de course* was in this instance strictly a courtesy one.

Rolls was criticized for not using a British car, but he was still of the opinion that Britain was not ready to launch out into the manufacture of competition machinery. He also took time out to write to the *Motor Car Journal* in January 1900, to reassure a correspondent that the French racers were not as herculean as rumour suggested. 'Though parts of a so-called

50-h.p. machine are in course of construction,' he wrote, 'it is only to be an experiment, while the 100-h.p. is at present "a castle in the air".' He was not far wrong, for the 1900 Gordon Bennett Panhards gave only 24 b.h.p. from 5·3 litres, while the Belgian Snoeck-Bolide disposed of a problematic 30 b.h.p., but required well over ten litres to achieve this. In any case, the British motoring fraternity had its hands full with the Thousand Miles' Trial, and no home-built competition machinery was forthcoming during 1900. But already there was hope of better things. In fact the 1901 race for the International Cup was even less inspiring than the 1900 event, but Edge and Rolls determined to carry out a reconaissance, with a view to serious British participation in the town-to-town races. They chose Paris–Toulouse–Paris in July 1900 as the venue for this, and naturally the car was a 16-h.p. four-cylinder Napier. Rolls acted as mechanic. The car retired after a collision with Jenatzy's Snoeck-Bolide: contemporary reports suggested cooling troubles as the car's principal stumbling-block, though Rolls himself made the surprising admission that they might have finished had the Napier been provided with standby tube ignition. It is on record, incidentally, that he gave his mother a ride on this machine. The best Britain could offer in the way of serious motoring competition—apart, of course, from the Thousand Miles' Trial—was the English Motor Club's hill-climb at Tilburstow, and Rolls did not enter for this, though he attended the dinner afterwards.

Edge has profited from his reconnaissance, and shortly after his return to England it was announced that Montague Napier had started work on three immense 50-h.p. racing cars. The 'Fifty', be it said, was a mistake on a gargantuan scale, and has since become the butt of generations of motoring writers. Still, it was better than nothing, and in the climate of late 1900 we should not sneer at Rolls or Count Zborowski for promptly placing their orders with Napier. Neither, of course, ever took delivery, and any hope of Rolls's taking part in the 1901 Gordon Bennett Cup Race faded when it became apparent that only one of the huge cars would be completed in time, and that even this would be far from ready for serious motoring. Rolls, however, was in Paris for the start of the race—run concurrently this year with Paris–Bordeaux—and elected to reserve his efforts for the more significant Paris–Berlin. His mount on this occasion was to be a 10·1-litre, four-cylinder Mors, disposing of some 60 b.h.p., and he was to be accompanied by Claud Crompton. This car was finished, if we are to believe *The Autocar*, in a fetching shade of 'Russian blue'.

But the choice of a tried make of car did not, alas! guarantee that it would be ready in time, and in fact work on the Mors was not finished until 11 p.m. on the eve of the race. As usual, there was an early-morning start. 'In the darkness of the night', recounted *The Standard*'s reporter, 'the big acetylene head-lamps of the automobiles and the smaller lanterns of the cycles gave the roads the appearance of a gigantic Venetian fair, but the illusion in that respect was, however, dispelled by the constant explosions of the gas in the motors'—in other words, the traditional vista of dust, exhaust smoke, begoggled drivers and mechanics, and the slow, portentous popping of really big engines ticking over at 400 r.p.m. Not that glamour in a more generally understood sense was absent, for Madame Camille du Gast was among the competitors, clad in 'a tailor-made grey leather costume', for which she received a well-earned ovation from the crowd. Already these races were becoming well-organized affairs from the manufacturer's viewpoint, and one maker was reported to have no fewer than seventy-seven mechanics on duty at Champigny, while one refiner had des-patched 1,300 gallons of petrol. The profiteers were also out in force, hiring out cars at £10 to £12 a time to those who wanted to see the start in style. National bitterness was in the air, and *The Times*'s French correspondent opined that the *tricolores* displayed on the German sections of the course were trophies from the Franco-Prussian War. One of the German competitors had his car stolen before the race, while the crowds were so dense at Champigny that Rolls had difficulty in reversing the Mors into its place.

At first all seemed to be going well for the British con-tingent, at any rate for Jarrott on the Panhard and Rolls on the Mors—the third British competitor was Edge, driving the 50-h.p. Napier on its second and last *grande épreuve*. At Luxem-bourg, Jarrott was running tenth, and Rolls twelfth, while

The Llangattock Stud. This photograph of the garage at the Hendre was taken about 1905, to judge by the presence of two Panhards, a Wolseley and an unidentified tricar, not to mention the absence of any Rolls-Royces. *Photo by courtesy of T. O. Smith.*

Advanced Service Methods, or how C. S. Rolls and Co. coped with hauling in the wrecks in 1903. Both cars are, of course, Panhards. *Photo by courtesy of* THE AUTOCAR.

The Thing from
Switzerland. An
unhappy crew
gather round the
26.4-litre Dufaux
racer at the
Brighton Speed
Trials, 1905.
*Photo by courtesy of
Rolls-Royce Ltd.*

Wearing the Green.
Rolls at the wheel
of his 1905 Gordon
Bennett Wolseley.
*Photo by courtesy of
Monmouth Museum.*

Charles Rolls
prepares to leave
Castletown Control
in the 96-h.p.
Wolseley. The
immense flywheel
is clearly visible.

The Wolseley at
full speed.

Last Race. Rolls on his way to winning the 1906 T.T. with the 20-h.p. Rolls-Royce. Platford, his mechanic, is leaning out for the corner motorcycle-and-sidecar style. *Photo by courtesy of Rolls-Royce Ltd.*

What The Other Competitors Saw. Rolls and Platford sail past a group of eager photographers on their way to victory. *Photo by courtesy of Rolls-Royce Ltd.*

Practice makes perfect. Rolls and Platford (left) and Northey (right) try out their 1906 Rolls-Royce in the Isle of Man. At this stage, artillery wheels are still worn. *Photo by courtesy of Rolls-Royce Ltd.*

Second Time Lucky. Rolls with the Rolls-Royce with which he won the 1906 T.T. *Photo by courtesy of Rolls-Royce Ltd.*

American Excursion. Rolls with the 'Light Twenty' stripped for action at the Empire City Track, New York, 1906. ▽

WELBECK PARK SPEED TRIALS, 1900

The Racing Cars prepared to start.

△   Dispatching the cars on Flying Start.

Stripping the cars for speed. *Photos by courtesy of the Misses Johnson.*   △

AUTOMOBILE CLUB 1000 MILES' TRIAL, 1900.

On the road out of Edinburgh. △

△ Facing the gale out of Edinburgh.

Arrival Home. At Whitehall, 6.45 p.m. May 12th.
Photos by courtesy of the Misses Johnson. ▽

Demonstrator *par excellence*. Charles Rolls puts the demonstration 'Silver Ghost' through its paces at Cannes, 1909.

Will she make it? *Photos by courtesy of Harry Fleck.*

Henri Fournier's Mors, the ultimate winner, was already in the lead. At Aix, Jarrott had moved up to ninth place, and Rolls to eleventh. In actual fact, about the only parts of the Mors that were trouble-free were the tyres, though, as Rolls remarked 'we stopped a number of times to extract nails, which we felt as we were moving along'. Misfiring dogged them; Crompton changed the coils, but all to no avail, so they struggled on on three cylinders to the nearest Mors depot, where the trouble was traced to an exhaust valve spring, which was replaced. This failing was to beset them again, though its impact was overshadowed by worse tribulation.

The second day was one of thick, wet mist, which failed to eliminate the dust menace, but merely plastered it on their goggles. The deplorable state of the *pavé* also slowed them up; and at Cologne the iron bracket supporting the rear-mounted water tank broke; this seems to have been an inherent weakness in the Mors design, since Rolls was to encounter this bother as well on the 1902 Paris–Vienna car. The tank dropped on to the back axle, and sprung its seams. Rolls and Crompton managed to plug the holes in the lower part, but the upper half remained porous, necessitating frequent stops for replenishment. At a hotel, they demanded *Wasser*, whereupon a misguided German waiter pressed glasses of wine upon them! By binding the tank up with wire, and lashing it to the frame, they managed to make the Düsseldorf control, where there was another Mors depot, but the staff were unhelpful, and could only recommend wiring Paris for a replacement tank. Crompton plunged his hand into the nearly boiling water, and was able to plug a few more holes.

The Mors crew at Hanover were equally discouraging, and in any case there was only a short interval of one-and-a-half hours before they had to be on their way again. Once again improvised repairs saved the day, and they staggered on to Berlin and the welcoming brass bands, having averaged 26·9 m.p.h. to take eighteenth place. Fournier's average, by comparison, was 44·1 m.p.h. The Mors had shown itself capable of 63 m.p.h., and Rolls considered that with better fortune he could have finished well up among the leaders. For several days afterwards the exhausted crew fell asleep, without warning, irrespective of where they were or what they were doing, Rolls even 'talking in my sleep (about the car, of course), a thing I have never been accused of before'. He paid generous tribute to Crompton, who seems to have been something of a superman, especially if we believe Rolls's later story that he fixed a defective sparking plug by climbing on the bonnet while the car was in motion! This gem, needless to say, comes from that classic of motoring lore, *Some Roadside Experiences*, and I strongly suspect that Rolls's anecdotes of the early days lost nothing in the telling.

The big race of 1902 was, of course, Paris–Vienna, and with it was combined the third contest for the Gordon Bennett International Cup. But before we pass on to Rolls's adventures during the 1902 racing season, it would be apposite to clear up the complex story of his three Mors racers. The first of these was, of course, the Paris–Berlin car, which he seems to have purchased at the beginning of 1902, since it was on the Mors stand at the 1901 Paris Salon. According to Henri Fournier, Rolls paid £1,200 for it—a fairly modest sum for a racing car at that time. It was used for Rolls's first attack on the kilometre record at Achères in April 1902, and he kept it until the late Summer, when he disposed of it for a tidy profit. In 1904 it was still running in the hands of Montague Grahame-White, who rebodied it and modernized it by fitting a contemporary Mors radiator.

The Paris–Vienna car was a slightly smaller machine with a 9,236 c.c. engine, and cost Rolls £2,000. This was rebodied by a small firm—Moss & Co., whose shops were in Fulham, near Rolls's own garage—with 'upturned boat' coachwork for the record attempt at Welbeck, and it was known to the staff of C. S. Rolls and Co. as 'The Easter Egg', a nickname usually associated with Léon Serpollet's sprint car of the period. Rolls modified the engine as well: reports speak of 'new cylinder heads', which may be a partial explanation of the cylinder dimensions quoted by Lord Brabazon—186-mm. bore and 150-mm. stroke, which would give a capacity of close on sixteen litres. Brabazon also says it had 'cylinders like tubs', and 'the timing of the low-tension magneto was achieved by striking the make-and-break tappet with a hammer'. Its last appearance in Rolls's hands was during the Irish Fortnight of 1903, when it ran in its original form with conventional Mors bonnet.

At the Southport Speed Trials that year, however, he had discarded this car in favour of a 1903-type machine similar to those which had run in Paris–Madrid and the Gordon Bennett Cup, with an 11·6-litre four-cylinder engine and mechanically-operated overhead inlet valves. He retained this Mors throughout 1904, and it seems to have been borrowed from its makers, for Harry Fleck remembers it lying in the blacksmith's forge at Lillie Hall for many weeks before it was finally shipped back to France. The Mors entry in the 1905 Brighton Speed Trials, incidentally, had nothing to do with Rolls, but was nominated by Louis Carle and driven by J. T. C. Moore-Brabazon. Some reports credited the 1903 racer with 110 b.h.p., but Georges Prade strenuously denied this in *L'Auto-Vélo*, and 100 b.h.p. seems a more reasonable estimate.

Rolls was off to a good start in 1902, with an entry in the Welbeck Speed Trials in January. His 20-h.p. Panhard was beaten only by Mayhew's similar car. And, despite the inauguration of C. S. Rolls and Co. in the same month, he was off to Achères in April in the newly-acquired Paris–Berlin Mors for an attack on the kilometre record. The valves had not even been ground in since its last race, so that his time of 35·4 sec. (63·1 m.p.h.) over a notoriously bumpy surface is more than creditable: Rolls had to hold on hard to save himself from being thrown out. As Léon Serpollet had already recorded 29·8 seconds over the kilometre, this was not a record; in fact it was appreciably slower than the unofficial speeds put up by Rolls and Edge at Chartres the previous year, despite the fact that he was now driving a more powerful car.

As for the *grandes épreuves* 1902 was a poor year for Rolls. He had long shown an interest in the use of alcohol fuel, and proposed the Prince d'Arenberg, donor of the famous Alcohol Cup, for membership of the A.C.G.B.I. Thus nobody was surprised when he entered the Mors for the *Concours du Ministre* in May: this race was restricted to cars running on alcohol, the object being to encourage the sale of that fuel, and thus solve the headache of a glut of beetroots that was bedevilling French farmers at the time. A broken connecting-rod prevented him from starting.

Nor did he fare any better in Paris–Vienna. At Gretz, his Mors got out of control on a difficult corner. It left the road, leapt a couple of gullies, regained the highway, shot across it, and ended up by making violent contact with a tree.

In the meantime he had declined a challenge from Serpollet for a speed match at Nice. He himself vouchsafed no reason, but Louis de Silva, who was by then working for him at Lillie Hall, explained in a letter to the *Field* that the two performances were not comparable, as Serpollet had been driving a current model under perfect road conditions, whereas Rolls had been using a year-old model on a bad road. He also pointed out that steam cars were not capable of sustained speed, which was perfectly true, though Serpollets had done well in the *Concours du Ministre* and were to acquit themselves creditably both in the 1903 Paris–Madrid Race and in the 1904 French Gordon Bennett Eliminating Trials. Though Rolls and Serpollet did meet at Bexhill, their cars ran in different classes, and Rolls's subsequent high-speed runs were conducted at Welbeck, and were thus debarred from international recognition.

At Bexhill Rolls, or rather his firm, entered various cars, and the record is complicated by the reluctance of the contemporary press to tell us exactly who drove what. However he did enter a 20-h.p. Panhard, a car which later became the subject of a lawsuit: it was driven by Mark Mayhew, and won its class at 35·49 m.p.h., though his 10-h.p. entry in the light touring class was unplaced. The Mors ran well: reverse was inoperative on this occasion, but it was beaten only by Jarrott's Panhard in the 1,000 kilogram class, the remaining opposition consisting of a brace of Mercédès and Herbert Austin's 30-h.p. Gordon Bennett type Wolseley. In the special class for 'big racers', irrespective of weight, Rolls trounced Edge on the 50-h.p. Napier with a speed of 48·61 m.p.h. It is interesting to note that Serpollet, who was made to run in a different category, for steam-powered racing cars, was fastest of them all, with a speed of 54·53 m.p.h., contrasting with Jarrott's best run at 52 m.p.h., and Rolls's 49·69 m.p.h.

The 1902 competition season closed with the Welbeck

Speed Trials in August. In this event Rolls won both the class for petrol cars of over 17 cwt. weight and the General Handicap. However, a protest was levelled against his 20-h.p. Panhard and the runner-up, a 20-h.p. M.M.C., on the ground that the two cars had run with an inadequate complement of passengers. Rolls insisted that he had entered the Panhard as a two-seater, and added the entirely irrelevant rider that it was a 1901 model, anyway. This did not prevent the organizers from disqualifying him, the honours going instead to E. M. C. Instone's 28-h.p. Daimler, which had turned in a modest 38 m.p.h. to Rolls's 46·57 m.p.h. The Daimler's passengers must have been on the heavy side.

But if Rolls had failed to reach Vienna in June, Edge had won the Gordon Bennett Cup for Britain on his Napier, and this ensured that the 1903 Race would be staged on British soil. In addition, a truly gargantuan town-to-town event—a race to end all races—was scheduled for May. This was to run between Paris and Madrid, and it very nearly killed the sport. Rolls included both contests in his plans, but in the meanwhile he took the Paris–Vienna Mors up to Welbeck with two official timekeepers—H. J. Swindley and G. P. Coleman—to put it through its paces. On this occasion it wore Dunlop tyres (it had previously run on Continentals) and the new streamlined body. Like its predecessor, it suffered from tail-lightness, and the 56-lb. weights placed in the stern came adrift, playing havoc with the handling. They all but went through the floor, and the party had to adjourn to Mansfield, where, in the words of *The Autocar*, 'the services of a joiner were obtained to box these cavorting ponderosities more securely in their stowage'. In these circumstances a first run over the measured kilometre in 32·2 sec. was satisfactory. A second run was spoilt by a burst tyre and a spectacular skid. On his third and last attempt, 'the car seemed veritably to spin the road beneath it, as it came on with steering wheels lashing under it as though the myriad strokes of its engines maddened it to mighty leaps. The expression upon the comfortable face of the Duke's head keeper as the car whirled on to the end, its brakes squealing like griddled fiends, expressed more than can any words.' Rolls's time of 27 seconds (82·84 m.p.h.) for the kilometre was the

79

highest speed as yet recorded anywhere on the road, even if it could not rank as a record. There was no ban on the exhibition of racing cars at Motor Shows in 1903, so the Mors went straight back from Welbeck to the Agricultural Hall at Islington, there to take its place among the touring Panhards and the potted palms.

1902 can claim to be the year in which the Gordon Bennett really arrived, and with England defending the Cup in Ireland against contenders from France, Germany, and the United States, there was promise of a good race in 1903. Rolls was certainly anxious to try his luck, and he adopted the practice of 'hedging his bets' by approaching two companies in two different countries. This was permitted: Charles Jarrott was to take this course of action in 1904, driving a de Dietrich in the French Eliminating Trials, and a Wolseley in the British contest, while de Crawhez' failure to win a place in the French team that year with a Clément-Bayard was compensated by his inclusion in the Belgian Pipe *équipe*. And in 1903, the A.C.G.B.I. was the only Club to select its drivers by competitive examination.

Even so, the first two places had already been assigned to Edge and Jarrott, and so Rolls, Mayhew, and Stocks on Napiers, and Lisle on a Star were left to fight it out at Welbeck for the third place. Alas! Rolls's 45-h.p. car, which he described as 'a very fine little machine', failed to come up to expectations. Carburettor trouble, followed by a broken inlet valve, left him with only one hope, to redeem himself in the second part of the Trials, to be staged at Dashwood Hill on the High Wycombe–Oxford road. But, as he remarked ruefully, 'Welbeck gets twelve times as many marks as Dashwood', and in the end Stocks was chosen to race in Ireland.

This put paid to one of his hopes. But in the meanwhile he had been making overtures to Emil Jellinek at the Daimler Motoren Gesellschaft. Jellinek was at the time involved in a monumental dispute with the German Automobile Club, which insisted that he should employ 'amateur' drivers for the three Mercédès that were to represent Germany on the Athy Circuit. Not that the word 'amateur' had the same meaning then as it enjoys now; a member of the managerial classes engaged in the motor trade, like Rolls or Edge, was deemed to have amateur status, whereas paid works drivers such as Gabriel or Théry were rated as professionals. Jellinek had had the temerity to nominate as two of his team Hieronymus and Werner, neither of whom were amateurs, and neither of whom were Club members. As neither side would give way, it seemed that Jellinek might have to go outside Germany for men worthy of his confidence, and both Rolls and de Crawhez were considered. In the end, however, Mercédès turned up in Ireland with two Belgians (Jenatzy and de Caters) and an American (Foxhall-Keene).

In the meanwhile Paris–Madrid had cast a shadow over the whole sport. Lack of crowd control, heat, and dust had taken their toll, and put paid to town-to-town races. The race was stopped at Bordeaux, but Rolls, who had reverted to an 80-h.p. Panhard for this occasion, got no further than Barbézieux. Starting 36th, he had worked up to 28th by Chartres, 14th at Tours, and 12th (or, according to some sources, 10th) at Poitiers, 316 kilometres from the start. He had worked his way into sixth place by Angoulême, but engine trouble put him out (according to the *Daily Mail*, 'the engine actually parted from the frame'), and he and the faithful Claud Crompton scrounged a lift on the step of another competitor's car.

But if Rolls could not wear the green or the white in the Irish Gordon Bennett, he was certainly going to watch; and the A.C.G.B.I. had laid on an 'Irish fortnight' for its members, to follow the race. It has little significance in motoring history except that it served as a precedent for subsequent Gordon Bennetts, and thus landed the German club in some very expensive festivities in 1904. Apart from the odd sprints interspersed with the tourism, it was rather a dreary procession round the Emerald Isle, and as the tour dragged on the field thinned appreciably.

Moore-Brabazon accompanied Rolls and the Paris–Vienna Mors, paying his own expenses. Nor was this all, for as Rolls's mechanic, he was treated as a menial on occasions. A friend of Rolls asked if he could borrow his 'man' to send off a telegram, and Brabazon tramped two miles on a hot day, being rewarded with a sixpenny tip. He was, however, to have his revenge:

meeting the man later at a dinner, he introduced himself with
the comment: 'Now that I know you, I'll do it next time for
nothing.' Rolls drove the Mors himself, C. S. Rolls and Co.'s
entry of a 20-h.p. Panhard being entrusted to C. W. Hacking,
who, to complicate matters further, also rode an Ormonde
motorcycle, though this was a private entry on its rider's part.
The Mors, incidentally, went through the whole tour under
its own power.

In the Phoenix Park Speed Trials at Dublin, the old Mors
was, of course, outclassed, as it was up against Hutton's 'Sixty'
Mercédès, similar to the car with which Jenatzy had won the
Cup, and de Forest on the 100-h.p. Mors driven in the race
by Gabriel. The other racing-car competition—Cramoisy's
Pipe and the Wolseleys of Austin and Smith-Cumming—does
not seem to have worried it, and Rolls did well to turn in a
time only $1\frac{1}{5}$ sec. slower than the Mercédès, while its speed
of 80·25 m.p.h. over the kilometre compares interestingly
with de Forest's 83 m.p.h. At the Castlewellan Hill-Climb,
Rolls came second behind another 'Sixty' Mercédès, driven
by Campbell Muir, but the stern could only be kept down by
setting the long-suffering Brabazon to balance himself on the
back tank, and hold on by rope. Like Crompton before him, he
found the Mors cooling arrangements irksome, especially
when he put his foot through the tank, and plunged into boiling
water. The winning Mercédès, incidentally, was none other
than Alfred Harmsworth's A.740, now on loan to the Montagu
Motor Museum, and my own mount in many a Brighton Run.

At Cork, Rolls took over the Panhard from Hacking for a
very gentlemanly match against my father's 22-h.p. Daimler.
No attempt was made to strip the cars, apart from the removal
of lamps and hoods, and the Daimler ran complete with two
horns, one of them a vast serpentine affair, in spite of which it
won. De Forest did not bother to compete for the *Cork Con-
stitution* Cup awarded for big racing cars, so Rolls had only to
cope with the Mercédès of Hutton and Higginbotham, and.
Austin's Wolseley, which it duly did, reversing the Phoenix
Park result. The Kerry Cup sprint, towards the end of the fortnight, attracted an even worse field, but de Forest was among
the competitors: in spite of which the older car managed to

win from scratch. One's respect for Rolls as a tuner is considerably enhanced.

Charles Rolls might be able to beat them on occasions, but now he preferred to join them, and his next appearances at a sprint meeting that October saw him at the wheel of de Forest's 1903 model Mors. In effect, the big racing car class at Southport was something of a Gordon Bennett reunion, for J. E. Hutton was running one of the French team's Panhards in place of his Mercédès, and Edge had the Napier he had driven in Ireland, while Lisle was at the wheel of the Star that had unsuccessfully contested the British Trials at Welbeck. As yet, the new Mors was not fully broken in, and suffered from fuel starvation. Not that Rolls was the only sufferer, for Edge was running on two cylinders most of the time, and the Panhard broke its throttle lever. Much burning of midnight oil in the Rolls camp failed to produce anything better than 62·44 m.p.h. 'It was quite pathetic', runs an eye-witness's report in the *Southport Visitor*, 'to see him hold up his hands in despair as he crossed the line'. Rolls even had the indignity of being defeated by the Star—a car scarcely capable of 50 m.p.h.—in the Mayor's Cup event for Unlimited Racing Cars.

Nothing daunted, he took the big Mors to Welbeck; in deplorable weather conditions he was lucky to find that the road was free of mud and despite a sticking inlet valve, he managed to record 84·68 m.p.h. Failing light prevented him from trying again once the car had found its form. The *Car Illustrated*—which referred to the machine confusingly as a 'specially constructed 110-h.p. Mors'—pointed out that it was now going faster than it ever had in de Forest's time, his best recorded speed in Ireland having been only 84·09 m.p.h. But while my father was correct in reminding his readers that this latest run was not a record, he was incorrect in ascribing the fastest official performance at that date to Augières, who had done 77·13 m.p.h. at Dourdan in November 1902. Already Duray had recorded 83·47 m.p.h. over the kilometre at Ostend in the redoubtable opposed-piston Gobron-Brillié. In Louis Rigolly's hands, incidentally, this machine was to attain nearly 95 m.p.h. at Nice in March 1904, and finally break through later in that year to the magic 'ton' with a speed of 103·55 m.p.h., by which time the Mors was too long in the tooth to be a serious contender, and in any case Rolls's thoughts were concentrated on the activities of a certain manufacturer of electric cranes in Cooke Street, Manchester.

1904 was a busy year for Rolls—with Panhards fading out of the picture in England, new agencies had to be negotiated for his motor business, while the Army Motor Volunteers also engaged a good deal of his time. C. S. Rolls and Co. involved themselves in a protracted lawsuit with Dr Rutherfoord Harris, M.P. Though he entered for the Ormonde–Daytona Speed Trials in Florida in January, he stayed in England. He ignored the Gordon Bennett Cup, and at the Bexhill Speed Trials he was content to serve as Chief Marshal. It was not until September that he reappeared in competition, running his Mors at the Portmarnock sprint in Ireland. He was promptly defeated in the first heat by Rawlinson on one of those big Weir-Darracqs which had enlivened the Gordon Bennett Eliminating Trials in the Isle of Man, and had spelt Nemesis for Alexandre Darracq's determined attempts to see his cars run under three flags at Homburg. This defeat was by no means as discreditable as the Darracqs' performance on earlier occasions would suggest, for they came to Douglas incomplete and unprepared, and once they had passed beyond the self-dismantling stage they were very fast. Rolls, however, was nettled and entered a protest on the legitimate, but rather petty ground that this match had not been held on the second day of the meeting, as per the published programme. His protest was allowed, but he was beaten in the final by Arthur Macdonald, driving the famous six-cylinder Napier L48; its first official appearance, though Edge had practised in it at Homburg.

At Blackpool the Mors—now described by *Motoring Illustrated* as a 1902 model!—competed against Rawlinson, Earp on the 80-h.p. Napier, one of the 1904 96-h.p. Gordon Bennett Wolseleys, and a 90-h.p. Mercédès. This was not a good day for Rolls, and the comment that the Mors was 'only less noisy than the Weir-Darracq' suggests that misfiring must have been the trouble. On his best run, he could not match Earp's performance, and his speed in the standing mile was a mere 57 m.p.h., as against the Darracq's 63·6 m.p.h., and the

62·2 m.p.h. recorded by the German car. One suspects that the Mercédès must also have been off form, for it was beaten by the Wolseley.

1905 was Rolls's last year as an independent driver, but even the rise of Rolls-Royce and his commitments on the new *marque's* behalf could not keep him out of the Gordon Bennett Cup. C. S. Rolls and Co. continued to support events at home. E. H. Arnott drove their entry of a 14-h.p. Minerva in the Scottish Reliability Trials in May, and there were entries of Orleans and Minerva (though not Rolls-Royce) at South Harting in June. At the Brighton Speed Trials in July he incurred the censure of *The Autocar* for entering seven cars under his own name, which the journal pointed out were strictly trade entries. In the circumstances, it was hardly fair that Rolls and other traders should go scot-free when the entrant of a F.I.A.T. had been disqualified because he had borrowed his car for the Trials. Of the cars sent down from Lillie Hall, the 30-h.p. six-cylinder Rolls-Royce was there solely to show the flag, but Orleans and Minerva touring cars competed seriously, a 14-h.p. example of the latter make being beaten in the £250–£300 class by the then unknown Louis Coatalen, driving Adams's 8–10-h.p. Humber. Claude Johnson competed in a special scratch contest for 15-h.p. Orleans cars— it speaks volumes for his public-relations ability that such a relatively obscure breed should have merited a 'one-make' event—but was defeated by W. H. Astell, who was also professionally connected with the Twickenham factory.

Charles Rolls's personal contribution to Brighton was the 150-h.p., 26·4 litre Dufaux from Switzerland. We shall hear more of the Dufaux when we come to consider the affairs of C. S. Rolls and Co. But for the time being let it be recorded that it was an even worse, and less excusable blunder than the 50-h.p. Napier of 1901. 'For all its infernal power', it achieved nothing, making only one complete run in the 1,000 kilogram class; its speed was a pathetic 49·24 m.p.h., in contrast with the victorious Earp's 90·87 m.p.h. on a Napier. Even the Rochet-Schneider, considered a slow car by the standards of the day, managed 64·98 m.p.h. 'Mr Dufaux' reported the *Morning Leader*, 'had a cold, or indigestion, or something mortally wrong inside. He came up the course making more noise than an infuriated Snark. He was firing like a Maxim gun, roaring like a bull, and covering himself and his driver with clouds of black smoke.' Evidently this automotive nightmare had been driven down from London, for it bore the registration number LC1504. It had already failed to appear at Filey Speed Trials, leaving Rolls to circulate the neighbourhood in quest of staider business with a six-cylinder Rolls-Royce. Though, as we shall see, Rolls continued to hedge his business bets for a few more months, he opted for confections less outlandish than those of Frédéric Dufaux.

But the big racing events of 1905 were, of course, the sixth Gordon Bennett Cup Race and the first Tourist Trophy. The latter is properly part of the story of the Rolls-Royce, and will be dealt with in that context. But the International Cup was now at the zenith of glamour and acrimony alike. The French were protesting over the unfairness of the regulations, the English were telling everyone that the French attitude was just not cricket, Frédéric Dufaux was protesting over the parsimonious attitude of his national Club, and when the contestants finally assembled at Clermont-Ferrand there were all the usual attempts to persuade the stewards that rival competitors were illicitly installing components of nationality other than their own. The Auvergnat peasants did not bother to protest: they simply made themselves tiresome in other ways.

This year, Britain had at least one really fast car, in the shape of the six-cylinder Napier, but it was to Wolseley, rather than to Napier, that Rolls turned. We may only conjecture why, but Cecil Bianchi is of the opinion that Herbert Austin approached Rolls on the advice of Charles Jarrott. The intermediary may well, however, have been Harvey Du Cros, Junior, who held the Panhard concession for England, and would thus have had business dealings with Rolls during the first years of the latter's business career. Du Cros was, of course, to be closely associated with Austin's own car-manufacturing venture, founded late in 1905 after his resignation from Wolseley. Austin certainly would have welcomed Rolls's support, for his own relations with his directors were strained by his obstinate adherence to the horizontal engine: already

Wolseley were not only launching a series of vertical-engined cars designed by J. D. Siddeley, but, worse still, an example of Siddeley's work had been entered for the British Eliminating Trials by Lionel de Rothschild; and in the Isle of Man the preparation of this car was to be entrusted to Siddeley, and not to Austin. The two remaining Wolseley contenders were, however, the same old 96-h.p. 'Beetles' that had run in 1904, though they had somehow lost six (nominal) b.h.p. in the course of development.

In any case, the Eliminating Trials in the Isle of Man were not only good practice for the forthcoming Tourist Trophy to be run over the same circuit, they were also good publicity for C. S. Rolls and Co. The astute Johnson had loaned a 20-h.p. Rolls-Royce to the A.C.G.B.I. for official duties, and the *Car Illustrated*'s staff were as appreciative of this gesture as they were of the spectacle of the Napiers, Wolseleys, Stars and Guinness's solitary Weir (née Weir-Darracq) contending for the right to wear the green. Rolls and Johnson, though they did not know it, had made an important conversion, since a year later my father, hitherto a dedicated Daimler owner, took delivery of his first Rolls-Royce, a 'Light Twenty' with *roi des belges* bodywork. According to family legend, it was by no means all we have come to expect of a Rolls-Royce, but it served its purpose, and up to his death in 1929 my father never owned any other make—except as a second car.

The story of the Eliminating Trials has been told in full in my previous book, *The Gordon Bennett Cup Races*. Suffice it to say that crashes eliminated the strong challenge of Macdonald's six-cylinder Napier and Girling's Wolseley-built Siddeley, while mechanical disorders disposed of Cecil Edge's hoary old 1903 Napier, Hargreaves on the Acton firm's only new car, and Guinness on the rebuilt Darracq. The two Mercédès-like Stars of the Goodwin brothers were never in the picture, which left the slow, but reliable old-school Wolseleys to fight it out with W. T. Clifford Earp's 1904 100-h.p. Napier. In fact, only Earp and Bianchi completed the full six rounds, and there were some complaints when the A.C.G.B.I. decided to give second place to Rolls rather than to his teammate. Nobody, however, was in a position to argue, since the

Club adopted their usual obscurantist attitude to these Trials, and did not publish detailed results until September, which time the Gordon Bennett was dead, and nearly buried.

But Rolls certainly had his share of troubles: two dogs had gone to the Happier Hunting Ground, the low-tension wires had parted from the commutator when the car hit a bump, and the spare tyre had made violent contact with the pressure pipe. As a replacement piece of rubber tubing of correct length could not be found, Rolls was obliged to reduce speed. To cap everything, the over-zealous constabulary had tried to stop all the competitors when Cecil Edge was in trouble on the mountain section of the course, and Rolls had been the principal sufferer, as is shown by the fact that his fourth lap was 12 m.p.h. slower than Bianchi's, and 14 m.p.h. slower than Earp's 49·5 m.p.h. As Rolls was appreciably faster than Bianchi in the timed hill-climb, however, the Club's decision was perhaps not as unfair as it sounds.

But the Wolseleys had little chance in the race proper against the Brasiers of Théry and Caillois, and the formidable Mercédès team spearheaded by Jenatzy. There were also three dark horses in the shape of the Italian F.I.A.T.s to be driven by Lancia, Cagno and Nazzaro. While the Wolseleys lacked speed, the Napier was handicapped on a mountainous course by its two-speed gearbox.

None the less, Rolls tackled the job with determination, as is confirmed both by H. J. Swindley and Massac Buist, who accompanied him during his practice circuits. These were conducted both on the big 'Beetle' and on a 20-h.p. touring car. To quote Buist:

> Many times he would stop the car, shift the broken branch of a tree, and set it up at a point on a curving gradient, which was to be a sign to him on the day of the race precisely where he was to change into a certain gear—provided a peasant passing meantime had not thought the tree likely fuel for the winter.

The expertise with which Rolls coaxed the Wolseley over a course blessed with 177 major corners left a deep impression on Swindley, who ended his report in *The Autocar*: 'The recollection of this trip will be long in fading from my mind, but that which will remain still longer is the cool, adroit, and masterly handling of the car.'

Rolls himself confessed that he would have been 'glad of more power', and complained that he had only been able to make twenty circuits before the race.

On the day of the race, the Wolseley pit crew sent the car off with too high a pressure in the tyres, and after a lap of distinctly skittish handling, Rolls found it expedient to let some air out. Dirty French oil (the lubricant sent out from England failed to arrive in time) clogged the lubricators, so that he had to stop on the third round and clean the system out. The off-side rear tyre blew some distance from the Pontgibaud depot, and Rolls limped in on the rim. The driving-seat broke up, and the car finished with the driver supporting himself on the steering wheel and brake lever. At the end, he was over an hour behind the winner, Théry's Brasier, but his eighth place was the best that Britain could manage, and an average speed of 40·4 m.p.h. was no mean feat anyway on one of the most difficult courses yet encountered in the history of motor racing. In any case, Wolseley had had the last laugh, which must have delighted Austin, after enduring so many of Edge's jibes against his cars.

Thus Rolls's swan-song in the *grandes épreuves* of the heroic age of motor racing proved worthy of his reputation.

But since 1902 he had been devoting more and more of his time to the sale of motor-cars on a commercial scale, and it is now time to trace the story of C. S. Rolls and Co. up to Rolls's meeting with Royce.

CHAPTER FIVE

An Etonian in Fulham

Do not purchase imitations of Panhards when we can supply Panhards at low prices.
C. S. Rolls and Co. advertisement, March 1904

C. S. Rolls and Co. have had practical experience for many years with all the leading makes of cars. Until recently they have specialized in Panhards which, in their opinion, were among the best and most reliable on the market.
C. S. Rolls and Co. catalogue, 1905

In January 1902 Charles Rolls went into business as an automobile agent with premises at Lillie Hall, Fulham.

Though this may seem a remarkable departure for the son of a peer in those days, it was, like all Rolls's activities, an entirely logical step in his self-appointed mission to convert Britain to the motor-car. He also needed a livelihood in order to support his personal motoring and ballooning programme. Neither sport was exactly cheap; an annual mileage of 6,000 on such a vehicle as a 20-h.p. Panhard could land its owner with a tyre bill in the region of £200, while the incidental expenses of a single balloon ascent could add up to £6, including gas, inflation, and the hire of helpers at start and finish. Rolls's basic allowance was £500 a year, and while this was amply sufficient to enable him to live the life of a gentleman of leisure in either Monmouth or London, it could not support his experiments in transportation.

Nor, incidentally, was Rolls the only Old Etonian in the trade, for Claude Watney, a contemporary of my father's, was also selling Panhards and Mercédès from showrooms in Wardour Street. None the less, the *Car Illustrated* found the fact worthy of comment in June 1903, when my father observed:

Both these young men, with no need, so far as money is concerned, to work, are throwing themselves heart and soul into the business of this great automobile movement. Both of them were at Eton with me, and several other old Etonians are also interested in the motor trade in one way and another.

Not that the motor trade was necessarily taboo for a young man of Rolls's upbringing in 1902, and entry into it was not comparable with such a situation as would confront a duke's daughter were she to join the chorus at a suburban music-hall. Engineering, after all, was more than respectable, and a training in the railway workshops was an eminently suitable background to a gentleman's career, in the same way as an apprenticeship with one of the leading motor-car manufacturers would be today. My father passed from Oxford to the London and South Western Railway's shops at Nine Elms, and was later able to put his knowledge to good effect in the General Strike of 1926. In a slightly later generation, such distinguished designers as W. O. Bentley and H. F. S. Morgan had a background of locomotive engineering. Further, to a young man anxious to make his living in the infant motor industry, the sales side was a better proposition at a time when imported cars far outnumbered the domestic product, and Britain's manufacturers were operating on too small a scale to venture into serious apprentice-training schemes.

One would also be guilty of judging the events of 1902 by the standards of the 1960s were one to suggest that there was anything disreputable about second-hand cars at this time. In an affluent society, the ownership of a second-hand vehicle suggests the antithesis of Jonesmanship—as one social commentator has put it, 'the world of the cheap edition'. The dealer has become a caricature, and unjustly so. True, the car-coper pure and simple is almost as old as the wares he cries: in 1896, Rolls was telling his father of an acquaintance who was already making a good living out of used cars, and in the Williamsons' classic novel, *The Lightning Conductor*, published only a few months after Charles went into business, there is a delectable portrait of one of these unscrupulous gentry—surely the prototype of those 'Yiddisher Guardsmen' who cashed in on the car shortages of 1920 and 1946 with their sawdust-packed back axles, and wooden pistons.

Nor is the used car, even now, inherently a sign of the

disreputable or the world of the second-rate. Within that ridiculous stratum of society created by those who persist in Keeping Up With The Joneses, there are still those who prefer a five-year-old thoroughbred to the latest product of the presswork industry, and are unworried by the presence of names other than their own in the registration book. The Edwardians cared not a whit for the Jones taste in motor-cars, and had no inhibitions whatever about buying second-hand. Phil Paddon, later known as a Rolls-Royce specialist, did a flourishing trade in high-class used machinery with an illustrious clientele; and many discriminating motorists bought their cars second-hand, especially the Continental models. Import duties were low, and many of the bigger and more covetable sporting types were not listed by their English concessionaires. Rolls-Royce certainly sold cars second-hand to customers who might have been expected to buy new. Sir Oswald Mosley, Bart. (father of the Fascist leader), bought a 'Thirty' second-hand, while Sir Gerald Du Maurier, the celebrated actor, was the third owner of his 'Twenty'. Even Lord Llangattock's first six-cylinder Rolls-Royce, a 'Thirty' supplied by his son, had originally belonged to a Mr Furber.

Rolls's garage in the pre-Rolls-Royce days was a relatively small enterprise, despite its excellent reputation. A man of Charles's standing within the motoring fraternity could be assured of maximum publicity from the trade press: while as Lord Llangattock's son he could also bank on support from the Society papers. There was also, of course, a vein of hostile publicity inspired by the anti-motorists, and hysterical followers of the creed that fast driving is the one unforgivable crime. Dame Grundy has always nursed a prejudice against fast cars, as witness her practice of naming the make of car in court cases which involve sporting machinery (and seldom on other occasions) and the ludicrous outburst of mass indignation that attended the high-speed testing of the Le Mans A.C. 'Cobras' on M1 in 1964. Rolls had always been a butt for such journalism, as witness the strictures on his performance in the Thousand Miles' Trial, while the Motor Volunteers, as we have seen, had been maliciously laughed off as a party of young bloods amusing themselves at the expense of His Majesty's

Government. C. S. Rolls and Co. was, as we shall see, a remarkably progressive organization for its time, but up to 1904, when Rolls took Claude Johnson into partnership, it was somewhat of a one-man band, with no co-directors. To the end of its days, in December 1906, it never acquired the status of a limited liability company, and in fact the financial administration during the latter part of the 'Rolls-Royce period' was in the hands of a holding company going by the name of the Rolls-Royce Distributing Co. Ltd.

The Fulham venture was, of course, financed by Lord Llangattock. Charles, after all, had no source of earned income apart from the odd prize money his racing might bring in—and in this respect, as we have seen, both 1900 and 1901 had been barren years—plus the odd few guineas he might pick up from motoring articles. But with the exception of a short period of writing for *The Throne* in 1908, he was never a regular motoring correspondent. The series he contributed to the *Daily Mail* on topics of aviation in 1908 and 1909 did not involve a regular contract. As to books, his sole efforts in that direction were his piece on motor vehicles in the 1903 edition of the *Encyclopaedia Britannica* (which, incidentally, the *Automotor Journal* damned with faint praise), and the delectable *Caprices of the Petrol Motor* which he wrote for the Badminton series. And, in any case, authorship is seldom a lucrative pastime!

I have, perhaps, stressed the family trait of parsimony in the Rolls family in so far as it helped to accentuate Charles's loneliness. But it did not manifest itself in Lord Llangattock, where his son's professional future was concerned. Throughout, he showed both generosity and foresight. A note in the family papers dated November 1905, reveals that an initial payment of £6,500 was made to launch the motor business in Fulham, and this was to be deducted from the legacy of £20,000 which was to come to Charles immediately upon his father's death. But in the meantime it had been found necessary to raise another £11,000—West End showrooms were expensive, and by this time C. S. Rolls and Co. had premises both in Conduit Street and Brook Street—plus a £10,000 bank guarantee. Had his father died while this huge loan was still outstanding, not only Charles, but quite possibly the future of the young Rolls-Royce business would have been jeopardized, so Lord Llangattock thoughtfully arranged that repayment of the £21,000 would not fall due until his wife's death, when Charles would receive a final legacy of £50,000. While he kept a watchful eye on his son's financial affairs, he never refused help if he felt it were needed, though we can see in the abandonment of a plan to open West End premises in Down Street as early as July 1902, a hint of paternal caution. In fact, the company's first Mayfair showrooms at No. 28 Brook Street were not opened until December 1903.

Yet even with the strong backing that Charles could command, the finances of C. S. Rolls and Co. were not always secure. In April 1903 he writes to his solicitor admitting that he is running too big an overdraft: 'It is due to Panhard having lately delivered my cars in big batches of 4 or 6 at a time which does not give me a chance to dispose of them, and has necessitated a large outlay to meet the amounts due on each car.'

He goes on in more cheerful vein which indicates the extent of the business he had built up in little more than a twelvemonth. There were outstanding orders on hand for nine Panhards, total retail value £4,409, plus a verbal order for another 15-h.p. car, 'value £885, which I haven't counted'.

Charles was already finding a new *métier* as demonstrator and salesman. It has been pointed out, with more than an element of truth, that his abilities in this direction went little further, and that the Rolls-Royce image was solely the creation of Claude Johnson. To Rolls, selling the car was the job in hand: had it been suggested to him that something should be done to render his showroom more congenial to his lady clients, he would have sent out to an ironmonger's for a seven-and-sixpenny mirror, whereas it is to Johnson that we owe the dignified aura, untrammelled by commercialism, that is No. 15 Conduit Street today. But it should be remembered that for two whole seasons—1902 and 1903—there was no Claude Johnson on the staff, yet the company's reputation grew to the point that Rolls could claim, in a 1904 advertisement, that he had 'the best motor workshops in London', and also win the official approval of the Automobile Club de France. The lawsuit between Rolls and Dr Rutherfoord Harris in 1904 revealed a more than slightly casual attitude towards customers' cars that Johnson would never have tolerated, but then the idea of a combined policy of sales and service was scarcely understood in 1902, when well-to-do owners installed screw-cutting lathes in their motor-houses, so as to be able to make those spare parts that the agent or concessionaire could not or would not supply.

From earliest days there had been emporia selling anything that could be unloaded on gullible purchasers without fear of infringement suits, but service facilities were apt to be limited to a cramped yard behind the potted palms, where mechanics of dubious qualifications ministered, sometimes by trial-and-error methods, to the plaints of customers. Often the best mechanics, in the case of imported cars, came direct from the factory and thus had but a limited command of English. Direct factory branches were rare, and were to be a development of future years. Panhard, though their affairs in England were in the capable hands of Harvey Du Cros, Junior, did not open a branch over here until 1904. Judged by the standards of the time, the facilities installed in the former skating-rink at Lillie Hall, Fulham, near the site of Imre Kiralfy's famous Big Wheel and the present Earls Court Exhibition Hall, were on a grand scale. This part of Fulham, incidentally, had a peculiar appeal for car manufacturers. Not far away from Lillie Hall were the workshops of the Roadway Autocar Co., the Mors concessionaires, a juxtaposition which may have given rise to the oft-repeated assertion that Rolls sold this make as well as racing it. Rolls-Royce Ltd. used Lillie Hall itself as a service station for some years after the absorption of C. S. Rolls and Co. Renault's English headquarters were close at hand until their removal to Acton in the 1930s; in the 1920s and 1930s Hispano-Suiza of Bois-Colombes maintained a depot in nearby Rickett Street; and Rovers are still in Seagrave Road.

In October 1902 the *Automotor Journal* inspected the works, which occupied an area of 30,000 square feet, and had space for 200 cars: an important factor in an era when cars could not readily be parked in the street, for reasons both of cold starting and the hazard to valuable brassware, and when many high-class terrace houses lacked a convenient mews behind, with stables that could be converted into motor-houses. The paper praised Rolls for planning his business on 'a thoroughly broad basis', and already, in addition to regular repair work, the firm was training and supplying drivers, charging batteries for electric cars, and hiring cars out (with chauffeurs, of course); only Panhards were used for this purpose. (There seems to have been some rather unofficial self-drive hire, as we shall see, but only to personal friends of the principal!) The only agency held was for Panhard. With a humorous touch typical of Rolls, the firm's telegraphic address was 'Sideslip'. J. E. Hutton, be it said, went one better, and telegraphic communications were addressed to him at 'Horselaugh, London'!

Mr Clough Williams-Ellis, owner of the Portmeirion Estate in Wales, recalls that a friend of his, then an undergraduate at Oxford, once found Charles's hire service a very present help in trouble. While on an unauthorized visit to London, he was unfortunate enough to encounter his tutor in Piccadilly. He kept his composure, and strode past the don without a flicker of recognition. There were several hours to wait before the next express from Paddington, and a motor-car seemed the only hope. He duly repaired to Brook Street, whence he departed shortly afterwards in a Panhard driven by one of Rolls's chauffeurs. Safely arrived in Oxford, he paid off his driver, and was able to face that evening's tutorial with equanimity.

In June 1903 Rolls sought to drum up business by staging an Open Day, to enable his customers to see the works, the equipment of which now included some recently installed electrically-driven machine tools of American origin. Both his Paris–Vienna Mors and a Panhard that had run in Paris–Rouen in 1894 were on show; for the competition-minded there was a 'cinematograph film' of Paris–Madrid, hot from the developing-room, while 'for those less seriously inclined' Rolls had provided light refreshments to the accompaniment of a Viennese band. Such extravagance on his part suggests that he was optimistic of the outcome of this press party!

Even then, the sale of accessories was a lucrative sideline, and though he could not hope to compete with Dunhill's

Motorities, who supplied 'everything but the motor', or Gamages, who were prepared to throw in the motor as well, he did market a useful little chemical fire-extinguisher and an engaging 'spark jumper'. In 1905 he made a brief excursion into lunacy by taking on the sale and promotion of one of those curious spring-wheels with which Edwardian inventors sought to consign the pneumatic tyre to limbo. (Their spiritual successors a decade later were preoccupied with devices intended to oust the poppet-valve.) This one was the brainchild of Clifford Hallé, son of the famous conductor, and Rolls submitted it to a 4,000-mile Automobile Club trial in October. The results were hardly encouraging. Not only had these contraptions to be lubricated twice daily, but one of the rear ones failed at 1,501 miles, and its replacement needed 'a new rim, tyre, and spokes' only 1,362 miles later. The other rear wheel, admittedly, lasted just over 3,000 miles, but *The Autocar* remarked sarcastically: 'The test was for reliability alone. The comfort of the wheel is not mentioned.' Rolls apparently regretted that he had allowed his name to be associated with this curiosity, as well he might.

According to Harry Fleck, who was working at Lillie Hall in the early days, insurance repair work 'practically kept us going', and St. John Nixon, who was in the insurance business, remembers taking a lot of work to E. T. Arnott, the manager there, in 1906. This indicates that Lillie Hall, unlike the sales department, did not immediately concentrate on Rolls-Royce to the exclusion of other makes when the firm's Orleans and Minerva agencies were dropped. In 1903 a Panhard chassis was fitted up as a breakdown truck: there was no crane, and ropes were slung under the dumb-irons of cars that could not be towed on their four wheels. In the same year Rolls published an instruction book for the Krebs carburettor fitted to Panhard cars: as yet handbooks were the exception rather than the rule, though F. W. Lanchester had already issued—in 1901—excellent 'descriptive', 'driving', and workshop manuals for his productions. 1905 saw the creation of a department 'to advise on the fitting up of private garages', in which we can detect the influence of Claude Johnson. But perhaps the most startling step taken by C. S. Rolls and Co. was announced in May 1903, when the world was informed that new Panhards could be bought on hire-purchase. The terms were to be 25 per cent down, the balance to be paid in four quarterly payments—no nonsense such as 'easy terms spread over three years'. Five per cent interest was charged. The fact of hire purchase is not, perhaps, surprising: but that *The Autocar* should give publicity to such an announcement at a time when sordid questions of money were taboo speaks volumes for Rolls's persuasiveness.

Rolls did all the demonstrating himself. His quickness of wit could match his skill behind the wheel on occasions, and this stood him in good stead when showing off the paces of a Panhard to a lady customer. Approaching St. Giles' Circus from Tottenham Court Road, he became aware that the police-man on point duty had suddenly shot up his hand. On a wet asphalt surface, Rolls had only one course open to him. He jammed on the transmission brake, whereupon the car turned right round. Rolls checked the skid, and motored smartly back the way he had come. 'See', he remarked casually to his fair passenger, 'these cars are so handy you can turn them on a sixpence.'

Shows must have been expensive as well as arduous. The Great Show Question was as yet unsolved—it was not until the first Olympia Motor Exhibition in February 1905 that this venue, sponsored by the Society of Motor Manufacturers and Traders, became 'the London Show'; and Rolls, though he became a signatory to the Show Bond, under which manu-facturers and agents undertook to support only one official function per annum, soon backed out when he found that the dice were loaded against older firms with a longer record as bondholders. For a while he rented stands at both the Crystal Palace and the Agricultural Hall, the latter being the scene of his first display. On this occasion only one of his exhibits—a Panhard *tonneau*—was for sale, the remaining space being occupied by a Mulliner-bodied 40-h.p. Panhard lent by his ballooning friend Leslie Bucknall, and that faithful old work-horse, the Paris–Berlin Mors. The Crystal Palace Show in 1903 was a preview of his Open Day, with both the 1902 racing Mors and the 1894 Panhard on exhibition, and it was not until the Islington display two months later that the Rolls stand contained only new cars. By 1904 he was showing no fewer than six vehicles, all Panhards, and was proudly telling visitors that all of them were already sold. This exhibition, incidentally, marked the début of the 8–10-h.p. three-cylinder model, a vehicle for which he had a peculiar affection. Maybe this was because by this time his company was making a speciality of 'doctor's single landaulettes', a style of town carriage to which this type of Panhard lent itself.

Apart from his occasional balloon ascents, and outings with the Motor Volunteers, the activities of Lillie Hall kept him fully employed, and out of racing, in 1904. He flirted briefly the following year with an ephemeral organization known as the British Empire Motor Trade Alliance, which claimed that it was not in any way competitive with the S.M.M.T., and attracted support from such personalities as Jarrott, Edge, Instone, and Austin. As its objects consisted of 'discussing how the interests of British motor builders may best be served', it is hard to comprehend what qualities it possessed which were lacking in the senior association. Mere talk never appealed to Rolls, and his membership lasted but a few months.

He experienced no difficulty in attracting illustrious clients, and his consistent use of the motor-car for his weekend visits enabled him to combine business with pleasure, though at this stage in his career they amounted to the same thing! He sold Lord Rosebery a 10-h.p. Panhard in January 1903, as a coming-of-age present for his son, Lord Dalmeny. The following month he was demonstrating another Panhard to the Crown Prince of Rumania, and was rewarded with an order, while other customers that year included Lord Willoughby de Eresby, Lady Beatrice Rawson, Vice-President of the Ladies' Automobile Club, and the Duke of Sutherland. A 1905 list of patrons published in an early Rolls-Royce catalogue (though clearly covering pre-Rolls-Royce days), proudly recorded four members of foreign princely houses, two dukes, two earls, a viscount, seven British barons, two foreign barons (De Zuylen, the President of the A.C.F., and de Forest, the wealthy Austro-Hungarian who had been his rival in the Irish Fortnight), three baronets, and two High Court judges. To this score was to be added during 1905 a very illustrious name in motoring circles, the wife of that great pioneer the Hon. Evelyn Ellis, who had brought a Panhard to England in 1895. She bought a 10-h.p. Rolls-Royce.

And also, of course, there was Lord Llangattock. That 'model of a motoring peer' had taken the plunge, and in March 1903 Charles wrote to him:

> Are you likely to be in Town soon? We have got a *tonneau* body within a short time of being ready to put on your chassis, in place of the present body, but before taking delivery of the latter, I would rather have liked you to see it, for although you have to open the front seat to get through to the back, you have more room in the back and more comfort once you are there, for there is no door like in the *tonneau*, and you are facing quite forward.

This delectable piece of confusion by science presumably refers to the 15-h.p. Panhard His Lordship was running in January 1904, rather than to its stable-mate, a formidable eight-seater omnibus on the 24-h.p. chassis.

More usually, however, the son's advice was briefer and more to the point, and in January 1908 Lord Llangattock is treated to a lesson in the wording of a classified advertisement. At the time, he was contemplating the sale of his 20-h.p. Rolls-Royce, and Charles writes:

> I would also recommend your advertising it for two or three weeks in the *Car* and *The Autocar*, offering to send photograph, also offering to give a trial to anyone, and would give as a reason for selling that you are buying a six-cylinder car of the same make.

There were hazards even in the sale of horseless carriages, as witness the lawsuit brought by Rolls against Dr Rutherfoord Harris, M.P. in 1904 for the recovery of £1,500 owed on a 20-h.p. Panhard which Rolls had sold the doctor, taking his 7-h.p. car in part exchange.

Rolls's case was that on completion Harris had found fault with the car and refused delivery. Charles Jarrott had been called into consultation as an independent expert, but had found nothing amiss, whereupon Dr Harris had sought a second opinion from a Mr Harrison. This time the car was adjudged to be sub-standard, and Rolls agreed to carry out another £40-worth of work. As if this were not enough, Dr Harris now decided on a new style of body, so a new contract was drawn up. When the customer changed his mind on the coach-work a third time, Rolls put his foot down, and was answered with a letter repudiating the contract of sale unless the car was completed by a specified date.

Harris maintained that the car had been raced without his permission—in fact Mayhew had driven it on Rolls's account at the Bexhill Speed Trials. Rolls admitted this in the witness-box, but denied that he had ever told Harris the Panhard was new; further admissions extracted from him revealed that it had been used to drive Santos-Dumont from London to Aldershot on the occasion of the famous aeronaut's visit to England, and that it had also been hired for a day to Lionel De Rothschild, who had been charged £9 for the pleasure. During Rolls's cross-examination by Mr Rufus Isaacs, K.C., we come across the following passage, which merits quotation in full. Mr Isaacs was investigating Mayhew's exploits at Bexhill.

ISAACS: What did he win?
ROLLS: Something.
ISAACS: Was it a race?
ROLLS: Well, it was not racing like they call it on the Continent.
ISAACS: No, no, it is not a race on the Continent, it is a holocaust.

It is hard to know where one's sympathies should lie. Harris was clearly an irritating client, but using a customer's car in a sprint without his knowledge or permission is not likely to inspire confidence. The court clearly felt the same way, for they allowed Rolls to keep the car—by now a victim of sub-stantial depreciation, no doubt—but let Harris off with a payment of £600 instead of the £1,500 the plaintiff had claimed. Each had to pay his own costs.

Initially, Louis de Silva, whom we have met driving Rolls's cars in sprints, was works manager, but he left to join Osborn and Lord, who were the importers of Grégoire cars. Both Osborn and Lord, incidentally, were also former Rolls employees. Later the workshops were in the care of E. T. Arnott; this made for a confusing situation, for his brother Ernest worked at the West End showrooms, where he looked after Minerva sales. Johnson solved the problem by christening Ernest 'Are-Nott', and E. T. 'Were-Nott'.

Panhards were the staple of the company until the latter part of 1904; in fact C. S. Rolls and Co. were still selling a few as late as mid-1905, but in the meantime circumstances had forced them to look elsewhere. Rolls might assure his solicitor in the spring of 1903 that the latest Panhards were a great improvement on their predecessors, and that the new engines would run up to 1,800 r.p.m.; he went as far as to add that 'the Panhard does what the Mercédès does, and more, at about half the price'. This was true, for the 15-h.p. Panhard sold at approximately £560, by comparison with the £1,100 asked for an 18–22-h.p. Mercédès. Further, Panhard's smaller models came into a sector of the market untouched by the German firm. But even in 1903, there was a noticeable drop in sales, and when, a year later, Panhard lowered their prices, Rolls was left with more than a dozen chassis on his hands. Fortunately, they were chassis and not complete cars, and he was able to recoup some of his losses by increasing the prices of the bodies he was fitting to them. The plain fact was that Panhard was no longer the premier *marque*. The writing on the wall had been there to see in 1902, and the Mercédès victory at Athy had clinched matters. Even if Mercédès had failed to distinguish themselves in Paris–Madrid—in fact the best Panhard, de Crawhez', finished fourth, ahead of J. B. Warden on the best Mercédès— the victory had gone to Mors. Even Rolls's favourite, the three-cylinder 8–10-h.p., was hard to sell.

Thus a second line of defence was indicated. At the end of 1903 Rolls was toying with the idea of marketing a 6-h.p. light car to sell for £150. Reports in the daily press suggested that this would be capable of 100 m.p.g.—a claim we need not take seriously—but the *Motor* went so far as to publish a brief description. This one does not seem to have progressed beyond the drawing-board, nor is it clear whose drawing-board was involved. Rolls and Johnson also negotiated for the selling rights of an electric brougham. In view of the limited appeal of this class of vehicle, it is as well for all concerned that in the meantime Henry Edmunds had introduced Rolls to Royce. Henry Royce was never interested in anything he had not designed himself, and specifically he saw no future in electric cars; even if in early years he had supplied a motor for use in a Pritchetts and Gold electric carriage.

This historic meeting, of course, took place in May 1904 and its implications will form the subject of a subsequent chapter. The advent of Royce had furnished Rolls with a long-term solution for his problems, but there was still a gap to be filled. Even at the end of that year, the new make from Manchester existed mainly on paper. Rolls might be publicizing four models, from the 10-h.p. 'twin' to the 30-h.p. six-cylinder, but the only cars in existence were the three prototype Royces, and perhaps two of the 10-h.p. cars. However good Henry Royce's designs might prove to be (and Rolls, certainly, had no doubts on this point from the start), the volume of sales yielded by them could not, on their own, possibly match the potential number of Panhards that Rolls might unload in a good year. And there were very few Rolls-Royces before the advent of the 40–50-h.p. car at the 1906 Olympia Show. True, total production of the earlier types added up to an impressive 102 units, but some of the later 'Twenties' and 'Thirties' were not delivered until 1907 or even 1908. That Rolls himself was proceeding with caution is shown by the text of his statement when he resigned from the British Empire Motor Trades Alliance in May 1905. 'I consider', he wrote, 'that my trade interest at the present moment does not justify my continuing as a member, but I hope at a later date to increase my British interests sufficiently to rejoin and become an active member.'

So other agencies had to be sought. One suspects that the Whitlock-Aster and the Serpollet, which Harry Fleck recalls from his days at Lillie Hall, were handled only in very small numbers. Not so the Minerva, a medium-priced Belgian car for which Rolls acquired the agency in November 1904. In those days, these products of Antwerp were a long way from their zenith, and nobody, least of all Rolls, would have suspected that one day they would be among the small *élite* of makes that could be mentioned in the same breath as the products of Derby. Sylvain de Jong has started very humbly with the manufacture of motorcycles and motorcycle engines, followed by a spidery single-cylinder *voiturette* known as the 'Minervette'. These were still being made in 1904, but Rolls was content to leave their representation in the hands of Minerva Motors Ltd., then under the management of David Citroën, a relative of the famous André. He did, however, contract for the sale of the English market's entire quota of two models, a 10-h.p. 'twin' and a four-cylinder 14-h.p. which sold complete for £285. Minerva affairs were kept separate from the Rolls-Royce business, and were the responsibility of E. H. Arnott. He drove a 14-h.p. with overdrive top gear in the 1905 T.T., but retired with ignition trouble at the end of the first lap.

In the meanwhile Claude Johnson had made arrangements with W. H. Astell, the Orleans company's managing director, to distribute their 15-h.p. four-cylinder car. By now the Orleans had shaken off its Vivinus ancestry, and was a straightforward machine which Harry Fleck recalls as 'a nice, ladylike car'. It sold for £500, and Johnson promptly organized a competitive demonstration of the 1905 model against an older Orleans and a 15-h.p. Panhard. On the climb to Hindhead on the Portsmouth Road, the contemporary Twickenham product, driven by Astell, managed 25·75 m.p.h., the 1904 Orleans 24·35 m.p.h., and the Panhard a staid 20·27 m.p.h. The age of this last-mentioned machine is nowhere specified; we are only told that it weighed a good hundredweight more than the Orleans which had supplanted it in the showrooms at Brook Street. Johnson's publicity was always masterly, and when he issued a challenge to other makers, it was so couched as to deter acceptance. Thus Rolls could face 1905 with an impressive range of cars, suiting every pocket from the 10-h.p. Minerva at £200 to the 30-h.p. Rolls-Royce at £890, albeit deliveries of this costly carriage were not to start for some months to come. Only Rolls-Royce and Minerva featured on the company's stand at Olympia in February 1905.

As Harry Fleck tells us, Rolls handled the French side of the business himself, making regular visits to the Paris Salon, held in those days just before Christmas. In May 1905 however, he also visited the Geneva Show, which in pre-1914 years was an unimportant affair, and of purely national interest: not the great international market-place it now is. Shortly afterwards the British motoring press published photographs of him at the wheel of the 100-h.p. straight-eight Dufaux racer, and it became apparent that he proposed adding a fourth string to his bow.

The Dufaux enjoyed the unhappy reputation of a professional non-starter. In 1904 it had arrived at the weigh-in for the Gordon Bennett Cup Race at Homburg, resplendent in the Swiss racing colours of red and yellow, only to be withdrawn with a broken wheel. In 1905 the solitary eight-cylinder car had been joined not only by a similar machine, but also by a gargantuan 'four' said to develop 150 b.h.p.: but this time the whole team had non-started owing to a dispute between the sponsor and the Swiss Automobile Club. However, the straight-eight made a great impression on Rolls, and he opened negotiations with Frédéric Dufaux for an agency in England. He also proposed to enter the big Swiss car in sprints, as a replacement for the now elderly 100-h.p. Mors.

Unfortunately he got, not the straight-eight, but the fearsome 26·4-litre four-cylinder device that was to have been the mainstay of the Swiss effort at Clermont-Ferrand. It had four separate cylinders of 225-mm. bore and 166-mm. stroke, no radiator in the accepted sense, and no starting handle at all, while the carburettor air intake was six inches from the ground. Neither Cyril Durlacher nor Harry Fleck, who had to work on it, recalls the monster with any affection. 'The example we had', Fleck says, 'was a weird-looking job. . . . Things were always going haywire, the cooling system was copper pipes in festoons brazed into the copper jackets on each cylinder head. The pipes came adrift, and the water was lost; and the flywheel and clutch cone seemed to be the receptacle for any stray nut or bolt which shook off; and bits got embedded in the clutch fabric, and she screamed to a standstill.' It was also Fleck's job to tow-start this alarming device behind a Panhard—though the Dufaux was allegedly built in conformity with the 1,000 kilogram Formula, it weighed more than its tug, and Fleck remembers being butted in the stern on several occasions.

It appeared once only in England: at the Brighton Speed Trials in July 1905, where, as we have seen, it was the laughing-stock of the meeting. Rolls sent it back to Switzerland, allegedly for 'adjustments', but he had had enough of Frédéric Dufaux's masterpiece. Interestingly enough, when South Lodge was cleared out after the death of Lady Shelley-Rolls, a number of patterns relating to this engine were unearthed, giving rise to the suggestion that Charles himself might have been the designer. I think this unlikely in the extreme: the most probable explanation is that the Dufaux*, as we are told, had to be completed on the boat *en route* for England, and that Rolls had possessed himself of the patterns as an insurance against any missing or improperly assembled parts.

But Rolls's visit was to have further repercussions. On 25 November, 1905, readers of *The Autocar* noted an announcement to the effect that C. S. Rolls and Co. would in future concentrate their entire effort on the promotion of the Rolls-Royce car. All orders on hand for the 1906 Minerva models would be taken over by Minerva Motors Limited. No mention was made of the Orleans, which leads one to suppose that this had never been a major seller. But while plans were going ahead for this change-over, *Motor Transport* was publishing an illustrated description of the new 'Rolls' commercial vehicles, made in 30-cwt and four-ton forms, and also suitable

---

* Since going to press, I have had access to the Dufaux papers, which indicate that Rolls gave a trial order for five cars and an omnibus chassis on 4 May 1905, guaranteeing orders to the tune of 750,000 Swiss francs if these gave satisfaction. On 8 June Dufaux was reporting that Rolls had told him that he was giving up the Panhard agency, and would in future handle only Minerva, Rolls-Royce and the Dufaux vehicles. Two cars and the 'bus should have been shipped in August, but the bodywork of the former was not finished to schedule, and on 17 November Rolls was complaining that deliveries were so far behind the promised dates that he could not commit himself during 1905. 'Ils se proposent', ran the final minute 'd'exposer un omnibus, bien qu'ils trouvent le changement de vitesse trop faible'—rather a serious fault, one would have thought, on a public service vehicle!

for omnibus use. These Rolls vehicles had, of course, nothing to do with Henry Royce, but were merely Swiss C.I.E.M.s renamed for the British market. In December the Associated Omnibus Co. was trying one out on their route between the Edgware Road and the Law Courts: it wore the trade-plates of C. S. Rolls and Co., but no mention was made of any sponsors, and its make and nationality were now correctly stated.

Rolls's handling of his motor business can certainly not be termed impulsive. If the Rutherfoord Harris affair reveals a certain casualness, there is no doubt that Rolls had been careful to avoid putting all his commercial eggs in one basket until Henry Royce's products had proved themselves, and until they proved that they would be able to maintain the volume of sales from Conduit Street at a satisfactory level. But it should be remembered, lest Rolls's caution should appear to betoken a lack of enthusiasm, that it was he who, on his return from the famous meeting at the Midland Hotel, dragged Claude Johnson out of bed with the excited words: 'I have found the greatest motor engineer in the world'.

It is now time to explore the meeting, and the effect it had on Charles Stewart Rolls.

CHAPTER SIX

Mr Rolls and Mr Royce

Those Who Try The Rolls-Royce Buy The Rolls-Royce
Those Who Buy The Rolls-Royce Will Buy None Other Than
* The Rolls-Royce*
And Give Repeat Orders For Rolls-Royce.
    C. S. Rolls and Co. advertisement, September 1906

Charles Stewart Rolls and Frederick Henry Royce met for the
first time at the Midland Hotel, Manchester, during the early
part of May 1904.

Many motoring historians delight to minimize Rolls's part
in the story of Rolls-Royce. They argue that he was no designer,
and that his involvement with Royce's cars amounted to little
more than a protracted honeymoon, fading first into a coolness
and ultimately into a divorce still cunningly concealed at the
time of his death in 1910. Royce designed the cars, Johnson sold
them, and Claremont kept vigil over Johnson's more alarming
exuberances: therefore, it is said, only alphabetical precedence
has kept Rolls's name alive in the world of motoring as well
as in the world of aviation. Rolls, they would have us believe,
picked up Royce's motor cars, played with them for a while,
and then cast them aside carelessly in favour of the aeroplanes
of Wright and Short.

There is an element of truth in this. We have seen that in
1904 Rolls was looking to the new Royce car to help bolster
up his shaky business at Lillie Hall and Brook Street—but
that as yet he was prepared to pursue other agencies until he
could satisfy himself that the Rolls-Royce alone would be an
adequate replacement for the Panhard. But can we blame him
for this attitude? He could always bank on parental support for
his business ventures, but already Lord Llangattock's loans
had reached formidable proportions. Royce was utterly unknown outside the world of the dynamo and the electric crane;
although his reputation in this particular field stood high.
C. W. Morton has told us that the first 10-h.p. Royce engine
ran for the first time on its test-bed on 23 February 1904, a

bare ten weeks before the meeting in Manchester. Though the complete Royce made its first public appearance in April at those A.C.G.B.I. Anti-Skid Trials that Rolls had dismissed so cursorily, this fact was not officially recorded until H. Massac Buist published his *Rolls-Royce Memories* in 1926: contemporary reports allude to a '10-h.p. car' without specifying the make, and the Parsons Chain Company, whose non-skid chains were tested on the vehicle, have expressed doubts whether it was in fact used for this purpose. On 17 September, *Motoring Illustrated* mentioned that Charles Rolls had attended the Army manoeuvres at Colchester with a 10-h.p. 'Rolls-Royce' (it was actually still a Royce), but this passed without further editorial comment. Interestingly enough, old employees from Cooke Street recall that one of the three prototypes was always known as a Rolls-Royce, though it had the Decauville radiator.

It would be a foolish historian who based all his deductions on what he read in the contemporary press: but we know that this journalistic ignorance was shared by the motor-fanatics who congregated at the Automobile Club in London or in the shadow of the potted palms at the Crystal Palace and the Royal Agricultural Hall. They knew nothing of the cars from Cooke Street, Manchester, until that first week in December 1904, when C. S. Rolls and Co. announced that they would be exhibiting at the Paris Salon; and, further, that the machines on their stand would be one hundred per cent British.

What is more, the Rolls-Royce was only one of many new makes that year: true, in those days, one could become a motor manufacturer without a superabundance of capital, but with so many contenders, survival depended upon an energetic publicity campaign, especially if the product hailed from the North. The motoring press operated from London and Coventry, and cars made in the neighbourhood of these two centres could count on the lion's share of journalistic support. Who, for instance, knew anything of the Salisbury-built Scout, the Rothwell from Oldham, or the Ryknield from Burton-on-Trent? Their sales were regional, with little chance of expansion, even if they made their annual appearances at the Crystal Palace, Islington, or Olympia. Admittedly, Crossley were already on their way to a place in the sun with a Mancunian motor-car, but then Crossley's sales were directed by Charles Jarrott and William Malesbury Letts, both old hands in the promotion stakes. More typical were the efforts of the brothers Benjamin and William Jowett, who were in production with their little flat-twins as early as 1911, but were not to attain nation-wide recognition until the early 1920s: and even then motoring writers were apt to dismiss the Jowett's remarkable hill-climbing capabilities as just another Tall Tale.

Not only was Royce unknown: Claude Johnson's reputation was anything but commercial. He was rather an elder statesman of motoring, remembered for his sterling work as Secretary of the A.C.G.B.I. between 1897 and 1902, for his successful organization of the Thousand Miles' Trial, and for the diplomacy with which he kept the peace between the various motoring associations. Rolls, however, had been the embodiment of the spirit of motoring since the 1890s. He may have forsaken racing temporarily in 1904, but his energetic, if sometimes casual direction of the affairs of C. S. Rolls and Co. had kept him in touch with his potential circle of clients. He might reject the carefree social life of the Edwardian era, but as a peer's son he had the entrée to any home where the motor-car might find a welcome, while his ballooning exploits also helped to break the ice with people who otherwise had nothing in common with this reserved and single-minded young man. Few people ascended in balloons, and fewer still bought them, but a 'balloon house-party' attracted plenty of attention in its immediate neighbourhood, and among those who foregathered at the Hendre, or Pitmaston, or Avington to speed the balloons on their way were always some who would fall victims to Charles's charm, and thus enable him to return to Conduit Street with an order for a new Rolls-Royce in his pocket. The Hon. Mrs Assheton-Harbord, a fellow-aeronaut who became one of his few close friends, bought two 'Twenties' and a 30-h.p. six-cylinder.

Nor is there any doubt that Rolls worked unrelentingly, during the so-called honeymoon years, to promote Royce's cars. In those early days, he always preferred the rapid four-cylinder 'Light Twenty' to the first six-cylinder models, and left the promotion of the latter largely to Johnson, but T. O. Smith, his personal mechanic and later his right-hand man in flying days, has testified that Rolls's single-minded enthusiasm was thrown into the selling of Rolls-Royces in 1906. Nor was interest purely commercial, for Mr Smith remembers that Charles always carried a set of overalls in his car, and was prepared 'to take his coat off and get dirty', if there were adjustments to be made. 'No greater mistake', ran an advertisement published by C. S. Rolls and Co. in November 1905, 'can be made than to suppose that the older the manufactory the better the car.' This was Rolls's thesis: one can sense behind it a quiet 'dig' at Panhard, Daimler, and Napier, all of whom could claim nineteenth-century origins; but such a reminder was necessary, since in pre-'Silver Ghost' days the name alone was insufficient recommendation. The 'Thirty's' crankshafts undoubtedly gave a great deal of trouble, the eight-cylinder turned out to be a costly, if superbly executed blunder, and it was said that even Rolls found a silent gear-change impossible on the 'Heavy Twenty'—as it was also whispered that he was capable of giving ham-fisted treatment to the 'Silver Ghost's' box, this may have been the driver's fault rather than the car's. But in those first years Royce was feeling his way—the inspection scheme instituted in 1908 was very necessary so long as the majority of Rolls-Royces in private service were still the early types; and it would be fair to sum up the initial products of Cooke Street as cars of above-average performance, a very high standard of silence, and a great deal of potential. The turning-point in Rolls-Royce's fortunes was not Rolls's victory in the 1906 T.T., but the successful 15,000 Mile Trial of the 40–50-h.p. car in 1907, while in the opinion of Henry Knox the *marque*'s primacy dates from 1912 or thereabouts. Before that date not everyone who could afford a Rolls-Royce would automatically have bought one: and some, at any rate, of the credit for setting Manchester, and later Derby, on the road to the summit must go to Rolls, even if we must disbelieve the nonsense perpetrated by the motoring press when they discovered Henry Royce's creations. Illustrative is this excerpt from the *Car Illustrated*'s report on the Paris Salon (21 December, 1904):

111

His long connection with the motor car industry and his intimate knowledge of all the best-known foreign and British automobiles have, no doubt, proved invaluable to *Mr C. S. Rolls in perfecting the design and details of the new all-British car* which his firm, C. S. Rolls and Co., have put on the market under the name of the 'Rolls-Royce' car. [The italics are mine!]

We have already explored the road which led Rolls to Royce, and their meeting is now a legend comparable with anything that has been written about W. O. Bentley or Ettore Bugatti. The story of Frederick Henry Royce is equally familiar. In 1884 he and a fellow electrical engineer, Ernest Claremont, had pooled their savings of £70, and set up a small business in Cooke Street, Manchester. This venture prospered: in 1894 F. H. Royce and Co. became a limited liability company. By 1897 they had orders on their books amounting to £6,000: this figure had risen to £9,000 by the spring of 1898, and to £20,000 in 1899. The name of the company became Royce Ltd. in 1900. In 1902 Royce bought a twin-cylinder Decauville car and was so appalled by its crudity that he determined to make an automobile himself. So runs the legend, and throughout his career Royce was to be a ruthless perfectionist; but if the Decauville was so bad, why is there so much of the French *marque* in the make-up of the first Royce? It even looked like a Decauville—the classical Greek profile of the radiator found on today's 'Silver Clouds' and 'Phantoms' did not appear until the name of Rolls was linked with the venture—so much so that Charles Rolls, confronted with a Royce for the first time outside the Midland Hotel at Manchester, actually thought it was a product of the Decauville factory. But the role of catalyst in the partnership was to be taken by Henry Edmunds. Edmunds, a founder-member of the A.C.G.B.I., had naturally been acquainted with Rolls for some time, and, as we have seen, had sampled his style of driving at Lady Georgiana Curzon's charity fête in 1900. He came into contact with Henry Royce through the purchase of a block of shares in Royce Ltd. Royce, knowing Edmunds to be an enthusiastic motorist, asked him to try the experimental 10-h.p. car.

Royce had a car to sell: Rolls was on the look-out for a vehicle to recapture the market lost to him through Panhard's failure to march with the times. On 26 March, 1904, Edmunds took the plunge and wrote to Royce from London:

I saw Mr Rolls yesterday, after telephoning you, and he said it would be much more convenient if you could see him in London, as he is so very much occupied: and, further, that several other houses are now in negotiation with him, wishing to do the whole part of his work. What he is looking for is a good high-class quality of car to replace the Panhard, preferably of three or four-cylinders. He has some personal dislike to two-cylinder cars. I will do all I can to bring about this arrangement with Mr Rolls: for I think your car deserves well: and ought to take its place when it is once recognized by the public on its merit.

This oft-quoted letter reveals much of Rolls. Ever-busy, he would be a difficult man to nail down to a specific time and place, especially if it were not of his own choosing. His addiction to three-cylinder engines was no singular quirk, for Vauxhall, Standard, and Arrol-Johnston, as well as Panhard, were interested in them at this time. There is also a hint of a 'hard sell': though in fact the 'other houses' to which Edmunds alludes were promoting that dubious commercial asset, the electric brougham, he was not going to miss any opportunity of pressing for the most advantageous terms in a deal with Royce.

Edmunds replied by posting specifications of the Royce car to Rolls, and added a note of personal confidence—'knowing, as I do, the skill of Mr Royce as a practical mechanical engineer, I feel one is very safe in taking up any work his firm may produce'. This approach might well have failed. Royce was not one to be distracted from his beloved workshops on a fool's errand, and Rolls liked to have his own way, that way favouring a meeting in London, not Manchester. However, Charles was hooked. On 29 April he sent a terse note to Edmunds, asking him to come up to Manchester 'any time next week'. It is interesting to note that the two motorists travelled up by train, and Edmunds recalls the almost prophetic conversation he had with Rolls *en route*. Rolls told him that he wanted a car connected with his name that would become as much a household word as Broadwood was among pianofortes, or Chubb among safes.

No record has been kept of the meeting. It must, however, have been satisfactory from Rolls's viewpoint, for notwithstanding his professed dislike of twin-cylinder engines, he agreed to handle the whole output of Royce cars. These cars were to bear his name as well as their maker's. He also borrowed one of the prototypes for his own use; as we have seen, H.R.H. The Duke of Connaught was to ride in it.

Royce's task (if at this stage he had any commercial ambitions for his cars), may not have been as difficult as Edmunds had anticipated. Rolls had a reputation for 'being unable to say no', provided his pocket was not involved, and this is borne out by the apparent ease with which he was talked into the sponsorship of such musical-comedy items as the Dufaux and the Hallé spring wheel. Further, the two men seem to have taken an instant liking to each other. Royce might laugh at the 'playboys of Conduit Street', and maintain that he did all the work, but those who saw him at the time of Rolls's death in July 1910, have testified to his genuine and unconcealed grief. After all, both were single-minded, though Royce, surprising as this may seem, had a greater capacity for relaxation, however seldom he permitted himself this luxury.

In 1964, a television programme on the story of the Rolls-Royce hinted at a possible earlier contact between Henry Royce and the Llangattock family. In this script, Royce was cast in the role of telegraph-boy who, in 1877 delivered to Mr H. A. Rolls's London home the announcement of his third son's birth. Alas! there is no proof of this: but the fact remains that Royce was a messenger at Mount Street at that time, and the future Lord Llangattock's house would have been on his 'beat'.

To revert to 1904—as yet there was no fusion between Rolls's business in London and that of Royce in Manchester. The first step towards amalgamation took place in November 1905, when Rolls jettisoned Minerva and Orleans in favour of Rolls-Royce. In March 1906 Rolls-Royce Ltd. came into

114

being with a nominal capital of £60,000, and the motor and electrical interests were divorced, Royce Ltd. continuing as an entirely separate concern until shortly after Royce's death in 1933, when it was wound up. Rolls's London business, though controlled through a holding company, Rolls-Royce Distributing, was to retain its identity until the end of 1906.

In December 1904 C. S. Rolls and Co. were still selling Panhards, and along with the press releases on the 10-h.p. Rolls-Royce they sent out photographs of a 24-h.p. Panhard landaulette that had recently been delivered to a customer. Rolls and Johnson, however, were in attendance in Paris, Rolls conducting the demonstrations, and Johnson talking to the press. The *Car Illustrated* was most favourably impressed, praising the 'flexibility, extraordinarily quiet running, and the unusual comfort of the body'. The highlight of Rolls's performance on this occasion was a getaway using top gear only. Knowing as we do the Edwardian dislike for the use of the indirect ratios, this would have been a strong selling-point, even before that rash of crazy marathons 'on the direct drive' which was to punctuate, not only the Battle of the Cylinders, but also the motor industry's career in public relations right up to the 1930s. This misguided style of sales promotion was, however, usually confined to six-cylinder cars, and it is doubtful whether any other 'twin' then on the market could have rivalled the Rolls-Royce in this respect. Top-gear starts were, of course, more a test of the driver's skill than of the car's flexibility, but most competing vehicles would have moved off to the accompaniment of labouring engines and groaning transmissions.

In those days, of course, journalists were driven, and not invited to take the wheel—most of the early first-hand reports of Rolls-Royce motoring came from members of the Fourth Estate like my father and H. J. Swindley, who bought cars themselves. Harry Fleck cannot recall journalists actually driving during his years with C. S. Rolls and Co., and I was told by Rolls-Royce Ltd., that neither Rolls, nor Percy Northey, who took over the task of demonstration from him when aviation became his predominant interest, were over-tolerant of drivers who made messy gear-changes. Further, Charles's style seems to have mellowed since the days of the Thousand Miles' Trial and the incident with Vera Butler at Barnet, if we are to judge from an account which survives of a drive with him late in 1905.

This trip covered the familiar route from South Lodge to the Hendre, and the car used was a 20-h.p. Rolls-Royce; it makes an interesting contrast with the nineteenth-century epics enshrined in early issues of *The Autocar* and *Some Roadside Experiences*. Henry Royce's sporting four-cylinder machine was, in any case, a far cry from the twin-cylinder rear-engined Peugeot with its handlebar steering, and the Paris–Marseilles–Paris Panhard with its tube ignition, temperamental water pump and incandescent brakes. Rolls was quick to demonstrate its flexibility by changing into top gear as they drove out of the gates of his London home, and C. A. E. Winnington, his passenger, recorded the manner of its going as follows: 'I had heard that the Rolls-Royce car was a quiet car, but I think that I can safely say that the mechanism of this car was literally inaudible, for one could hear nothing but the swish of the tyres along the wet surface.'

The journey itself merited little comment. Instead of the slow and painful progress involving a night's rest with 'Aunt Annie' at Purton, they did not stop at all until they had reached Swinford Bridge, a few miles west of Oxford. Birdlip was, of course, by-passed, but hills are not mentioned at all. They left Kensington at daybreak, arriving at the Hendre in time for breakfast at 9.15 a.m. No wonder the Llangattock family were incredulous.

Rolls was rated a considerate driver. We may question whether he passed *all* vehicles in neutral as Winnington tells us; this method in all probability applied only to horse-drawn traffic—but he certainly stopped the car for led horses, as well he might. No longer was he issuing tracts on behalf of the Church of England Society for the Promotion of Kindness to Animals, but in 1905 he had been a signatory to a petition drawn up by Old Etonians in favour of the abolition of the Eton College Beagles, 'a sport in which boys are encouraged to seek amusement from the infliction of pain on animals'.

With Charles Rolls at the helm in London, the Rolls-Royce

sold well, and it was Rolls's name, not that of Royce, which was stressed in all early advertising. The activities of Royce Ltd. are dismissed with the words 'Works, Manchester' in very small type on the title page of the 1905 catalogue. This volume, though it runs to one hundred pages (which must have strained the budget more than somewhat!), and contains comprehensive details of the full range of cars, reams of testimonials from the small band of owners, and potted biographies, with photographs, of Rolls and Johnson, ignores Royce altogether. The firm's mainstay was as yet the 20-h.p. four-cylinder, selling at a modest £735 complete, for the six-cylinder 'Thirty' was still in the teething stage. But even if the cars were easy to sell, Rolls was flinging himself heart and soul into his task. Financially he might be involved with Minerva and Orleans as well, and up to August 1905 he was still dividing his advertising equally between the three makes. Much midnight oil might still be expended on fruitless endeavours to make the Dufaux racer fire on all four cylinders for any length of time, but he was tirelessly at work, selling Rolls-Royces. If his support of the first two races for the Tourist Trophy in 1905 and 1906 gave man and car alike the run of the headlines, there were other lesser activities calculated to promote the make of which he had said 'Others may equal it, but they'll never better it.' In June 1905 we find him taking his Rolls-Royce on a 'midnight motor meet' to Maidenhead with a theatrical party. The actors and actresses posed in their cars outside Skindles Hotel, and the results were rushed back to London to be processed in time for the following night's 'biograph show' at the Alhambra; not, I hasten to add, for an early example of those tedious 'commercials' that interrupt one's enjoyment of the cinema today, but none the less good publicity. At that time the 'biograph' earned its living as a species of *entr'acte* in the more sophisticated music-halls.

He worked hard on the press. Foster Pedley of the *Car Illustrated* rode as his mechanic on the 'Twenty's' preliminary trials in the Isle of Man, and the august W. Worby Beaumont, engineer to the A.C.G.B.I., sat beside him on the way up to the Motor Union's rally at Eaton Hall, Cheshire, in July 1905, noting that 'Mr Rolls had very little more to do than to steer.'

This particular rally, be it said, was used by Rolls and Johnson to assemble every Royce and Rolls-Royce made to date, nine of them all told. 1906 saw a 'Twenty' loaned to the A.C.G.B.I. for trials with the Collier tyre, while C. S. Rolls and Co., also supported large-scale demonstrations of the automobile to the sub-editors of the London newspapers, and to the International Parliamentary Union. As yet, we may note, such chores were not assigned to junior P.R.O.s—the principals personally drove their wares, and the cast of the latter demonstration reads like an excerpt from a contemporary 'Who's Who In The Motor Industry'. Frederick Coleman brought along a brace of Whites, Captain H. H. P. Deasy, though already a manufacturer in his own right, was there in the interests of Martini of Switzerland, and George Lanchester had one of his own cars. Frank Wellington drove a Spyker and F. R. Simms a Simms-Welbeck. Edge, of course, took charge of Napier's entry, and Jarrott of Crossley's. T. B. Browne had a James and Browne, J. W. Stocks two De Dions, and F. S. Bennett a Cadillac. Other familiar figures were Jarrott's partner W. M. Letts with their firm's other *protégé*, the De Dietrich, D'Arcy R. Baker of F.I.A.T. Motors Ltd., and J. D. Siddeley who had replaced Herbert Austin as General Manager of Wolseley. Percival Perry, already well-known in motoring circles, and shortly to direct Henry Ford's first major attack on the British market, drove a mysterious obscurity rejoicing in the name of Sorex.

At the Motor Show staged at Olympia in November 1905, Rolls was seen in deep converse with the Prime Minister, Mr A. J. Balfour. He failed to shake the Premier's long-standing loyalty to Napier, but as a dutiful son he turned up at a big pre-election Unionist rally in London at which Lord Llangattock took the chair, and lent cars to the Party canvassers in the election itself. At this Show, interestingly enough, the Hallé wheel was still featured, and C. S. Rolls and Co. continued to advertise it for another year. T. O. Smith, however, has no recollection of seeing a set of these oddities installed on a Rolls-Royce.

At this stage most bodies fitted to Rolls-Royces were the work of Barker and Co. of North Kensington: chassis were delivered from Manchester without lamps or other fittings, these being added by E. T. Arnott's department at Lillie Hall. There seems to have been some difficulty with Barkers' over prices, as Lord Llangattock complained of their high charges in November 1905 and was answered sympathetically by Charles, who reminded him that 'there are a lot of extras required and included in your carriage, and their work is, o course, very good'. These extras included a card-case and an umbrella-holder, but the invoice still came out at only £802 for a complete 'Heavy Twenty', plus £17 10s. extra for a 'specially low gear' to cope with gradients stiffer than 1-in-7·2. (Evidently Lord Llangattock's mountain-moving days were over!) Charles personally tested his father's car, and reported (17 March, 1906) on 'a very fierce clutch'. He also referred a request for giant Palmer tyres to Royce, and tried to dissuade his parent from fitting them, 'as they do not give a good ride'.

As yet there was no thought of a one-model policy. In addition to the 10-h.p. 'twin', there were a 15-h.p. three-cylinder, two versions of the four-cylinder 'Twenty', and the 30-h.p. six-cylinder. For 1906, the unfortunate Vee-Eight was added to the range. Certainly the 20-h.p. seems to have been the principal seller, and Harry Fleck remembers the staff at Lillie Hall toiling for three days and three nights on the repair of a 'Light Twenty' that had come into collision with a milk float in Kingston Vale on its delivery run from London.

The influence of Rolls on design was, of course, limited to general advice on what C. S. Rolls and Co. could sell; apart of course from the special case of the 'Light Twenty', where the two partners worked in close liaison to evolve a T.T.-winner. We cannot trace his hand, for instance, in the 'Invisible Vee-Eight', which was, after all, only a superior example of that unhappy fad of the period, the petrol brougham. By concealing the mechanism under the floor, makers hoped to combine the virtues of the electric carriage with none of its limitations of range or snail-like progress. Such firms as Napier and Minerva tried their hand at such devices, but problems of control-linkage were never solved. The eight-cylinder Rolls-Royce of 1905–06 must be regarded as one of Claude Johnson's rare errors of judgement. I have been told, incidentally, that the instigator of the whole idea was none other than my father.

By contrast, the 15-h.p. three-cylinder was clearly produced by Royce at Rolls's behest. This configuration had quite a following: as late as 1907, Louis Coatalen was to incur William Hillman's censure by producing a 'four' when he had been specifically asked to evolve a 'three', and Rolls had done quite well with the little 8–10-h.p. Panhard. This was probably the consequence of one of his firm's specialities, those 'doctor's landaulettes' that fitted the Panhard chassis admirably. The twin-cylinder Rolls-Royce, with its short wheelbase of 6 ft. 3 ins. could not accommodate chauffeur-driven coachwork, but the 'Fifteen's' wheelbase was 9 ft. 7 ins., and with such a body it sold for a mere £695, or £145 less than the comparable 'Heavy Twenty' model. However, the car did not catch on: and though Rolls took one on the 1905 Army manoeuvres, and engineered the presentation of another to Dr Warre, the Headmaster of Eton, we hear no more of it.

But by far the most important work that Rolls undertook for Rolls-Royce in the years before the advent of the 'Silver Ghost' concerned the Tourist Trophy Races of 1905 and 1906. His approval of the race was shared, surprisingly enough, by Claude Johnson; though probably 'CJ's' dislike for competitive events has been exaggerated. We know, for instance, that he supported whole-heartedly Rolls's record run from Monte Carlo to London in May 1906, despite the fact that less than a year earlier he had urged the Automobile Club of Great Britain and Ireland 'to do everything in its power to prevent the high speeds of automobiles being brought before the public notice'; the publicity value of such a demonstration of performance was too high to be spurned. In any case, the Tourist Trophy represented a new kind of sport. By the summer of 1905, Rolls had sloughed off all his affiliations with supporters of the 1,000-kg. Formula, and he therefore had no qualms about writing: 'Racing, pure and simple, has served its purpose, and the construction of special racing machines, which are of no use to the ordinary motorist, involves competing firms in enormous expense.' The object of the Tourist Trophy was, however, 'the improvement of motor cars of a type which is useful to the ordinary purchaser', and certainly the event in its original guise lived up to Rolls's assessment. Prototypes were permitted, but each car had to carry driver and mechanic, plus a load of ballast equivalent to the weight of two more adults. Unladen weight must not be less than 1,300 lbs., or more than 1,600 lbs. The fuel allowance was also limited, though until the last moment the A.C.G.B.I. did not specify the exact ration that they would permit. Any doubts the organizers might have entertained as to the popularity of such an event were dispelled by the number of *marques* which supported it. Along with Napier, Daimler, Wolseley, Siddeley, Spyker, Star, Argyll, White, Clément, Renault, Dennis, Darracq, and Peugeot, all of whom had some degree of interest in the sport, there were Thornycroft, Vauxhall, and Humber, who were new to this aspect of motoring, and breeds such as Cadillac, James and Browne, and Swift, names seldom, if ever, associated with other circuits. The regulations were intended to exclude freaks, but Johnson was not worried even if some peculiar designs managed to pass the scrutineers. He opined that they would soon be exposed as impracticable the moment they reached the customers. In fact, the T.T. was not long to remain a race for 'catalogue' machinery: it might become even more 'tourist' in 1907, when cars in the 'Heavy' class had to sport enormous vertical screens to simulate the drag of landaulette coachwork, but 1908 was to see a 'Four-Inch' formula and a spate of special cars: and in later years not even the ban on superchargers imposed in 1934, and the continuance of handicap rules favouring the smaller machinery could save the T.T. from becoming just another race for 'sports cars'.

Rolls, as we have seen, went about his preparations meticulously. His preliminary reconnaissance in the Isle of Man was conducted on an open-bodied 'Heavy Twenty', and as a result he was able to recommend to Royce those gear ratios best suited to the requisite combination of speed and fuel economy. The petrol allowance ultimately fixed for the race was $9\frac{3}{4}$ gallons, and this would demand a fuel consumption of at least $22 \cdot 5$ m.p.g. if a car was to be able to complete four laps of the course. In fact, Rolls managed $27 \cdot 5$ m.p.g., while trials on the London–Oxford Road revealed 28 m.p.g., thanks to a new gearbox evolved by Royce. This incorporated a geared-up top which Rolls termed his 'sprinting gear', and was to feature not only on production 'Light Twenties', but also on all 'Silver Ghosts' made up to the summer of 1909. Of the two cars entered for the 1905 Tourist Trophy, one, to be driven by Percy Northey, had the standard engine of 95-mm. bore and 127-mm. stroke; the other, which Rolls would drive himself, had the cylinder bore enlarged to 100-mm.

By the end of August, the multifarious field, now reduced by defections from 54 to 42, had assembled in the Isle of Man. Among those who had withdrawn were Daimler, Deasy, Renault, Bristol, Crossley, Germain and Enfield. Of the others, the Vauxhall had a three-cylinder engine and an overdrive gearbox: the Simms-Welbeck wore bumpers: the Arrol-Johnston had an opposed-piston twin-cylinder power unit on that firm's accepted lines, albeit mounted in a modern chassis utterly divorced from their traditional dog-carts: and F. S. Bennett's little 9-h.p. Cadillac was an example of the indestructible 'single' that was as yet Henry M. Leland's staple product. The first arrival in the Island was Rolls's second string, the Minerva entrusted to Ernest Arnott. Champagne was flowing freely in the Rolls camp, and they had reason to be sanguine, for not only had Arnott set the ball rolling with a very fast lap, but Rolls was timed over the course at 33 m.p.h. Even more encouraging, the fuel consumption on this occasion worked out at 26 m.p.g. Victory seemed within their grasp.

The cars were towed to the start behind horses, to conserve precious fuel. Rolls and Johnson were amassing some useful publicity behind the scenes, for one of the official cars was a 30-h.p. Rolls-Royce lent by their firm, and spectators were being issued with score-cards inscribed with the name of C. S. Rolls and Co. Wolseleys, incidentally, adopted the same expedient.

Nemesis, however, was to intervene. The cars coasted away downhill from the start, and Rolls was the first off the line. He attempted to engage third gear, and failed. He then tried his 'sprinting gear' with equal lack of success, and returned to the attack with third once more. There was a loud crack, and the car coasted to a standstill.

Not that he was the only unfortunate. As competitors in the veteran-car classes at Prescott know, wooden wheels do not take kindly to energetic cornering techniques, and disregard of this simple little rule eliminated Warren's Speedwell, Rawlinson's Darracq, and Bennett's Cadillac, all on the first round. Hadley, who had already experienced a crash on the circuit while acting as Sidney Girling's mechanician in the 1905 Gordon Bennett Eliminating Trials, put his Wolseley into a hedge. Arnott's Minerva retired with disorders of the ignition, and the Vauxhall 'rammed a tree near Ramsey and neither ran nor rammed any more'. First casualty of petrol rationing was the Dixi, which expired on the third lap. But in the meanwhile Percy Northey was circulating steadily on the second Rolls-Royce: his third circuit was the day's fastest, with a speed of 34·1 m.p.h., better than Rolls's more powerful machine had achieved in practice. He was first across the line, and for a moment the Rolls *équipe* hoped that the disaster to their principal had been avenged. The victor was, however, J. S. Napier on his own design, the 18-h.p. Arrol-Johnston, his average speed being 33·9 m.p.h. to Northey's 33·7 m.p.h., and the 33·3 m.p.h. of the third man home, Norman Littlejohn on a Vinot-Deguingand.

Rolls was furious. He did not wait to see the finish of the race, but had his car shipped straight back to the mainland. In a statement issued at the time, he announced:

> I found a certain number of broken loose nuts at the bottom of the gearbox, which, so far as I can see, must have been put in through a hole at the top. This is a sort of thing that happens frequently in France, but I hardly thought it possible that it could occur in this country. The effect was that as soon as I started running by the gravity of the car down hill, using no power, the pieces caught in the gearing and broke the gear wheels.

Though sabotage was common in Continental events, the *Car Illustrated* was not among those who took Rolls's allegations seriously, for the magazine drew a parallel with a story told in the paddock 'concerning a certain Manx cat which committed suicide by jumping into the gearbox' of one of the official cars whilst this was being driven round the circuit. It

seems certain from what we know of the driving techniques of
the period that Rolls tried to engage a gear while coasting
with a dead engine—a practice that is not recommended unless
one's car is blessed with synchromesh. And synchromesh was
not to appear until 1928!

When this wild charge failed, Rolls launched a protest
against the victorious Arrol-Johnston, on the pretext that its
silencer had come adrift during the race. To drive around with
this component dragging on the ground was, he contended,
unsafe; further, the absence of a silencer infringed the
A.C.G.B.I.'s regulations for touring cars, and it caused the
engine to develop more brake-horsepower than it would when
fully silenced. Napier had several good answers: he had stopped
to fix the offending component shortly after it detached itself;
the engine had *lost* power since he had designed his exhaust
system to enhance the performance, and, as a Parthian shot,
he reminded Rolls that there were no regulations governing
the construction or use of silencers. The A.C.G.B.I. must have
considered Rolls's protest a reasonable one, though they dis-
allowed it; for they returned his statutory cash deposit with
their refusal. Perhaps they felt that to deprive the parsimonious
Rolls of cash would have exacerbated the situation too far;
they had already had unhappy experiences with S. F. Edge
during the Gordon Bennett Eliminating Trials of 1904. Once
the bitterness of defeat was over, we find Charles in a far
mellower mood, and on 18 September he summarizes the result
of the T.T. in a letter to Captain Lionel Spiller, his father's
secretary:

> The smaller of our two cars did well on Thursday, making
> the fastest non-stop run in the Race, and averaging $33\frac{3}{4}$ miles
> an hour for $208\frac{1}{2}$ miles without a single stop of any kind,
> and on a consumption of $25\frac{1}{2}$ miles to the gallon. My own
> car was considerably faster and consumed less, and must
> have won, but the gear was broken up at the start, owing,
> I think to some loose pieces having got into the gear some-
> how.

No mention of sabotage here—Rolls's bouts of irritability
and anger were as brief and sudden as his gales of laughter, and

valuable lessons had been learnt. A Rolls-Royce had come in second, and the car that had beaten it was not a competitor in the same market. As yet, the standard Arrol-Johnston was an enormous dog-cart on solid tyres, with underfloor engine, started by an arrangement of pulleys, and crowned with varnished-wood bodywork. It is only fair to point out, though, that their 18-h.p. T.T. type subsequently went into production.

None the less, some vindication was indicated, and further tests were carried out with the two cars on that familiar stamping-ground, the London–Oxford road. Rolls recorded 23·3 m.p.g. on his 'Twenty', now repaired, while Northey's machine managed 24·9 m.p.g. in Johnson's hands, thus proving that the high gearing had no adverse effect on the 'Twenty's' hill-climbing capabilities—as if the mountain section of the Isle of Man course had not already clinched this point.

For the 1906 Race, weight restrictions were abandoned, but the maximum permissible fuel consumption was set at 25 m.p.g., and an attempt was made to deter makers from the adoption of freak gear ratios by stipulating that competing vehicles must be able to cover a measured half-mile at a speed not higher than 12 m.p.h. in top gear, and also to undertake a stop and re-start on a gradient of 1-in-6. Rolls-Royce were sitting pretty this year—on test Northey and Royce (who was trying out Rolls's car for him) were getting 50 m.p.h. and 28 m.p.g. Nor did the new rules worry them. Rolls and Johnson demonstrated the flexibility of the T.T. cars by driving them down the Mall in London, the less flexible of the pair covering the measured distance at 9·04 m.p.h. 1-in-6 hills were child's play, and to show his contempt for them Claude Johnson took a 'Light Twenty' down to Jasper Road in Sydenham, and accomplished the stop-and-restart with nine passengers on board! The car was also demonstrated up the 1-in-4 gradient of Cudham Hill in Kent. Anyone who still believed that the cars were grossly overgeared could be shown a 'Light Twenty' chassis with a cabriolet body, a combination actually delivered to a customer late in 1905.

In May 1906 it was announced that Rolls and Northey had left for Monte Carlo in the two T.T. cars for a 'general appraisal' of their behaviour. Curiously enough, this does not seem to have been an anticipation of the later Rolls-Royce practice of rigorous Continental tests for every new model. This stemmed from two factors, Henry Royce's nearly fatal illness in 1911, and the failure of James Radley's 'Silver Ghost' on the Katschberg Pass during the Austrian Alpine Trials of 1912. Johnson, in his determination to preserve Royce's health, installed him in a villa at Le Canadel on the Riviera, and Royce wintered there every year until his death, with the exception of the 1914-18 period. He was, of course, active throughout this period, and cars were constantly being brought down from Derby for inspection and trial.

The Radley affair has to my mind been grossly exaggerated, though it alarmed Rolls-Royce to the point of preparing a works team of the modified 'Alpine Eagle' models with four-speed gearboxes for the 1913 Alpine Trials, and this gearbox was subsequently fitted as standard to all 'Ghosts'. It certainly wrote a Continental testing routine into the methods of Derby, and this routine led directly to perhaps the most remarkable performance ever achieved by a Rolls-Royce product on the circuits—H. S. F. Hay's sixth place at Le Mans in 1949 on a *ten-year-old* 4¼-litre Bentley with 60,000 miles to its credit. But as one Edwardian motorist told me: 'The improvements in 1913 did not *save* Rolls-Royce; the car was first-class before, and with the four-speed box it became perfect.'

Rolls, however, was not thinking nearly so far ahead. France, as he knew of old, was free of those irritating speed limits that destroyed the publicity value of high-speed runs at home, where to claim an average speed in excess of 20 m.p.h. was to invite prosecution. He also had his eye on a 'record' set up the previous month by Charles Jarrott on a 40-h.p. Crossley. Jarrott had averaged 24·2 m.p.h. between London and Monte-Carlo, despite several *détours* that had increased the distance appreciably beyond the 1,242 kilometres of the direct route. Further, the 7-litre Crossley was a much bigger and more powerful car than the 4-litre Rolls-Royce, which the contemporary press credited with an output of 32 b.h.p.—Henry Royce, needless to say, was reticent on this point! The original plan was to drive home in convoy with both cars, but Northey had to return early, and went by train.

Rolls was supremely confident of his ability to beat Jarrott, and though the attempt was given no advance publicity, it is clear from Massac Buist's account in *Rolls-Royce Memories* that the whole affair was carefully planned. Buist was required to memorize landmarks on the run south, and found Rolls's tastes in this direction peculiar. Mountains and aqueducts failed to appeal; instead 'he wanted to know how many kilometres it was since the last Michelin tyre advertisement had been passed, and when the next would be espied. Apparently nothing else was of any use to him.' Level-crossing keepers were tipped in advance (not, one suspects, by Rolls) so that they would open their gates promptly, and not delay the record seekers. Buist tells us that he had to dissuade Rolls from sending a whole sheaf of telegrams reporting their progress across France to Johnson before the car had even left Monte Carlo.

His crew, of course, were not pampered. Jarrott had regaled his passengers with cold cutlets in aspic and curried chicken (not very digestible, one would have thought, in the *tonneau* of an Edwardian tourer). Rolls took champagne and cold tea, but flabbergasted his companions by telling them that the former was for his own consumption; they must make do with the temperance beverage. They must have rejoiced when the *octroi* officials at Nice, not content with unpacking the car's entire load, charged him duty on the champagne. For the rest 'we existed', wrote Rolls cheerfully, 'almost entirely on Plasmon lunch packets, and on soup, coffee, cocoa, etc.' This contrasts with Mr T. O. Smith's memories of motoring with Charles, for he recalls that Rolls, however hurried he might be, always made sure that his mechanic never went without a meal.

Troubles were few. Within six miles of the start, the bulb horn detached itself—this was only to be expected on rough *pavé*, and by 1906 Rolls had dropped the habit of issuing a spare one to his back-seat passengers. At the first big town they stopped to buy a replacement, but Rolls objected to the price asked, and they continued without making a purchase. The 'Light Twenty's' direct third gear sufficed for the ascent of the Esterels, and despite a puncture and an encounter with a thunder-storm they maintained an average speed of 30 m.p.h.

as far as Lyons. Vision was obscured by torrential rain, which also kept *octroi* officials and level-crossing keepers within doors, irrespective of the *pourboires* they had already received. Rolls praised his 'electric breast lamp' as an aid to map-reading, but Buist remembers clasping the pulpy remnants of a map under one of the oil sidelamps, and trying to decipher it by the flickering light. They overshot an important fork in the road, and the impatient Rolls refused to retrace his steps, with the consequence that by Dijon they had lost two hours on their schedule. In spite of this, their time from Monte Carlo to Boulogne was 28 hr. 4 min., representing an average speed of 27·3 m.p.h. So far they had beaten Jarrott by a handsome margin, but they then had to cool their heels on the quay for more than three hours before the next boat sailed for Folkestone. They would not have beaten the Crossley's record at all, had not Rolls cold-bloodedly disregarded the 20 m.p.h. speed limit on the road to London. When they reached the Crystal Palace, they found that the anxious Johnson had sent a driver out on a 30-h.p. Rolls-Royce to convoy them into the West End. By this time Charles could no longer contain his impatience, and he started to harangue the unhappy escort. Johnson's chauffeur, demoralized by this display of temper, promptly led them into a blocked road. This was enough for Rolls, who determined to do his own navigation. But for all his experience of demonstrating Panhards at the old Crystal Palace Shows, he was unfamiliar with the maze that was (and is) South-East London, and his route to Blackfriars Bridge was peculiar and devious. However, the Rolls-Royce managed to lop one-and-a-half minutes off Jarrott's time.

Jarrott was not amused. He told *Motoring Illustrated*:

I strongly object to his making capital out of a comparison with my London–Monte Carlo performance. There is nothing relative between racing and touring conditions, and my run was made under the latter purely and simply. All the way I observed the decencies and courtesies of the road, and went through towns such as Lyons, Macon, and Dijon very slowly. It is quite evident that Mr Rolls stopped for nothing: with him it was a speed record.

Jarrott further reminded the magazine's readers that with a less powerful car Rolls would have to have driven flat out in order to equal the Crossley's performance; a contention which, to my mind, does not stand up to close scrutiny, for in the Rolls-Royce's overdrive ratio 45–50 m.p.h. could be sustained, whereas the greater weight of the Crossley would result in a formidable consumption of tyres were the car cruised on its limit of perhaps 55 m.p.h. Further, Jarrott had no record to beat, apart from a very unofficial 48-hour run of which I have been unable to trace any details. But then the first decade of the present century was an era in which the promoters of the automobile did better out of the free advertising they earned through the correspondence columns of the motoring press than ever they did from mere paid insertions. Edge was anything but verbose in his display advertisements for the six-cylinder Napier, but any controversy with a motoring flavour was sure to be turned into a propaganda campaign for the products of Acton. Jarrott might assert that if he went out again in the Crossley to break the record, he would 'knock five hours off the time at the least', but he never substantiated this claim. Within a month Rolls's record had fallen to H. R. Pope on a 7½-litre Itala, and Jarrott's next bid, in March 1907 (again on a Crossley), resulted in a time of 35 hr. 20 min., or two hours and eight minutes less than Rolls's 1906 performance . . . and, be it said, he needed six and three-quarter litres to achieve even this.

Nor was the testing programme complete, for C. S. Rolls and Co. supported the Scottish Reliability Trials in June. Rolls was ballooning elsewhere, so Johnson drove a 'Thirty' and Northey the 20-h.p. T.T. car, which created a favourable impression in an event where high gearing was anything but an asset. A 'Twenty' also ran at Shelsley Walsh, but by now Rolls was too busy to appear in person at such a relatively unimportant meeting.

In July Rolls and Northey were already practising in the Isle of Man, the cars still wearing wooden wheels. Charles Rolls had, however, not forgotten the disasters that had overtaken some of their competitors in 1905, and advocated the adoption of wire wheels. Royce expressed his reluctance to squander £40 from the young company's limited funds on such an improvement, whereupon Johnson, whose desire for good publicity sometimes overran his economic principles, offered to put up the money from C. S. Rolls and Co.'s bank balance. This time Royce gave in, and the cars ran in the Island on wire wheels. This year, too, the chassis frames were liberally drilled and the toeboard lined with asbestos to save the occupants' feet: some of this work was carried out at Lillie Hall from plans drawn up by Royce in Manchester.

Once again Johnson was doing things in style, and lent two 30-h.p. Rolls-Royces to ferry journalists from London to Liverpool; not an unnecessary luxury, be it said, for on the occasion of previous motoring events in the Isle of Man, a certain lack of co-ordination had been noted between the railway and steamship companies. John De Looze, the Secretary of Rolls-Royce Ltd., had arranged to send lap-by-lap results by telegram to Conduit Street, where they would be displayed on a special blackboard.

Fewer cars faced the starter this year, 31 as against 42 in 1905. Such old friends as James and Browne, Darracq, Argyll, Arrol-Johnston and Thornycroft were back again, as was Minerva, though this *marque* no longer wore the colours of C. S. Rolls and Co.: the *Automobile Club Journal*, incidentally, considered Wright's example of the Belgian *marque* to be 'a standard touring car in every sense of the term', a phrase which indicates that some of its rivals were suspect, even if they had successfully crept over a measured half-mile at twelve miles an hour. Arrol-Johnston were, of course, defending the Trophy, while newcomers included such well-known names as Berliet and Bianchi, as well as real obscurities of the stamp of the Climax, Vici, and Hardman. James and Browne's entry was their first car to have a vertical engine. Tom Thornycroft arrived at the start with a knee out of joint, this injury having been incurred in the pursuit of 'a wild Manx cat'. Perhaps it had developed an affinity for the inside of his Thornycroft's gearbox!

Rolls was sent on his way to the accompaniment of cries of 'better luck this time', and in the event it was Northey who was to encounter trouble on the first lap. He came to a standstill near Sulby Bridge with a broken front spring. J. S. Napier was getting round at 39 m.p.h. in the Arrol-Johnston, but Rolls was 59 seconds ahead of his nearest rival. Already one of the Minervas was out with clutch trouble, and Lascelles' Vici was in the ditch at Keppel Bridge.

On the second lap, Rolls overtook Napier, who had started ahead of him. Tyre trouble was beginning to dog the Scottish car, which was cruel luck, as the Arrol-Johnstons were certainly faster than the Rolls-Royces, as is shown by Napier's final lap at 40·2 m.p.h., the best circuit of the whole race.

The third lap put paid to George's challenge on the Argyll; his floorboards fell out, and the unhappy driver had to disentangle an assortment of apparel from the propeller-shaft. Browne's Minerva succumbed to the same disorders as had its team-mate, and a S.C.A.R. ran out of petrol. As Rolls lapped McConnell's Bianchi, a stone smashed his goggles and cut his face. Eric Platford, his mechanic, handed over his pair. Rolls wiped his face, and they continued without a stop. Despite the Arrol-Johnston's superior speed on the level, Rolls was being timed on the mountainous section of the course at 26 m.p.h. as against Napier's 25·1 m.p.h., and tyre trouble finally put the Arrol-Johnston out of the running, though it struggled on to take seventh place. Now Bablot was lying second with a Berliet, but he was a good ten minutes behind. Towards the end, the French car was speeding up, and the British car slowing down. The gap was too wide to bridge, as is shown by the times of Rolls's last and slowest lap (1 hr. 3 min. 35 sec.) and Bablot's final circuit, which took three and a half minutes longer. As Rolls himself said: 'I had nothing to do but sit there and wait till the car got to the finish.' His average speed for the four laps was 39·3 m.p.h., compared with Bablot's 35·4 m.p.h., and Napier's winning speed of 33·9 m.p.h. on the Arrol-Johnston in 1905.

It is characteristic of Rolls that, immediately after winning his last motor race, he went straight from Douglas to Paris to take part in the first race for the Gordon Bennett Balloon Cup. I feel it is also in character that he told reporters that the credit for his victory in the Isle of Man was 'obviously due to Mr Royce, the designer and builder' of his car. From Paris he was to go on to America, there to promote Rolls-Royce sales.

While Rolls had been working hard on his beloved 'Light Twenty', the 'Battle of the Cylinders' had been developing. It is irrelevant to delve deeply into the origins of the six-cylinder engine—Spyker, Napier, Sunbeam and Brooke were among the claimants to primacy, and even the protagonists of the 'six' were not above changing sides. Until 1913, S. F. Edge was Napier's sole selling agent, and during this period he missed no opportunity of telling the world, in and out of season, that Napier had pioneered the six-cylinder engine. In 1922, however, we find him promoting Spykers in London, and championing the cause of the Dutch *marque*, despite the fact that this engaging device with four-wheel-drive had been, on its maker's admission, a 'one-off'. Johnson, by contrast, started by defending the Spyker claim, but then backed down graciously on the ground that the car had never progressed beyond the prototype stage, whereas six-cylinder Napiers had been delivered to customers as early as 1904.

Napier had turned to six cylinders in quest of smoothness, silence, and flexibility, and these were the advantages stressed by the more intelligent converts to multi-cylinderism. Unfortunately, for every one manufacturer who adopts a design for logical reasons, there are often ten who sense the emergence of a new fad or fashion, and jump smartly aboard the bandwagon. Thus we find no fewer than fifty-seven different brands of six-cylinder car listed early in 1907, though some of these existed only on paper. One cannot see a Rolls, an Edge, or a Johnson losing any sleep over the Londonia, the Wasp, or the Empress. Further, by no means all these 'sixes' possessed any of the advertised virtues of the breed. Karslake and Pomeroy, in their admirable book, *From Veteran to Vintage*, opine that such Continental monsters as the $11\frac{1}{2}$-litre Panhard of 1905 merely served as pretexts for 'making a fast car larger'. The Mercédès and Hotchkiss, which were among the better specimens, suffered from acute crankshaft vibration, while the 70-h.p. F.I.A.T. was merely that company's big 'four' with two extra cylinders added, and 'yards and yards of shivering crankshaft'. As for some of the smaller and cheaper offerings, these were, as Henry Knox recalls, 'nasty and undergeared', as small sixes so often are—witness the rash of 1½-litre machinery inflicted on Europe in the early 1930s.

With this first wave of six-cylinderism, which reached its climax in 1907, there came also the introduction of the top-gear marathon as a proof of flexibility. Cecil Edge set the ball rolling in September 1905, when he drove a six-cylinder Napier all the way from Brighton to Edinburgh on the 'direct drive', and in the same year Claude Johnson was conducting a 30-h.p. Rolls-Royce up the Cat and Fiddle Pass, also on top. This peculiar and pointless exercise was to develop into what can only be termed a feud between Napier and Rolls-Royce, and the idea received a new lease of life in the exploits of Miss Violet Cordery on sundry Invictas in the 1920s. I have no doubt that, but for the widespread acceptance of automatic transmission on the bigger cars of today, some enterprising manufacturer would have rediscovered this stunt in the post-Hitler era.

The six-cylinder Rolls-Royce remained Claude Johnson's preserve as long as 'fours' were being produced at Cooke Street, and thus Rolls played but a small part in the 'battle'. Most of the letters from Conduit Street to the press on this subject came from Johnson's pen, and it was Johnson who proposed, contested, and won the celebrated match against Captain Deasy's 30–40-h.p. four-cylinder Martini in 1906. This was hailed as a glorious victory by the supporters of the 'six', even if 390 of the 396 marks which separated the two contestants were the result of an unlucky fuel-feed blockage on the Swiss car.

Rolls's case, when he bothered to argue, was simple and to the point. To the gibes of J. E. Hutton, who attacked the complexity of the six-cylinder engine ('My 29th valve has stuck'), he retorted:

The arguments that Mr Hutton puts forward against the six-cylinder car are precisely what he used against the four-cylinder car when he was selling 5-h.p. and 7-h.p. Panhards. If Mr Hutton will give himself experience with a high-class and properly-designed six-cylinder car, he will find, as other users have, that the six-cylinder car is no more liable to break down than a four.

He could not resist reminding Hutton of his own abortive attempt to produce a team of six-cylinder cars for the 1904 Gordon Bennett Eliminating Trials. These were to have had automatic transmissions, and (reputedly) hydraulic brakes with push-button control, but they never materialized. To Rolls, the proof of the pudding lay in the eating, and the six-cylinder Rolls-Royce was a *fait accompli*. Crankshaft vibration might still be troubling Cooke Street, but as yet it was troubling everyone else. In any case, this secret was well-kept as far as Rolls-Royce were concerned.

The controversy dragged on; it culminated in a debate staged at the Automobile Club in February 1907, but though Rolls re-entered the lists on his return from America that month, he said nothing new. The significance of this 'battle' to Rolls lay in the decision that he and his partners, Royce and Johnson, were in process of reaching. They had committed themselves to the six-cylinder engine, and eighteen years were to pass before any other type of power unit was installed in a catalogued Rolls-Royce model. Though as yet the public had not been told, the exciting side of motoring, such as the Tourist Trophy, was now a thing of the past where Manchester and Conduit Street were concerned, and in its place would come a process of steady, unspectacular evolution. Rolls might agree with the new policy in his capacity of Technical Managing Director of Rolls-Royce Ltd. but it could never appeal to his restless, questing spirit for long.

But as he boarded the S.S. *Baltic*, *en route* for the United States in October 1906, the affairs of Rolls-Royce Ltd. were still uppermost in his mind. Stowed in the ship's hold were three of the cars that bore his name—two 'Light Twenties' and the 'Thirty' with which Johnson had won the 'Battle of the Cylinders'. At Manchester, Royce was putting the finishing touches to the new 40–50-h.p. model that was to set Rolls-Royce on a course leading straight to the pinnacle of success. Plans for the fusion of C. S. Rolls and Co. with Rolls-Royce Ltd. were going ahead, and Charles had granted his father a power of attorney. If he had any misgivings, they were financial, as is shown by a letter he wrote on board ship on 11 October:

It is principally a matter of bargaining for the best price we can get for CSR and Co.'s business and goodwill. ... There is probably no doubt that the manufacturing end will in any case enlarge, and if they make 260 cars p.a., we, CSR and Co., if we remained separate, would have to have more cap[ital] to sell that number, so on the whole the amalgamation seems good as it does not involve having to find any cap[ital] at my end, and I should have a good share holding in the Co., with a certain salary plus comm[ission] on profits, and to be released of a great am[oun]t of responsibility.

It is interesting to note that already he was seeking relief from the daily round of demonstrations and other sales-promotion activities. His thoughts were turning to the air. He had told the press that he hoped to fit in some balloon ascents in America, and in fact he did compete in an 'Aero-Auto Race' at Pittsfield, Massachusetts, within a week of his arrival. But he had also been experimenting for some time with models based on the Wright type of aeroplane, and had expressed a desire to meet the Wright brothers. Thus his American trip not only marked a turning-point in the fortunes of Rolls-Royce, but also a turning-point in the life of one of its sponsors.

It is now time to turn the clock back to 1901, to his friendship with Frank Hedges Butler, and to the events attendant on the foundation of the Aero Club of Great Britain.

CHAPTER SEVEN

The Balloonatics

Ballooning ranks as one of the most delightful and exhil-arating pastimes of the twentieth century, in which women, without loss of dignity or 'mannishness', can share; and it has always amused me that whenever I confess to an unalloyed delight in the pastime, people should still regard me as avowing myself endowed with a spirit of foolhardiness and unconven-tional love of adventure beyond the average of my sex.
Mrs Vera Iltid Nicholl (Vera Butler), *The World*,
July 1906

We have already seen that Charles Stewart Rolls was endowed with the outward urge to a greater degree than were his contemporaries. The late Lord Brabazon of Tara has described his outlook as 'almost prophetic'. Unlike many prophets his world was the world of practice and not that of theory. His native shrewdness told him that the motor-car had passed from revolution to evolution, and thus he was content to let the affairs of Rolls-Royce settle down to a steady process of con-solidation. The 40–50-h.p. car represented a 'new look' in luxury vehicles, even if there were no startling technical departures to be found under its bonnet; but while Rolls might welcome that settled state of affairs at Conduit Street that he was forecasting to Lord Llangattock in October 1906, he was bored by business for its own sake. And already he had been turning his thoughts skywards.

Not that he was unique in this respect. Between 1906 and 1909 other motorists began to think of aviation, and when the French abandoned their Grand Prix in the latter years, the new movement received a further fillip. W. F. Bradley has testified that in the early days of flying many of the faces to be seen at Issy, Pau, and Le Mans belonged to old friends from the town-to-town races and the circuits, such as Rougier and the brothers Henry and Maurice Farman; while in Britain motoring sport and aviation were to grow up side-by-side at Brooklands. Men graduated from road to air: Louis Paulhan, who learnt to fly before he could drive, was a rare exception. J. T. C.

136

Moore-Brabazon, the first man to fly in his own country on a British-built aeroplane, had served his apprenticeship, first as 'gentleman mechanic' to Rolls, and subsequently at the wheel of Mors, Minerva, and Austin cars: T. O. M. Sopwith, whose name was to become a household word as the progenitor of some of the greatest British aircraft of World War I, also graduated to the air via the motor car, though he was never, as has been stated in print, an 'articled pupil' at Lillie Hall.

In 1906, however, when Rolls was crossing to America in the S.S. *Baltic*, powered flight existed largely on paper. Orville Wright's successful hop at Kitty Hawk in 1903 had been followed by a long silence. True, lighter-than-air dirigibles had been flown successfully: the first of the Graf von Zeppelin's rigid giants had made its début over Lake Constance as early as July 1900, but he was still struggling against prejudice, and was a long way from the role of commercial ambassador for his country which he was to enjoy during the heyday of the *Graf Zeppelin* and the *Hindenburg* in the 1930s. In England both E. T. Willows and Dr Barton had coaxed their non-rigid airships off the ground, but though these flights made nonsense of the claim subsequently lodged in 1907 by Rolls and Frank Hedges Butler to have been 'the first Englishmen to go a voyage in a private airship', they met with questionable success. For all practical purposes, the world of flying was the world of the balloon: and the balloon was a typically Edwardian phenomenon. Its progress was leisured and, in good weather, carefree. The sport could be pursued in privacy, undisturbed by the ministrations of the police, or the intrusion of the populace: and to those innocent of mechanical knowledge, there was not much to go wrong. The virtues claimed for the sport by its protagonists are curiously redolent of the publicity campaigns that launched preselective gearboxes in the 1930s, and automatic transmissions in the 1950s.

Even the craft's technical progress had been so gentle as to be imperceptible. Beside a Rolls-Royce of 1906, Karl Benz's 1893 'Velo' reminds one of a small dinosaur in the lion-house, but beyond the displacement of hot air by gas, the balloon had changed little since Pilâtre de Rozier had persuaded the Montgolfier brothers to let him make the first human ascent in 1783. Two years later Blanchard and Jefferies had completed the first Channel crossing, while in more recent years mails had been conveyed from beleaguered Paris in the Franco–Prussian War of 1870. The Japanese were using balloons for artillery observation during the Siege of Port Arthur in 1904. Thus one may be surprised to find Charles Rolls observing in 1906 that 'so far as ballooning is concerned you still have to get a machine that you can steer where you like', when, four years before, he had been present at a ceremony commemorating the hundredth anniversary of the first ascent to have been made from the City of Bath! The *Daily Mail* was even more scathing: after a century of so-called development, the paper opined, 'no real progress had been achieved in the art of directing or controlling it'. Edwardian gentlemen might suddenly discover that their unsolicited vista of bilious-green gasholders had its compensations, but even the technical press regarded the gaseous spheres as more or less a joke. The *Car Illustrated*, whose readers surely included over ninety per cent of the ballooning fraternity, faithfully reported the International Balloon Race at Hurlingham in 1908, but it also poked fun at the stars of the show. 'They looked such fat, good-natured things,' it remarked, 'one longed to make them a mouth to smile with.' The Gordon Bennett International Balloon Race outlived its sponsor by a good eleven years, but nobody paid much heed to it, and America's outright victory in the third series at St. Louis in 1929 sent balloon racing to its grave all but unsung. The private individual might be fed up with traffic jams, but by then he could, for the expenditure of nine hundred pounds, acquire far more predictable air transport in the form of a De Havilland 'Moth', a German Klemm, a French Caudron, or one of the vast family of 'Cub' monoplanes inspired by Mr C. G. Taylor. Primitive these may have been in comparison with the 'executive transports' of today but, unlike the balloon, their navigation no longer depended on hope. True, the movement has been kept alive by Clubs and individuals in various countries since then—a balloon race was even staged in Britain in 1965—but it is now agreed that the balloon's practical value is limited to research, a field whence it is being ousted rapidly by the advance of rocketry.

But if this is and was so, why did Rolls, who had little use for dead ends, and extricated himself smartly whenever he encountered one, not only engage actively in the sport, but maintain his interest for nine years? Electric broughams and the saurian Dufaux were jettisoned, but not the balloon. The simple answer is—that he liked it. It is also clear from his writings even at the turn of the century that he recognized the conquest of the air as the next logical step after the conquest of the road. We have seen from his career as a racing motorist that he believed in meticulous preparation and it would therefore have been obvious to him that he must come to terms with the new element. He must learn his way about the sky as he was to learn the intricacies of the Auvergne Circuit and the T.T. course in the Isle of Man. To Rolls, personal conquest was not enough: if flying was to be sold as motoring had been successfully sold, the fear of the sky must be vanquished. Had he lived, one can almost see him chaperoning County Councillors into aeroplanes as he had demonstrated the motor car to their predecessors in his Locomobile in 1902. When he started his gliding experiments at Eastchurch in the summer of 1909, he was no tyro: eighteen months previously he had celebrated his hundredth flight as a passenger in the French airship *Ville de Paris*.

The leisurely progress of a balloon was its principal charm. 'There is no giddiness', wrote Frank Hedges Butler, 'no movement, only a sensation of perfect quiet and restfulness.' Rolls, whose interest in the camera was otherwise casual, became a connoisseur of aerial photography. Even the drearier appendages of cities took on a new glamour from the air: though Vera Butler might remark that subtopia from a thousand feet up 'looks even less attractive and more dismally formal than at near sight', a reporter who ascended with Rolls became rhapsodic, comparing tombstones in a cemetery to 'a giant double-six at dominoes', and Sir Thomas Sopwith has memories of a night flight over London in which road-works gave the impression of 'one continuous strip of light from Hounslow to the City'. In these days of air travel, the lights of London are a commonplace to many of us, but one must remember that they were a novelty to the Edwardians.

So was the cloudscape. Butler, who was an experienced traveller, and could have been forgiven a *blasé* approach, wrote: 'One never has two ascents alike; the ever-changing panorama of clouds sometimes resembles glaciers, and snow mountains, sometimes the rolling billows of the sea.' In this still naïve age, the amateur aeronauts were also fascinated by the changes in weather and temperature to be found above the clouds: one ascent made in December furnished such a contrast. On the ground ice predominated, so much so that the balloon's envelope burst on contact with a frozen ploughed field: but at 4,500 feet brilliant sunshine made conditions 'so warm and balmy that fur coats were discarded'.

A balloon's envelope protected its occupants from rain and wind alike. Even during a long-distance race we read of the crew's dining off 'cold chicken, cake, pears, and white wine' over Lake Constance, a far cry from those Plasmon biscuits hurriedly munched in a Rolls-Royce speeding northward up the *routes nationales* of France. Ladies, in summer anyway, had no need to masquerade as bears or arctic trappers: where there was no dust, fetching costumes were the order of the day. In 1907 Mrs Assheton-Harbord competed for her own Cup in 'a large-brimmed flat crowned brown hat, trimmed with hydrangeas and green tulle, a dainty white muslin blouse, and a cream serge skirt'.

If becalmed, the crew could anchor, as Frank Hedges Butler did over the Devil's Dyke one night in 1906. 'In the early morning', he records on this occasion, 'the notes of the cuckoo were heard, and the songs of the nightingale and other birds afforded a concert which was indeed as unique as it was enjoyable.' Over open country at three thousand feet, the sounds of the farmyard filtered gently through, geese being the most audible. Oswald Short remembers watching the track of a torpedo under water while crossing the Solent with Charles Rolls in 1909. From rather lower altitudes communication with fellow-humans on the ground was possible, though during the 1906 Gordon Bennett Race Rolls's appeals for directions in his 'atrocious French' were misconstrued as signals of distress. On another occasion a balloon's crew unwittingly subjected a scarecrow to a lengthy inquisition, while a literal-minded yokel answered the question 'Where are we?', with a truly teenage retort: "Why, you are up in a balloon'!

These were the splendours of ballooning in favourable conditions. The miseries could take on peculiar forms. Hazards often attended the ascent, for an unkind gust of wind could blow the balloon into a factory chimney or gasholder, as actually happened both at Monmouth and Battersea in 1906. At Hurlingham one was liable to take off into a tree. There were hazards coming down: Rolls once disrupted a cricket match, and even when the cricketers had been mollified, their spiked boots played havoc with the balloon's fragile envelope. The hop poles of Kent, Hampshire, and Herefordshire were a nightmare to aeronauts: uncomfortable to land upon, they were also death to the trailrope, a sixty-foot length which was thrown out to help maintain equilibrium at low altitudes, and also to serve as a brake. The French aeronaut Jacques Faure, confronted with a bill for damage incurred when 'trailing' near Alton, was heard to mutter darkly: 'How the blazes was I to know that the English grew their —— beer on trees'? On one of Rolls's ascents from Avington, his sister's home, a youth in a Hampshire village seized hold of the trail-rope, giving the crew some anxious moments.

Ice was no problem, but the weight of snow on the envelope could force a balloon down. Heavy passengers could prevent it from lifting at all, and on the Aero Club's first official ascent in 1901, Rolls had to stand down so that the burly Frank Hedges Butler could go aloft. Upward and downward movement was controlled by the use of ballast, which was jealously guarded. If a sack spilt, the passengers were set to work sweeping sand off the floor of the car, and when the supply ran out, inessential articles had to serve instead. Princess Teano, writing of her experiences in the first Balloon Derby held at Ranelagh in 1906, recalls that one of the first casualties when ballast ran short was 'Bradshaw'—as we shall see, an important item in the amateur aeronaut's kit. On another occasion Rolls adjured his passengers not to throw their chicken bones overboard after lunch: 'they might be needed as ballast'.

Fifty thousand cubic feet of gas in a silk envelope were a handful on the ground on a gusty day: it took thirty men to hold down a single balloon at Hurlingham in 1908. Occasionally a handler would become airborne, as happened at the start of the 1921 Gordon Bennett Cup Race. An even more embarrassing fate attended a 'peasant' whose aid was enlisted to hold Rolls's balloon down during a temporary landing he made with T. O. M. Sopwith in Surrey. The man's curiosity got the better of him, and he took a look inside. Coal gas is an admirable anaesthetic, and he took no further interest in the proceedings for some considerable time! Spectators often had to duck out of the way of flailing trail-ropes and falling sand at the start of balloon-races. Dr Barton, the airship designer, was once fired on by 'a drunken Volunteer'. While on occasions balloons could cover the ground quickly—in 1908 Griffith Brewer flew the 52 miles from Hurlingham to Castle Hedingham, Essex, in 65 minutes, an average of 48 m.p.h., and Rolls put nine miles into less than eleven minutes on *Britannia*—progress could be painfully slow, and craft were often reported missing, only to turn up after a circuitous passage. The Aero Club de France's balloon *Sonia II* drifted for 24 hours over Paris in May 1908: not that this worried the crew, who had provisioned themselves hopefully for a long voyage.

Despite the discomforts of sitting under large quantities of inflammable gas in a thunderstorm, and the constant risk of being blown out to sea, fatal accidents were rare. 'With ordinary precautions', wrote Rolls in 1903, 'ballooning is no more dangerous than any other kind of sport', and he pointed out that during the year of the Paris Exhibition over 600 ascents had been made without a single hitch. That winter, however, a half-filled and derelict balloon was found in the Apennines near Campoli, and it was feared that the crew had been eaten by wolves. The alarmists also made a great deal of capital out of the tragic disappearance of Lieutenants Caulfield and Martin-Leake, who were swept out over the Devon coast in May 1907.

There was, of course, the hazard of inadvertently crossing a frontier and being arrested as a spy. The Franco–German border was never a wise place to go ballooning, and Oswald Short suspects that at least one German aeronaut in Britain combined pleasure with other activities, for he only ascended from Battersea when the prevailing wind blew in the direction of Chatham Dockyard.

The great years of ballooning as a fashionable sport were from 1905 to 1908. In 1901, when Charles Rolls took to the air, it was little more than a 'stunt' used to enliven the bigger fairs. Rolls's mentor was Frank Hedges Butler. Butler, a wine-merchant by profession, was one of those indefatigable globe trotters who are found in profusion during the Victorian era. In 1872, as a youth of seventeen, he had accompanied his brother on a walking-tour of Switzerland, and by 1880 he had added Scandinavia, the United States, North Africa, the West Indies, British Guiana, Venezuela, Palestine, India, and Ceylon to his score. A keen climber and hunter of big game, he was as gregarious as Rolls was solitary, and he chronicled his adventures in a formidable volume with the even more formidable title of *Fifty Years of Travel on Land, Air, and Water*. His chosen trade took him often to France and, like Rolls, he encountered the motor car for the first time in that country, though it was not until 1897 that he bought one for himself. This was a $3\frac{1}{2}$-h.p. Benz, of which he wrote: 'What we most enjoyed . . . was pushing the cars up the hills, so that when we did go down the other side, we had the satisfaction of pleasure well earned.'

Frank Butler was somewhat of a *bon viveur*, and never went motoring without 'a box of Bath Oliver biscuits and one or two bottles of sherry'. He was not blessed with a mechanical bent and, according to Rolls, coped with a breakdown by planting himself on the running-board of his car, and waiting till he could bribe a passing tramp to summon assistance, or fetch supplies of water. From 1896 onwards, his constant companion on his travels had been his daughter Vera, an amazonian young woman, who was equally happy sharing a cycle tour from Aix-les-Bains to Geneva, or an ascent of Mont Blanc. Vera became a motorist in her own right, buying a $4\frac{1}{2}$-h.p. Renault in 1901. She seems to have comprehended the automobile better than did her father, for she celebrated this purchase by a test-drive from Paris to Nice, and later contributed an article on her favourite *marque* to the 'Cars and How to Drive Them' series which my father published in the *Car Illustrated*.

According to Butler, his famed balloon trip with his daughter and Rolls in 1901 was fortuitous. Vera's Renault suffered a *contretemps*, 'caused by an escape of petrol', thus depriving the Butlers of a projected motor tour. As compensation for this, the adventurous Vera suggested that Spencer, the aeronaut, be commissioned to take them up in the balloon *City of York*. At this time the Spencers and the Shorts were the only balloon manufacturers in Britain, but whereas the still unknown Short brothers were already displaying a scientific approach, their rivals seem to have derived their income from 'stunt' ascents at charity fêtes. Rolls was invited along for this trip, which took place on 24 September, 1901.

The party landed at dusk near Lee Green, but not before Rolls and Vera Butler had taken a number of photographs, or before a momentous conversation had taken place over London. As Rolls later put it: 'One said: "Let us get up some sort of balloon club." "Good idea", was the reply, "open the valve and let us go down and set to work." So we opened the valve, came down, and in a week or ten days we had a hundred applicants for membership.'

The idea, be it said, came from Vera, though it was her father who conducted the campaign which launched the Aero Club. The first prospectus was sent out on 30 October, and on 13 November the first meeting was held, attracting such eminent motorists as Colonel R. E. B. Crompton, my father, W. Worby Beaumont, Charles Cordingley, Sir David Salomons, Alfred Harmsworth and Henry Sturmey. As the birth of the Club coincided with the presence in England of the famous Brazilian aeronaut Santos-Dumont, he was duly fêted, and driven down to Aldershot to see what the Army was doing with balloons.

Inevitably, there had been some mild bickering. While Rolls and the Butlers had been discovering the delights of aeronautics three thousand feet above London, F. R. Simms, the founder of the A.C.G.B.I., had been pondering similar ideas from the ground, and had gone so far as to register a company under the name of the Aero Proprietary Ltd. He protested that the Standing Committee convened by Butler had no right to form their Club, but his resistance lasted only a week, and in the end the only token opposition came from the Aeronautical Society, a scientific body formed in 1866. Though the Society had staged an exhibition at the Crystal Palace as early as 1868, its interests remained mainly theoretical, and in the end, when the International Aeronautical Federation (F.A.I.) came into being, it recognized the Aero Club as the body governing aerial sport in Britain. On 15 November, 1901, the new Club got away to a good start by organizing its first official balloon ascent.

Progress was, however, gradual, and the Club did not appoint its first full-time Secretary till 1905—Rolls interviewed applicants at his office in Conduit Street. In the same year it issued its first certificates to aeronauts, though curiously enough neither Rolls nor Butler claimed theirs for some time. Nor, of course, did Spencer, who as a 'professional' was debarred from Club membership. Certificates were awarded immediately to C. F. Pollock and Professor A. K. Huntington; Butler, who had by this time some fifty ascents to his credit, did not qualify until February 1906, while Rolls did not follow suit until July, which time it must have been a matter of some urgency if he were to take his place in the British team for the first Gordon Bennett Cup Race. This delay resulted from a clash between his two prevailing interests—ballooning, and the development of the 'Light Twenty' Rolls-Royce, which was to culminate, as we have seen, with a victory in the second race for the Tourist Trophy.

By this time, of course, ballooning had become fashionable, and in April 1906 the Aero Club was able to announce that its own balloon would make regular ascents every Saturday from the Crystal Palace 'until the end of May—thereafter on occasional Thursdays and Saturdays'. Short Brothers offered a new service, too: those who kept balloons at their works at Battersea could now have their craft ready within an hour of a telephone call. By 1908 the Club had come to an arrangement with the Gas Light and Coke Company, whereby that concern agreed to lay down a twelve-inch pipe capable of supplying 100,000 cubic feet of gas per hour to the Hurlingham Club Grounds, which had supplanted the Crystal Palace and Ranelagh as the fashionable headquarters of the sport. But by then the craze had nearly spent itself—there might be an international race in 1909, but before the year was out the Club's own balloon had been sold for £25.

Rolls, of course, sat on the Club's Committee, but Club politics interested him not at all. He was a member of the British delegation to the F.A.I. conferences staged at Brussels (September 1907) and London (January 1909). The latter was exacerbated by a British protest against the award of the first prize in the 1908 Gordon Bennett Race to Colonel Schaeck of Switzerland, despite the fact that he had contravened the rules of the contest by landing at sea. The protest failed—and it must have grieved James Gordon Bennett to realize that by transferring his interests to the sky he had not circumvented the interminable altercations that had punctuated the series of motor-races associated with his name.

Even at its zenith, ballooning had some insurmountable limitations. A balloon could only start its voyage from the vicinity of a gas-works, and thus participants in 'balloon house-parties' had to desert the drawing-room and the croquet lawn for the less salubrious atmosphere of the local gas company's premises. True, when Rolls, Butler, and Pollock ascended from Bulwell Hall, Notts, in July 1906, the authorities were kind enough to lay gas-pipes up the drive, but the ascents 'from the Hendre' were in fact conducted from the Monmouth Gas Works in the town, while Lady Shelley-Rolls's guests at Avington Park travelled two miles by car to the Winchester city gasholders at Winnall Moors before ascending skywards. The Short brothers operated from the gas-works at Battersea. We may safely ignore such outbursts of journalistic exuberance as the assertion that Rolls's ascents from Cowes started 'from a boat'. Imagination boggles at the thought of yards of gas-pipe bucketing betwixt ship and shore!

Nor was the sport a cheap one. As one was at the mercy of the elements, the place of descent was unpredictable, and the intelligent aeronaut always packed a copy of Bradshaw's Railway Guide in his basket, and arranged for a party to follow him by road. Harry Fleck, who followed Rolls on several occasions, estimates that in five cases out of ten contact between balloon and car was successfully achieved: he used to ascertain the direction of the wind by watching factory chimneys, as blank stares were the likeliest response to such questions as 'Have you seen a balloon around these parts?' A balloon and its attendant impedimenta represented a bulky load, and cars were hardly ever used for retrieving. Rolls had his '70-h.p.' 'Silver Ghost' of 1908 2,000-Mile Trial type fitted up as a balloon tender, and replicas of this car have been made up by more than one veteran-car enthusiast, but Mr Smith confirms that it would only cope with very small balloons, such as the *Imp* of 17,500 cubic feet. He can only recall its being turned to this purpose on one occasion. Normally the motor party was concerned solely with tracking the balloon to its landing-place, and enlisting the help of locals who could furnish a cart for its transportation to the nearest railway station.

There were two methods of landing a balloon. One of these was to let the gas escape gradually by 'valving', and took some time: it was much simpler to bring the craft near the ground, and then pull the 'rip panel', a small section which would let the gas out rapidly. After use, the rip panel had to be sewn back again, a process which cost the aeronaut about ten shillings. Understandably, Rolls never 'ripped' if he could possibly avoid it. A four-seater car and equipment cost about £160, plus £90 for the envelope, and a typical budget for a flight from London to Brighton in 1906 was estimated as follows: £4 10s. for gas, £2 10s. for inflation, and another £1 for cartage to the gas-works. Provided that 'Bradshaw' was intelligently used, the hire of a cart to the nearest station once one had landed should not cost more than five shillings (happy days!), but the average aeronaut expected to dispense another five shillings in assorted tips. Not so Rolls: the farm labourer who helped him dismantle and pack up his balloon was lucky to receive sixpence!

With good organization, however, it could be a pleasant sport. When Rolls ascended from Avington in May 1907, his landing at Brockenhurst coincided with a convenient 'special' from the station, and he was back in London by 8.15 p.m. On a flight to Derby, Butler managed even better; he left Wandsworth at 12.30 noon, and touched down in time to catch the 7.15 p.m. dining-car train home.

No matter where one landed, everyone was friendly. The Aero Club might find it necessary to issue a stern and admonitory note on the indiscriminate use of trail-ropes in 1909, but their adverse effects were much exaggerated, thanks to their small diameter and light weight. Sir Thomas Sopwith remembers 'trailing' over greenhouses with no ill effect, and farmers were quick to accept reasonable compensation. Oswald Short recalls one who had no qualms in accepting an offer of £3 after a field of standing corn had been flattened by a rope. In the carefree world of the Edwardian house-party, even those die-hards who subscribed to Mr Cathcart Wason's view of the motor-car as 'a stinking engine of iniquity' would welcome fellow-Edwardians who 'dropped in' from the skies, as they were to welcome their sons and daughters in their 'Moths' in the 1930s. In March 1906 Rolls paid two unheralded visits to country-houses in East Anglia; and the Vicar of Shernbourne, Norfolk, put him and Colonel Capper up for the night when they landed at the conclusion of the first race for the Gordon Bennett Cup. Nor did it matter what time of day it was: a landowner at Horley entertained Rolls and his friends to dinner when he brought *Britannia* down after a demonstration flight from Hurlingham, while the Rev. F. S. Sclater of Newick Park, Sussex, found Rolls, Butler, Pollock, Mrs Dunville, and Mrs Assheton-Harbord on his front doorstep one fine morning in 1907. They got their breakfast 'on the house'. This hospitality was not confined to the moneyed classes either: when Princess Teano's party landed near a gipsy encampment in Essex, they were invited to partake of gin. None of the surviving aeronauts of those days can recall any hostility, and the only dissentient vote I can trace came from a barrister in the New Forest. 'That gentleman', reported *The Times*, 'preferred the descent should take place at another spot, fearing damage might be caused to his beautiful trees.'

By contrast to the motor-car, of course, the balloon offered little diversity in the way of sport. For a while balloon-parties were fashionable. These were staged at Pitmaston, J. A. Holder's home near Birmingham, where a model railway in the grounds was a further attraction to Rolls and his party: at Wickhurst, Leslie Bucknall's country house in Kent: at Avington on the Itchen, the home of Sir John and Lady Shelley-Rolls: and of course at the Hendre, where the long-suffering Lord Llangattock endured the incursions of his son's ballooning friends regularly every Easter and Christmas until 1909. Mr George Ward, who watched these ascents, remembers John Rolls as an unenthusiastic passenger. Lord Llangattock confined his participation to captive ascents from the gas-works, and to a cryptic request to 'give my love to those you meet above' as his son departed on a flight across the Bristol Channel. But his wife, notwithstanding her distrust of 'hazardous pleasures', allowed Charles to transport her from the town to her own front lawn ('Taking Mum Home By Balloon', as one irreverent journalist phrased it). One of the advantages of a feudal society was, of course, the ease with which gas companies acceded to the use of their facilities, and at Eastertide, 1906, a 'large concourse of people' attended the departure of the balloonists. In 1907 the programme was more ambitious: three balloons were fielded, a 'special saloon train' was chartered to take the guests down to Monmouth, and Oswald Short came down in person to provide technical assistance. No wonder the gas-holder at Monmouth was all but emptied. 1908 was even better, with four balloons, and an international flavour was lent by the presence of the Comte d'Oultremont, President of the Belgian Aero Club, and the Comte Castillon de St. Victor, of the Aero Club de France: there was also an untoward incident, when Rolls collided with some cattle-trucks at take-off. The last balloon-party at Monmouth was staged at Christmas, 1909: thenceforward aviation weeks were to be the order of the day, and sponsorship was to pass from the stately homes to the municipalities.

Avington, being close to Winchester and Southampton, attracted bigger crowds, some 2,000 people being present at the Winchester Gas Works at Whitsun, 1907, to see three balloons take the air. The *Hampshire Observer* contributes a curious footnote to these antics:

> The fact that three passengers were able to go is one of the most eloquent tributes to the quality of the gas. . . . This superiority in quality of the Winchester gas over that

of Chelsea is a matter upon which Mr Head and the water and gas company are to be congratulated, and one which should not be lost on gas consumers.

The significance of this diminishes when we find Rolls using almost exactly the same words of praise at Monmouth! Still, Mr Head's efficiency did not go unrewarded, for the following year he was taken up as a passenger in *Kismet*. On another occasion Rolls performed the creditable feat of landing on his sister's lawn at Avington after ascending from Chichester.

Of a more competitive nature were the car versus balloon matches. On the first occasion when this sport was tried, Charles and his Panhard were, however, among the pursuers, and the event received a somewhat jaundiced press, especially from Charles Cordingley of the *Motor Car Journal* whose big Mercédès limousine was scratched by overhanging boughs when he ventured off the beaten track. Both the local gas and Frank Hedges Butler were too heavy for the balloon, and 'four fifty-pound bags of ballast' had to be substituted for the founder of the Aero Club before it would consent to become airborne. A second chase, also starting from the Crystal Palace, followed shortly afterward, and this again ended in a victory for the balloon (*Graphic*, manned by Rolls, Butler, Vera Butler and Pollock). It descended at Herriard, near Alton, while the nearest car was some five miles away in the neighbourhood of Farnham. Warren Smith's Argyll became involved with a hunt at Oxshott, and the driver's chivalrous decision not to cross the scent, coupled with the stag's tiresome predilection for doubling back on its tracks, cost him precious hours. Bersey's Panhard bogged down altogether in a muddy lane near Guildford, which was bad luck; at one stage he had been very 'warm', and Rolls reported hearing the noise of his engine through the drifting fog. But in December 1902 another chase was staged, from Reading gas-works this time, and the motorists showed that at long last they had found their form. Rolls was caught by Mark Mayhew, who managed to save his car from being clouted by the trail-rope, and then took to the fields on foot to effect a successful capture. By 1904, when a chase featured in the programme of the Pitmaston balloon-party, the cars were clearly on top, though Rolls himself managed to evade his pursuers, and the motorists had a tough time contending with 'thick-headed drivers of horsed vehicles and stubborn cyclists', not to mention a cow which threatened to charge them, but thought better of it. There were also the peasantry: as the drivers penetrated into the Welsh Marches, they were greeted by such unhelpful comments on their quarry as 'I saw him throw out a lot of sand, look you.' None the less, Pollock and Huntington in *Norfolk* were cornered by George Lanchester's Lanchester and W. A. Brown's Renault.

There were also races between two balloons, a sport in which Rolls and Pollock specialized. The first of these was staged from the Crystal Palace in July 1904, with Rolls and Huntington in *Aero Club I* and Pollock in *Norfolk*. Pollock elected to 'trail' until a village got in his way, but Rolls found himself becalmed near Cambridge, and had to submit to the humiliation of capture by the occupants of a passing car on the Newmarket road. None the less, Pollock and Rolls again met at Oxford the following year, Moore-Brabazon being in Rolls's crew on this occasion, while the experiment was repeated in 1906. This contest turned out to be somewhat of a fiasco, since Pollock failed to take on sufficient ballast at the start, and had to make a hasty descent on the polo ground in Wimbledon Park, fortunately while it was unoccupied. One feels that cricket would have been a far safer game to disturb. Rolls, the pursuer, had nothing to pursue, but he continued 'at a regular altitude', and descended in Bulstrode Park, Gerrards Cross, where he received the usual welcome, and employed himself pleasurably by giving captive ascents to Sir John Ramsden's house-party. Shortly afterwards we find him again chasing Pollock, but this time he was combining business with pleasure by conducting the hunt from the wheel of a 30-h.p. Rolls-Royce.

The game of Hare and Hounds was Rolls's personal contribution to aeronautical sport. Though reports indicate that similar pastimes had a short vogue in both Switzerland and Germany, its pursuit in Britain was instigated by Rolls, who presented a cup to the winner of this event, and invariably acted as 'hare', using his small balloon *Imp*: this carried black and white streamers to assist in identification. The 'hare' was not allowed to make any intermediate descents, a privilege reserved for the 'hounds', who could make temporary landings should they overshoot the 'hare', or wish to stalk him. The balloon which landed nearest to the 'hare' was adjudged the winner. To avoid the risk of unhappy landings, it was ordained that the race should be declared null and void were Rolls to descend within a ten-mile radius of Charing Cross. The 'hounds' were also enjoined to ascend with their trail-ropes out so as to avoid bumping into each other at the start: collisions were bad enough, but there was the even more alarming risk that the crew of a balloon might be asphyxiated by the gas escaping from the valves of a following craft.

As played in June 1908, the game attracted a field of eleven 'hounds', their pilots including John Dunville, Mrs Assheton-Harbord, Colonel Capper (designer of the airship *Nulli Secundus*), Professor Huntington, Leslie Bucknall, Griffith Brewer and Frank Hedges Butler. On this occasion, the press were transported in no less a vehicle than AX 201, the original Rolls-Royce 'Silver Ghost'. If Claude Johnson read *The Times's* assessment of it as 'a splendid racing motor car', he must have blenched, but in the event it followed as well, if not better than the official 'hounds'. Rolls was nearly captured when his trail rope involved itself with some telegraph wires near Epsom, but he cut himself loose, and thereafter only Dunville in *La Mascotte* was ever close to him. Rolls came down at Amberley, near Arundel: Dunville descended amid a scene of rural peace some four miles away at Fittleworth, 'into Mr John Budd's meadow, all abloom with wild rose, foxgloves, and honeysuckle'. 'All the rustics and a cow or two', continued the report, patronizingly, 'crowded round to give assistance if any were needed.' Against such a pastoral background, one cannot marvel that motorists turned to ballooning to escape the police, whose campaign of persecution was even then reaching a climax: for those were the days when failure of an A.A. Scout to salute a member's car indicated one thing, and one thing only—the imminence of a speed trap!

Three ladies were among the ranks of the 'hounds' in the 1909 race, and this year Rolls was well and truly caught,

Mortimer Singer being the victor, and Pollock the runner-up. H. E. Perrin, writing in the *Car Illustrated* of a season that had seen the sudden and almost total eclipse of the balloon, commented sarcastically:

> The only achievement during the year which the writer can recall as a ballooning record was the landing effected by Mr A. Mortimer Singer within twenty yards of the Hon. C. S. Rolls's 'hare' balloon *Imp* in the Hare and Hounds Race at Hurlingham last June.

The sport of Hare and Hounds died with Rolls—and in any case balloon racing in England was moribund several months before his death.

For these diversions he used a small balloon of 17,500 cubic feet, which he named *Imp*. A minor mystery surrounds the balloons he was piloting at this time; officially *Imp* made its initial ascent from Shorts' works on 15 March, 1908, yet earlier than this Rolls had been using another small craft, said to have a capacity of only 11,000 cubic feet, to which contemporary reports give the name of *Midget*. But the provenance of *Midget* remains unsolved: Sir Thomas Sopwith confirms that he made a number of ascents with Rolls in a very small balloon before 1908—on the other hand, neither Oswald Short, who made Charles's balloons nor T. O. Smith, who was his personal mechanic at this time, can recall any small-capacity craft apart from *Imp*. Clearly, though, Rolls and Sopwith cannot have ascended *together* in an 11,000 cubic-feet balloon, as this would have given insufficient lift. As it was, the latter was in considerable demand as a passenger for *Imp* owing to his light weight. It is interesting to note that Sopwith's own balloon log records three ascents in *Midget*; this seems to prove that Rolls owned two small capacity craft.

I very much doubt if Rolls owned any of the balloons he piloted, apart from *Midget*, *Imp*, and *Britannia*, his entry for the 1906 Gordon Bennett Cup Race, though he may have had a stake in others. He certainly captained numerous craft, among them Mrs Assheton-Harbord's *Valkyrie* and *Padsop* (a joint venture by Sopwith and Phil Paddon), but it is hard to credit that his finances could have supported a whole stud of balloons on the salary and commission he was drawing from Rolls-Royce Ltd., much less so on the more uncertain arrangements that obtained up to the end of 1906, while C. S. Rolls and Co. retained its separate existence. Certain it is that his subsequent experiments with aeroplanes strained his pocket, and at the time of his death he was looking for backers to help launch an aircraft manufacturing business.

Serious balloon racing did not arrive until 1906, and Rolls's interest in the sport is reflected by the fact that in an exceptionally busy year he found time to watch the start of the French Balloon Grand Prix, shortly after his successful attack on the Monte Carlo–London record with the 'Light Twenty' Rolls-Royce. In July it was the turn of the British Aero Club, who organized an International Balloon Derby starting from Ranelagh. Though competitors were made to paint their name and nationality on their envelopes, the contest was international only in name, all seven starters being British. This was a 'fixed-point' race—the object was to finish nearest to an appointed spot, in this case near Ingatestone in Essex. Nobody was successful, the best performance being put up by the wily Butler, in *Enchantress*—he hovered low over the Thames Estuary, watching the sails of passing barges in order to ascertain more accurately the direction of the wind. Rolls suffered from 'too light a quality of gas' (O! to be in Winchester, or even in Monmouth!). He was flying solo in *Midget* —or so the reports stated—and was therefore compelled by the rules to carry sealed ballast equivalent to the weight of one passenger. This limited the amount of usable ballast he could take, and he was thus reduced to throwing out 'other dispensable objects'. By this time he must have been conversant with the railway system of Essex, and possibly would have lacked a copy of the faithful 'Bradshaw' to sacrifice in the cause of altitude.

But a truly international competition was at hand. James Gordon Bennett, disillusioned by the squabbles of the national motor clubs, had awarded a new Trophy for balloon racing, and for this event Rolls ordered from Short Brothers what was at the time the largest balloon in England, the 78,000 cubic

The Aero Club's first official ascent at Stamford Bridge in 1901.
Photo by courtesy of the Royal Aero Club.

Abandoned race. Hurlingham, 11 July 1908. △
Photos by courtesy of the Royal Aero Club. ▽

▽ Ascent of the *Mercury* at Monmouth, 26 December 1908.
Photo by courtesy of the Royal Aero Club.

◁ The *Mercury* lands at the Hendre, 26 July 1908.
Photo by courtesy of the Royal Aero Club.

Gordon Bennett Race, Paris 1906. General View.
Photo by courtesy of the Royal Aero Club.

Rolls ascends with Major Baden Powell.
Photo by courtesy of the Royal Aero Club.

Gordon Bennett Race, Berlin 1908.
Photo by courtesy of the Royal Aero Club.

A curiosity in the English countryside. *Photo by courtesy of the Royal Aero Club.*

Inauguration of the *Esperance* at Hurlingham, 23 May 1909. *Photo by courtesy of the Royal Aero Club.*

Flight with Wilbur Wright, 8 October 1908. *Photo by courtesy of the Royal Aero Club.*

The Wright brothers at Sheppey, May 1909. Orville is next to C.S.R. and Wilbur behind in bowler hat. *Photo by courtesy of the Royal Aero Club.*

The Eiffel Tower
from the air.
Charles Rolls took
this photograph
from a balloon.
*Photo by courtesy of
Rolls-Royce Ltd.*

Balloon tender.
Rolls's special
'70-h.p.' Silver
Ghost two-seater
with *Imp* stowed
astern, 1909. *Photo
by courtesy of
Rolls-Royce Ltd.*

foot *Britannia*. It was furnished with two alternative 'bodies', a ten-seater for touring, and a two-seater for racing, and made a test flight from Battersea to Maidstone just before the 1906 T.T. At this period, Rolls must have attained a state of perpetual motion, for his interest in ballooning was close to its zenith, and his determination to avenge the disaster of 1905 involved him in numerous trials with the 'Light Twenty' Rolls-Royce. No wonder he persuaded Royce to carry out some of the preliminary testing for him!

Each country could nominate a team of three balloons, and the British contingent was made up of Rolls, with Colonel Capper in *Britannia*, Butler in *City of London* and Huntington in *Zephyr*. The arrangements were complex, and rendered more so by the unpredictability of balloon flight. Thus every competitor's passport had to be visa-ed for France, Germany, Austria, and Russia, entry to this last-mentioned country demanding a special, additional passport. He was also furnished with a set of forms printed in four languages—English, French, German, and Latin!—which were to be presented to two 'responsible persons' upon landing. These 'responsible persons' would certify the place at which the balloon had descended. Also incorporated was a quadrilingual *questionnaire* full of practical requests such as 'Can we obtain a cart to carry this balloon to the railway station?' In Paris, at the start of the race, soldiers were in attendance to lay down the necessary gas pipes and walk the balloons out: but there were insufficient passes for the press, and Rolls sportingly lent his to journalists. The nations represented were Great Britain, France, Belgium, Italy, the United States, and Spain, and Santos-Dumont enlivened the proceedings by fielding a power-assisted balloon with a 6-h.p. engine. There was nothing in the rules to prohibit this, but the intrepid inventor caught his arm in the transmission shaft, and was forced to retire.

In the event, the multiplicity of visas proved superfluous, for the prevailing wind blew eastwards, and all those who cleared the Channel coast landed in England. The winner was Lieutenant Frank P. Lahm of the United States Army, who managed the 402 miles to Fylingdales in Yorkshire in 22 hrs. 5 min. Rolls made the headlines by disappearing altogether.

For the first thirteen hours he had flown a circuitous route over France: he had 'trailed' over the sea, and had all but 'bagged' three steamers for his pains: and he crossed the English coast at Hastings, where he threw a message overboard (The *Evening Standard* conscientiously recorded that it had been retrieved by a pet dog rejoicing in the name of 'Little Nell'). Thereafter nothing was heard of him.

Some strange reports came in. A 'yellow balloon with long trailing appendages and wings' was seen going south over Thetford, but this seems to have been an early case of 'flying-sauceritis', a disease not unknown even then. An outbreak in South Wales in 1909 was, of course, blamed on Rolls! He eventually turned up at Shernbourne, Norfolk, between Sandringham and the North Sea, explaining his failure to report by the fact that neither the village nor the nearby railway station at Dersingham possessed a telegraph office. He had been airborne for 26 hrs. 18 min. and nonchalantly remarked that he would have stayed up even longer but for the risk of falling into the sea. He ascribed the smoothness of his descent to the use of the rip panel—evidently the hope of an award justified the expenditure of ten shillings on this occasion. He was placed third in the Race, and won the Aero Club de France's gold medal for the flight of the longest duration as well as the Gould Cup for the best performance by a British competitor. Butler had failed to reach England, and Huntington in *Zephyr* had descended on the Kentish shore of the Thames Estuary. Though Rolls was cited as a prospective competitor in both the 1907 and 1908 races for the Gordon Bennett Cup, he did not compete on either occasion. Of the controversial 1908 contest he wrote to a friend: 'I think I was well out of the balloon race this year—the weather was so thick that it seemed a question of who could take the greatest risk without being carried over the sea.'

However, there were two major events in the British calendar in 1907 for Rolls to support. The first of these was the Harbord Cup, donated by the Hon. Mrs Assheton-Harbord, not only an enthusiastic aeronaut, but also a loyal supporter of Rolls-Royce to the tune of two 'Twenties' and a 'Thirty'. She had already won distinction in aeronautical circles in 1906 by winning the Krabbé Cup for the longest flight accomplished within the British Isles during the months of August, September and October: this, incidentally, had been donated by Miss Hilda Krabbé, another lady aeronaut, and later to become the wife of J. T. C. Moore-Brabazon. The Harbord Cup Race was run on the same principles as the 'International Derby' of 1906: Rolls piloted the donor's balloon *Nebula*, and was seen off by Lady Llangattock, who wore a white feather boa. Huntington and Brewer had difficulty in leaving the ground at all, and were seen frantically throwing out ballast, while the fashionably dressed ladies were (equally frantically) opening their parasols to protect themselves from this uncomfortable brand of manna. But while the sun shone at Ranelagh, competitors were battling their way through a heavy thunderstorm over Windsor. Butler was again the victor: Rolls could manage no better than third place. On this occasion he was accompanied by Lieutenant Caulfield, destined to die only a week later in an Army balloon.

Weather conditions played havoc with the race for Frank Hedges Butler's cup, and only Colonel Capper on *Pegasus* succeeded in clearing the London suburbs. Rolls, on *Britannia* this time, rammed Mrs Harbord's *Nebula* at the start, and though his ripped envelope failed to prevent him getting airborne, he had to land on Wimbledon Common.

1908 was little better. Both the 'Harbord' and the 'Butler' were blown and rained off, though seven aeronauts elected to give the crowd their money's worth on the day appointed for the latter, and Rolls got as far as Chipping Ongar, where he is reported as having 'an amusing and lively conversation with people in the town'. The balloonists had their compensation in a good race for the International Trophy. The 31 starters included eighteen from Continental Europe, but these were at a disadvantage in a 'fixed-point' event demanding skilled map-reading and a good knowledge of local topography. The route, incidentally, was marked by no less a person than Miss Dorothy Levitt in a Napier. A high wind at the start took its toll: Demoor's French *Aero Club IV* collided with another competitor, while the Belgian *Emulation du Nord* took off straight into a tree, and 'with its passengers was temporarily lost to view to the accompaniment of an alarming crashing of wood'. Ballast was hastily thrown out, and M. Crombez—later to be well-known as an aviator—departed skywards with a branch still entangled in his ropework. He came down for good at Harlington, near what is now London Airport.

Despite fears that the white course-markers might be confused with domestic washing, both Pollock and Griffith Brewer finished less than one and a half miles off the official 'set-point'. Rolls was not among the leaders—nor, understandably enough, were any of the continental contingent.

Rolls's last serious race was the 1909 International event, which started from Hurlingham. The decline in 'balloonacy' was apparent from the small field of only fourteen, all British apart from three Germans and a Belgian. The finishing point this year was near Billericay, and clearly the foreigners had been studying their maps carefully: the winner was von Thewald of Germany, but even he was a good three and a half miles from his target, thanks to a 'wilful and wayward wind'. Rolls on *Mercury* had difficulty in getting away, and sprayed the spectators with sand; in spite of this he was awarded fifth place. Unluckiest of all was Dr Hutz, a German competitor who descended on a house in Stratford, with the car of his balloon overhanging a canal bank. A mother and child imprisoned by the crash were rescued before they could succumb to the escaping gas. For the second year in succession the Harbord Cup was a casualty of the weather, but this did not stop Rolls from making an ascent in the Baroness Heeckeren's *Espérance*, another Short-built craft which he had lately test-flown for its owner. He landed safely at Littlehampton. This was almost the last time Rolls flew a balloon, for already he and Smith were working on a glider of Wright type, with which Rolls aimed to prepare himself for powered flight.

Even if his natural caution deterred him from making a return appearance in the Gordon Bennett Cup, he had always kept a careful eye on aeronautical, as well as motoring developments on the Continent. As early as December 1901, he went ballooning in France with the Butlers, and was caught in a snowstorm. Thereafter he seems to have fitted ascents in with his business schedule as best he could. He visited France in

May 1903, to take part in Paris–Madrid, and managed to make two balloon trips during this stay, one of which ended uncomfortably in a tree—he had to climb down the trail-rope to terra firma. Also abortive was a plan to cross the Channel in May 1904 with Pollock and Huntington in *Aero Club No. 1*: the party gave up at Heathfield. While selling Rolls-Royces in America in the autumn and winter of 1906, he made at least one balloon trip, and the International Aeronautical Conference staged in Brussels in September 1907 was made a pretext for yet another race. On this occasion he got lost again, and stayed up for twenty-five hours. Even this could only net him fourth place, for Erbsloh, who was to win that year's race for the Gordon Bennett Cup, remained in the air for more than thirty hours to win this event as well. Only sixty-three miles, incidentally, separated the first four finishers. Rolls commented favourably on the rubberized fabric used for the envelopes of the German balloons, and the following year the Anglo-German *Continental*, so equipped, was flying in England.

All Rolls's enthusiasms were communicated to his friends, and both Lady Brabazon and Sir Thomas Sopwith remember the zest with which he tackled ballooning—while his interest lasted. Among those he introduced to the sport were Moore-Brabazon and Warwick Wright, later a well-known figure in motoring circles. Others to receive their initiation at his hands were Captain Corbet of the London and Parisian Motor Company, then promoting the six-cylinder Hotchkiss as a rival to the Rolls-Royces; Lord Royston; and J. Lyons Sampson of the A.C.G.B.I., who had acted as starter for the Thousand Miles' Trial, and was to die in the same week as Rolls, victim of an accident involving a car and a traction-engine. 'Some members of White's Club' were taken up in 1907, while the theatrical profession was regaled with balloons as it had been with Rolls-Royces. In 1906 Mr Louis Bradfield and Miss Godwynne Earle, of the Coliseum company, accompanied him on an ascent which took them to Bognor, and he also offered to take the celebrated comedian Harry Tate up as a passenger, the idea being that Tate should prepare a 'ballooning' sketch to match his immortal skit on motoring. T. O. Smith, however, does not remember Tate's availing himself of this invitation.

When a party of senior French aeronauts visited London in 1908, Rolls was asked to show them the city from the air, and they duly ascended in *Valkyrie* with Butler and Mrs Harbord.

If his ballooning adventures had no technical value—we hear little of various schemes for meteorological research which were mooted during the early years of the Aero Club—they did at least introduce him to the Short brothers. Horace, Eustace and Oswald Short had been quietly making balloons in the obscurity of their small workshops under the railway arches at Battersea since 1899, and might have disappeared from business in equal obscurity, had not Rolls been on the look-out for a balloon manufacturer in 1905. But this time there was no Henry Edmunds to guide his steps. Instead, he asked his secretary, Miss Florence Caswell, to furnish him with a list of balloon makers culled from the directory, and set off to interview each firm in succession. The results were disappointing, for most of his subjects proved to be in the toy-balloon business; and Miss Caswell remembers his jubilation when he returned with the news that Shorts welcomed any orders he could bring them. By March 1906 the hither unknown little firm had at least three orders on hand—a small balloon (perhaps the mysterious *Midget*) for Rolls, a big craft for Professor Huntington, and another balloon commissioned as a joint venture by Rolls, Moore-Brabazon, and Warwick Wright. Thereafter Shorts never looked back, and Mr Oswald Short, the only surviving brother, pays tribute to Rolls in the following words: 'By his advice and by his actions he saved us from financial losses, which, in those early days, we might not have been able to recover from.'

We shall meet the Shorts again when we discuss Rolls's career as an aviator. Suffice it to say that he was to be among their first customers when they decided to transfer their allegiance from balloons to aeroplanes. 1909 was to mark the end of serious private ballooning, and Shorts made their last free balloon in 1914. Thereafter they specialized in marine aircraft, culminating in the 'C-boats' which introduced luxury to the long-distance airlines of the Commonwealth, and their military derivative, the indestructible 'Sunderland' of the Second World War.

In 1906 the *Motor* had said of Rolls: 'He is making an ascent every Saturday—his taste is insatiable', and ballooning was not only a genuine hobby, but one in which, singularly, he could meet the opposite sex on equal terms. In the world of the balloon, his solitary nature seems to have unbent for a while, and with Vera Butler, with Mrs Moore-Brabazon (Hilda Krabbé), and especially with Mrs Assheton-Harbord he enjoyed terms of easy friendship. When his balloon passed over Eton in May 1908, he waved cheerfully to Etonians on the ground, and even wrote to the local paper to identify himself. 'We thought perhaps they would be interested to know that it was an Old Etonian in the balloon.' His ability is demonstrated by the fact that he was in demand by private owners as a 'test pilot', and in 1909 he captained two Short-built balloons on their maiden ascents. If any proof is needed of his love for the sport, it can be found in the manner in which he contrived to spare the time for ascents even when the affairs of C. S. Rolls and Co., and Rolls-Royce Ltd., must have pressed him hard.

Not even his affection for balloons, however, could convince him of their utility. In 1906 he was writing enthusiastically of the French Army's experiments with observation balloons, but he clearly did not subscribe to Auguste Gaudron's grandiose ideas (expounded in a lecture to the Society of Arts in January 1908). The French aeronaut claimed that by sending ten troop-carrying balloons across the Channel daily it would be possible to transport 5,000 men for an outlay of only £60,000. Rolls had been nearer the truth when he had told the *Car Illustrated* that 'from the aeroplane you can drop a bomb into any fort you like'. Knowing him as we do, we need not be surprised that this observation was published in October 1906, on the eve of his departure for America.

From the moment he set foot in the United States and interviewed the Wright brothers, the balloon was doomed in his eyes. With the arrival of the Wrights in France in 1908, his involvement with this newest form of locomotion could not long be delayed. So far the conflict of interests had been three-cornered: the cars that bore his name, the balloons that gave him the nearest approach to relaxation he was ever to enjoy, and the aeroplane which he already saw as the weapon, if not the transport, of the future. He was not to abandon Royce and Johnson without a struggle, but though he was to make a balloon ascent as late as April 1910, his eyes were firmly turned elsewhere.

CHAPTER EIGHT

Towards Powered Flight

The sensation of flight was delightful and novel, and the fact of accomplishing what several eminent scientists have 'proved' impossible gave also an added satisfaction.
The Hon. C. S. Rolls, *The Times*, October 1908

When Curtiss's aeroplane rose, I had a feeling of ecstatic joy only comparable to the most intense, ideal sensations of art and love. The consciousness of the weight of one's body seemed gradually lost. The enchantment was so great that orally to express it I muttered Ben Jonson's verse: 'O! so soft, O! so sweet is she.'
Gabriele d'Annunzio, quoted in the *Motor*, September 1909

Thus a practical engineer and a poet recorded the sensations of powered flight.

Today the aeroplane, like the motor-car before it, has been integrated into our social structure. A generation that can contemplate with equanimity an air passage, if not the fare, to Sydney, Tokyo or New York, finds it hard to credit that in 1920 an early passenger on the scheduled service between England and France could summarize his journey in the words: 'They shut you up in a box in London, you are ill, and then it is Paris'! Even less could they realize the dramatic impact of flying in 1908, when Wilbur Wright demonstrated for the first time in Europe the practical possibilities of the new invention. Unless this is understood, we may well marvel at Royce's adamantine resistance to his partner's blandishments, and of his refusal even to consider an entry into the field of aviation, in which attitude he was staunchly supported by Ernest Claremont.

Such are the perils of judging past history by the standards of today. Rolls-Royce Ltd. was a young firm and had to resist diversification, even in its milder forms as practised by Napier: the Acton firm were to wait longer than Derby before embarking upon the manufacture of aero-engines, but by 1910 their

163

products embraced commercial vehicles as well as private cars, and the latter ranged from twin-cylinder 'Tens' up to the big 65-h.p. 'Six'. Even after the advent of the flying boom in 1909, aeroplanes were a chancy speculation, as both Humber and Star found to their cost. Herbert Austin's short-lived aircraft department contributed to his company's one brief period of receivership as late as 1921, when the aeroplane's practical value had been conclusively proved by the First World War. And even in 1906 no one had successfully flown a heavier-than-air craft in Europe. Clement Ader's experiments with the steam-driven 'Avion' had done no more than enrich the vocabulary of the Gallic tongue by one substantive, while as for the brothers Wright in America, their first hop at Kitty Hawk in 1903 had been followed by a lengthy silence. The layout of the twin-screw, tail-first pusher biplane as propounded by Wilbur and Orville was well known; indeed Rolls had experimented with models based on their ideas, but the scepticism that attended their efforts had hardened their attitude to the press, and they retired to the seclusion of Fort Myer, leaving public opinion to dismiss their aeroplane as a mere flash in the pan. To the vast majority powered flight was still synonymous with the airship.

The main reason for this was simple; as yet there were no aero-engines as such to power early experimental craft. Automobile power units had attained a reasonable level of efficiency: if the 1,000-kilogram formula had achieved nothing else, it had at least channelled principles of design in the right direction. Unfortunately, racing-car designers concentrated their main efforts on lightening and drilling components other than the engine, with the consequence that quite a few of their early creations literally disintegrated on the circuits. But Rolls was on the right track when he told the *Evening News* (in November 1901, over a year before the Wrights, or anyone else, had flown): 'No one has yet produced a machine light enough, car or engine, to defy that irritating law of gravitation, and be at the same time absolutely reliable.' He went on, prophetically: 'Hence the danger: the leaders, the first in ideas become the first in experiment. And so death may seize them before even the step they made is assured to us.'

Even in 1910, when Charles paid the price for being 'one of the first in experiment', engines were still too heavy. Designers were soon to surmount this problem—World War I was to see liquid-cooled units of the type of the Mercédès, Rolls-Royce and Hispano-Suiza, developing over 200 b.h.p., and capable of propelling nearly a ton of aeroplane at over 130 m.p.h.; but the disadvantages of using a converted car engine are illustrated by the Shorts' first effort, exhibited at the London Aero Show in the spring of 1909. It never flew—and no wonder, for its four-cylinder 40-h.p. Nordenfelt motor, complete with radiator, turned the scales at over 800 lb, ample for a good-sized touring car, but hopeless in the air. From the start the Wrights dispensed with some of this weight by adopting an air-cooled 'four' of their own design, while later the French firm of Gnome was to produce a series of efficient rotaries, also air-cooled. These were of constant-speed type, and the gyroscopic effect of a large rotating mass in the nose killed many an unwary pilot, but the idea at least relieved designers of the need to budget for a lot of ponderous plumbing.

Rolls's reaction to the Wrights' achievement once again shows him as a visionary. The brothers may have countered scepticism by retreat, but Charles was determined to meet them, and meet them he did when he visited America in 1906. We know even less of this encounter than we do of the meeting with Henry Royce in Manchester, and its circumstances render such a contact improbable. When Rolls accompanied Henry Edmunds northwards, he was perhaps Britain's best-known motorist. The self-styled 'mechanic' of Cooke Street might be tempted to pre-judge him as an aristocratic dilettante, but any contact with commercial interests in London was worth exploring. In America, however, Rolls was unknown. The Llangattock family's horizons did not extend beyond Europe, and in any case Britons did not look westward in 1906; for there was still a faintly nasty taste lingering from the days of the Civil War and the *Alabama* incident. Even in the world of motoring, Britain felt she had little to learn from America. What she had seen of the transatlantic automobile was not encouraging. Ransom E. Olds might be capable of turning out three thousand Curved Dash Runabouts in a single year, but the end-product had failed to acquit itself with distinction on British roads, while as for the bigger offerings, Birmingham, Coventry and Manchester could look back on the U.S.A.'s contenders for the Gordon Bennett races of 1903 and 1905, and titter gently. The American motorist had already recognized the snob value of the imported car, and European manufacturers had responded with a mild break-through into the market. Mors, Mercédès and Napier had tried their hands with branch factories in the New World, F.I.A.T. were to do so within the next few years, while Daimler and Humber, among others, were quoted in contemporary American 'automobile directories', and the American Locomotive Company's Alco was a thinly-disguised Berliet. *The Automobile* might greet Rolls's arrival with a longish article describing him as 'a manufacturer of automobiles, as a daring and skilful driver of high-powered racing cars, an authority on all subjects relating to automobiles, and an ardent devotee of the sport of ballooning', but one suspects that it was his title and his youthful enthusiasm that appealed to our transatlantic friends. They had never heard of the Rolls-Royce, and this ignorance was to persist in the minds of the vast majority for some years to come. Rolls's selling trip had no consequences comparable, even from the viewpoint of pure prestige, with, say, the impact of Sir William Lyons and his Jaguars in the 1940s and 1950s. Such a comparison is a trifle harsh, for America was no 'nation on wheels' in 1906, but one may be certain that, had *Time* magazine existed then, Charles would never have appeared on the cover as 'Rolls-Royce's Rolls'.

Thus it is remarkable that he should have come face to face with the Wrights, and almost as remarkable that the voluminous Wright papers carry no evidence of the encounter. Mr Marvin McFarland, who has edited these documents, has found but one oblique reference, in a letter from Octave Chanute to Wilbur Wright, dated 15 October, 1906: 'I enclose clipping from yesterday's paper noticing an interview with C. S. Rolls' —and this was, it would seem, intended solely to draw the brothers' attention to the aeronaut's presence in New York. Rolls was later to claim that he had met them first in 1896, but this was surely a misprint for 1906; and the only positive evidence we have is the testimony of Miss Florence Caswell, his private secretary, and Mr T. O. Smith, his mechanic, both of whom recall his alluding to such a meeting. He was not apparently on terms of great intimacy with either brother at any time—neither Lady Brabazon nor her sister-in-law Lady Lambart, both of whom were in close contact with him in the early flying days, remembers any special relationship. Mr E. Keith-Davies, who was associated with Rolls's flying exploits during the last few weeks of his life, gained the impression that Rolls had close contacts with Wilbur and Orville, but it should be taken into consideration that in 1910 the Wright biplane was becoming obsolescent, and Charles was by then one of its few remaining protagonists in Europe. Certain it was that Rolls was not singled out by Wilbur Wright when he flew for the first time with the American aviator in 1908. Six other people were taken up the same day. He acted as host and guide to the brothers when they came to England in 1909, but this was only to be expected at a time when the Short brothers' airfield in the Isle of Sheppey formed the headquarters of flying in this country. Rolls's long-standing association with the Shorts made him the natural cicerone. One must also remember that he would have seized on such an occasion to gain some extra publicity for the 'Silver Ghost' Rolls-Royce. An oft-published picture of himself with Horace Short and the Wrights is testimony that he did.

If Rolls's investigations into American aviation were of significance only to himself, his trip to the United States was nevertheless a serious endeavour to drum up export sales. The earnestness of his approach is shown by the fact that he took out a licence under the then omnipotent Selden patent. What is more, he exhibited his cars at the Association of Licensed Automobile Manufacturers' Show in New York's Madison Square Garden in January 1907, though of all the American motoring journals only the obscure and ephemeral *Motor Way* gave his stand a mention. He also made contact with a number of influential people. The *Manchester Evening Chronicle* was certainly exaggerating when it published an account of his American exploits under the headline 'Manchester's record order for America', but contemporary reports indicate that

Walter Martin, the newly appointed concessionaire in New York, agreed to take 17 cars in 1907, and fifty in 1908—impressive statistics if one bears in mind that Rolls estimated his firm's maximum productive capacity to be 260 vehicles a year; and in the early days of the 'Silver Ghost', it was appreciably less than this. What is more, many of these orders were for cars that the New Yorkers had never seen—the 40–50-h.p., for the samples he had shipped in the S.S. *Baltic* were two 'Twenties' and a 'Thirty'. Modest the export demand may have been, but for the time being it deprived Charles of a Rolls-Royce of his own. A very early 'Silver Ghost' had been earmarked for him, but in fact it was delivered to a Mr S. B. Stevens of Rome, N.Y. This car still exists, and was one of the stars of the Rolls-Royce and Bentley pageant staged at Goodwood in May 1964, in the hands of its owner and restorer, Mr Millard Newman of Tampa, Florida. Rolls was not to have a personal 'Ghost' until he took delivery of the so-called balloon tender in 1908. Three 30-h.p. cars were sold in the U.S.A., and a fourth in Canada, where Ketchum and Co., of Toronto, were signed up as agents. An early order for a 'Silver Ghost' was placed by the wife of Colonel John Jacob Astor.

Rolls also launched the obsolescent 'Light Twenty' on a brief but distinguished competition career in the U.S.A. It won a Silver Trophy in a five-mile race at the Empire City Track, New York, covering the distance in 5 mins. 51·8 sec. Rolls cornered savagely, resisting all the attempts of American drivers to jockey him out of the way. That Manchester had speed to sell as well as silence is demonstrated by the heavy metal the Rolls-Royce defeated—a 30-h.p. Packard, a 45-h.p. Peerless, a 60-h.p. Renault, and a 45-h.p. Westinghouse (despite its name, it hailed from France). Fastest of these was the Packard, but even this finished twenty seconds behind Rolls. Rumour said that S. B. Stevens would enter his 'Silver Ghost' for the 1907 Glidden Tour, but rumour was wrong, while a study of the contemporary American motoring press has failed to elicit any details of a mysterious 'sealed bonnet trial', staged by the Automobile Club of America, in which another 40–50-h.p. car allegedly won a Silver Trophy. None the less, a 'Twenty' was certainly awarded a Bronze Medal in the

'International Touring Car Championship'; for all its grandiose style, this contest, like all other events in the United States at this time, was not recognized by the Automobile Club de France. Peter Helck remembers seeing a 'Light Twenty' in action in the 24-Hour Race at Morris Park, N.Y., that September. Burne and Fuller, its drivers, put 468 miles into the first twenty hours.

The results of this sales-promotion tour hardly merited the acclaim it received in the British motoring press; but they formed the basis on which Rolls-Royce's present reputation in the United States was founded. This reputation was to lead to the manufacture of more than 1,700 'Silver Ghosts' and 1,200-odd 'Phantom I's' at Springfield, Massachusetts, between 1921 and 1931. Rolls also took a long, hard look at the American automobile industry, and his findings are of interest. The market, in his view, demanded light and powerful cars with long and strong springs to cope with the appalling road surfaces. Lubrication systems must be freeze-proof. Not only was a substantial clearance essential, but a minimum wheel 'tread' of $56\frac{1}{2}$ inches was imperative if a vehicle was to clear the streetcar tracks. He formed a low opinion of American tyres (the Yankees were astonished at the way his Dunlops lasted) and bodywork. The U.S.A. was ready for six-cylinderism, whatever the impassioned debaters of the A.C.G.B.I. might decide, and the correctness of this diagnosis is demonstrated by the fact that, whereas only six makers in the United States (one of them the American Napier Co.) were offering engines of this type in 1907, their ranks had swollen to sixteen by 1908. Among the more important converts we may note Oldsmobile, Pierce 'Great Arrow', and Peerless. Henry Ford, however, had had enough of his Model-K and was turning to simpler and cheaper motor-cars.

Rolls complained that British makers as a whole were apathetic over exports (not by any means for the last time!), and were not bothering to export their best wares. This was rather a harsh criticism, viewed against the background of the national economy in 1907, when only small countries like Belgium depended on exports to keep their car factories going. Certainly Continental makers did not invariably expose their most interesting types to the British market, with the consequence that many technically attractive designs of the 1908–14 era are unknown in these islands. Rolls further reminded would-be exporters that an energetic export policy must be matched by a network of good agents—Claude Johnson would have called these 'retailers', as Rolls-Royce still do. This point was apparently ignored by his audience, to judge from the plaints aired to this day in the correspondence columns of the more critical journals.

Britain's industry made no comment, but some Americans took exception to Charles's strictures on the native product. Marcus J. Brock of the A.L.A.M. claimed that home demand was still running too high to allow of any serious export drive, but J. D. Maxwell, maker of the car that bore his name, and, incidentally, a rebel against the blanketing tactics of the Selden faction, observed: 'We are far behind the foreigners in roads, but are more than their equal in mechanics, and we are about ready to prove our superiority by an invasion of foreign markets.' In the event, another three years were to pass before this prediction was realized.

Mr E. R. Thomas, manufacturer of the celebrated Thomas 'Flyer', was, however, prepared to match words with deeds, or so he said. 'Why', he asked, 'is it that every first-class foreign automobile manufacturer has his shops full of American tools, identical with those of American manufacturers, except some are not so modern or so good?' Though Mr Thomas probably did not know it, there was American equipment in the workshops at Lillie Hall. He challenged Rolls to pit a 'regular stock touring car made by the Rolls-Royce company' against one of his own productions, the course for the match to be from New York to Chicago and back. He stipulated that the contest should take place within thirty days of the date of his letter. 'As the Rolls company have machines in this country', he concluded, 'the short time will prove no hardship.' At no point, be it said, did either Mr Thomas or his opponents draw attention to the remarkable similarity between his car and those produced by the house of Brasier in Paris.

Rolls, like Johnson, was not interested in challenges unless he could dictate the terms. He also had an admirable excuse for declining—Martin had no cars to spare, and he doubted if any private owner would lend a Rolls-Royce for such antics. He reminded readers of *The Autocar* that Thomas had not supported the T.T., or indeed any other European event. Walter Martin piously echoed the sentiments of Conduit Street in a statement deploring this 'high speed mania'. 'If Mr Thomas desires to illustrate this point, such a contest would not prove anything.' Rolls might not play, but an old colleague, E. H. Arnott, offered to take up the cudgels on behalf of an equally familiar adversary, no other than the Arrol-Johnston which he was now promoting. Arnott's proviso, however, was that half the match should be contested over the Tourist Trophy or the Scottish Reliability Trials, and Mr Thomas of Buffalo ignored this proposition.

Meanwhile Rolls-Royce Ltd. had been reorganized, and the firm of C. S. Rolls and Co. absorbed into the new structure. C. W. Morton is of the opinion that the catalyst was once again Henry Edmunds, and the fusion was, in any case, accomplished without any of the friction that punctuated relations between Montague Napier and S. F. Edge. Though we find references to the old London company in the press as late as February 1907, thenceforward there was to be one organization only.

From Rolls's viewpoint this was a godsend. Finance had always been critical: his difficulties in settling for the large batches of cars landed on him by Panhard had driven him into the arms of Royce, and even after the 'outside' makes had been jettisoned he had still been dependent on his own resources and his father's generosity. Rolls-Royce were expanding, and absorption at their hands would save him again from tying up large sums in more expensive cars—the 'Silver Ghost' chassis *retailed* at £985. Further, the affairs of C. S. Rolls and Co. had been conducted on rather haphazard lines. Claude Johnson's superlative skill in the realm of public relations was accompanied by a carefree disregard of accountancy, and some of his more grandiose schemes must have horrified the cautious Ernest Claremont. There was the champagne liberally dispensed during the 1905 T.T., and an even more astounding proposition Johnson put to the Rolls-Royce board, whereby every 'Silver Ghost' chassis should carry an unconditional guarantee against obsolescence. Had this been adopted, an original owner would have the right to demand, *free of charge*, every modification introduced by Rolls-Royce Ltd., during the production life of the model. The 'Ghost' remained in production until 1925, and one can envisage cars coming back for three-speed gearboxes in 1909, for reconversion to four speeds in 1914, for the inclusion of an electric starter in 1919, and for front-wheel brakes in 1924, all at the maker's expense! Needless to say, this splendid if unrealistic gesture was vetoed.

The assets acquired in London also proved a disappointment to Derby, since they included a number of bad debts. Rolls borrowed T. S. Haldenby from Derby to reorganize the arrangements at Lillie Hall. As to Lord Llangattock, who had to be consulted as Rolls's power-of-attorney while he was in America, he welcomed the scheme unreservedly. 'We need fear', wrote Johnson, 'no opposition from that quarter.'

With an increased capital of £200,000, Rolls-Royce were ready to consolidate. Sacrifices were, however, demanded, and one of these was the racing programme. Rolls must have regretted the company's defection, and there is a hint that Royce shared his views. In October 1906, C. S. Rolls and Co. had announced their entry for the 1907 T.T., and as late as the following January we find Royce writing to the *Car Illustrated* to advocate a greater fuel allowance for six-cylinder cars in the race, in view of the type's superiority 'as regards silence and absence of vibration'. Some support is lent to this surprising attitude by Phil Paddon, who told Henry Knox that Royce and Rolls favoured the production of what we would now term a 'G.T.' The former even made four such machines, the two 70-h.p. 'Silver Ghosts' with overhead inlet valves prepared for the 2,000 Miles' Trial of 1908, and a brace of replicas. Johnson, however, overruled any further developments along these lines. He told the *Automotor Journal* that these exciting fast tourers were 'somewhat noisy . . . and not altogether offsprings of the Rolls-Royce house'.

Royce went no further with his feelers. In April 1907 *The Autocar* announced that Rolls-Royce were now making six-cylinder cars only, and cast doubts on the future of their T.T. entry. On 18 May the cat was out of the bag: Rolls had scratched, on the ground that Manchester was no longer able to supply duplicates of the 20-h.p. type.

The *marque's* racing days might be over, but it was to distinguish itself in the Scottish Reliability Trials of 1907 and the 2,000 Miles' Trial of 1908, though Rolls did not drive on either occasion. Rolls-Royce did not support the A.C.G.B.I.'s Flexibility Trials at the Crystal Palace in February 1907: Johnson disliked the regulations, which in his view favoured three-speed gearboxes unduly. But then the Battle of the Cylinders was an era of inacceptable challenges. No Crossleys or De Dietrichs took part, since William Letts dismissed the Club's criteria for flexibility with the scathing words: 'Of course it can be done, but I do not think anyone in his right senses would consider there was anything to be proud of in doing it.' No Argylls ran, either, for Alex Govan insisted on the insertion of a rule stipulating the use of standard gear ratios. Of the six-cylinder brigade, only Napier, Ford and Brooke competed. The former was, rather naturally, adjudged the victor.

Meanwhile Johnson was throwing out challenges that nobody accepted, and offering free demonstrations runs in the new 40–50-h.p. Rolls-Royce to anyone who had yet to experience six-cylinder motoring at its best. By March 1907 the one-model policy was approved by the board, though never officially announced: there were to be no deviations from this decision until 1922, when the general economic slump fathered the six-cylinder 'Twenty'. In July and August came the famous 15,000 mile observed trial of AX 201, the original 'Silver Ghost'.

Already such long-distance trials were in fashion. A 40-h.p. Wolseley-Siddeley car had lately been tested over 10,000 miles, and Captain Corbet, whom we have already met as one of Rolls's ballooning companions, was at this very time submitting a six-cylinder Hotchkiss to a similar, if hardly trouble-free demonstration. The 'Silver Ghost's' fifteen thousand miles, however, not only included the course of the Scottish Reliability Trials, in which Claude Johnson collected a Gold Medal, but were completed with only a single involuntary stop—when the petrol tap shook loose, and closed itself. The latter part of the Trial was run over a circuit in five stages. London Manchester was assigned to Johnson: Eric Platford took over from Manchester to Berwick-on-Tweed; then Macready drove the car from Berwick to Glasgow and back. The run from Berwick to Manchester was a second spell for Platford, and Rolls handled the final stage, back to London. The total value of replacements at the finish—none of them essential to the car's continued running—was £2 2s. 7d., and the running costs, inclusive of tyres, worked out at 4½d. per mile. Historians often ignore the fact that the name 'Silver Ghost' was first assigned to the car used for this Trial, and only subsequently became a generic name for all its 7,800-odd descendants.

If this oft-related exploit won Rolls-Royce the R.A.C.'s Dewar Trophy (the A.C.G.B.I. had been accorded Royal patronage during 1907), and paved the way to unchallenged supremacy, it also attracted a new kind of publicity. *The Autocar* wrote:

> Credit is heaped high upon the head of that retiring, studious man whose outward semblance suggests the philosophical thinker rather than the practical engineer, but whose immense capacity for pains and analysis, and absolute genius for material and its treatment has in the matter under review resulted in the manner of which all concerned have a right to be proud.

What a change from 1905, when Henry Royce was dismissed with a summary 'Works, Manchester', in Rolls's publicity material! Now the car was established, it was the creator, and no longer the publicist, who was to be regarded as indispensable. Rolls had played his part.

But there was still work to do, and through the period of expansion he took his duties as Technical Managing Director seriously. Though Johnson continued to sign the majority of the company's letters to the press, Rolls handled technical matters, and in May 1908, we find him querying the claim of an owner of a rival '38·4-h.p. car' to have done 19·96 m.p.g. In those days of high gearing and slow-turning engines such an impressive figure was no impossibility, but it furnished Rolls with a pretext for reminding readers of the *Automotor Journal* that the 'Silver Ghost's' *overall* consumption during the 15,000-mile trial had been 15·7 m.p.g.

Expansion also meant that the company was fast outgrowing its cramped quarters in Cooke Street, Manchester, and the proposed move to Derby was first announced in April 1907. This choice was governed by a number of factors: the modest price of land, the offer of a long-term contract for electricity at moderate cost, and a site already furnished with roads, gas, water, sewage, and railway sidings. The standard wage rate was appreciably lower than that obtaining in Manchester—a vital factor for a young company with limited capital, and the highest standards of workmanship. As Rolls said: 'The class of men who are quite acceptable for ordinary engineering works would be unsuitable for us and for our standard of work.' There was also plenty of room for physical expansion, which was out of the question at Cooke Street, though it would have been possible had the company moved out to Trafford Park, where the crane factory of Royce Ltd. was now located. My father opened the new Rolls-Royce works in July 1908, and Rolls made the introductory speech. According to the *Automotor Journal* he was entirely at his ease on this occasion, as might have been expected, 'taking the lead in the formal parts of the little ceremony, ever ready to answer all enquiries, and justly proud to a degree of what he and his associates had already performed'. Almost as soon as the party was over, he rushed back to London to take part in the balloon race for the Hedges Butler Cup at Hurlingham—though as it transpired, the weather put paid to this contest.

There was also expansion at Conduit Street, where 1907 had seen the addition of 20,000 square feet of floor space, and the installation of a lift, reported to be a product of Royce Ltd., and capable of accommodating the largest limousines in the 'Silver Ghost' range.

It is fashionable to regard Rolls in these later years as paying only lip-service to Rolls-Royce Ltd. This is far from the truth. The work was unexciting—a steady round of meetings and demonstrations, and not at all the life to be expected of one who had been the Golden Boy of British motoring. Such employment was no longer news: even if Rolls-Royce still had rivals for the title of 'The Best Car in the World', the 'Silver Ghost' needed no press after the successful completion of the 15,000-miles' trial. When changes—such as the replacement of the 'sprinting gear' by a conventional three-speed gearbox in the summer of 1909—were introduced, they were fully described and illustrated in the technical weeklies, but otherwise mentions of the *marque* treated of new body styles stately and exotic, and illustrious clients from all countries of the world. Where motoring was concerned, Rolls had settled down—or so it seemed. There were no more dashes down the *routes nationales*, for these were unnecessary. Unfortunately his minutes from Conduit Street to Derby have not survived, but Mr T. O. Smith has preserved a number of internal documents dating from 1908 and 1909 which give an insight into the busy and unobtrusive life Charles was leading at this time. Some of the later notes show that Percy Northey was handling an increasing volume of the work, but nevertheless Rolls was tirelessly demonstrating Rolls-Royces up and down the country. In May 1908 we find him at Tamworth: in December he has appointments in Atherstone and Norwich. At the beginning of 1909, he is off to Scarborough, but four days later, he receives a reminder from Conduit Street to be back in London 'on Thursday, in order that we may give a run to Mr Fletcher on Friday'. In February, Smith is instructed to have the demonstrator landaulette (chassis no. 541) at the ready for 'a very probable buyer'. By 24 March he is under orders to join Rolls in France for his tour of the flying-fields, which certainly had business connections, if we are to judge from the numerous photographs published of the 'Silver Ghost' negotiating the tortuous and hilly roads of the Riviera. There were more demonstrations in Wokingham and Tonbridge in June, and at Windsor in July, while at the end of the month Smith had to ship the 'Ghost' over to Cowes, 'together with four sets of literature'. A minute date 22 March confirms that the role of Technical Managing Director was no sinecure: 'When advising extra spares for people going abroad', Rolls writes, 'Macready says we should include piston rings in case of breaking one when lifting cylinders or after cleaning, also rubber insertion for joints.'

Rolls kept irregular hours. Miss Caswell remembers his disconcerting habit of appearing without warning, even at times when he had announced his intention of being absent for three weeks. He would forget appointments with the demonstration car, and his secretary would make frantic telephone calls to South Lodge. Neither his own meals nor anyone else's meant anything to him, and he would dictate cheerfully through the lunch hour, unlike Johnson, who lunched out regularly. His office hours became even more erratic when he took up flying in 1909. But he carried on until the conflict of interests became irreconcilable, both to himself and to his fellow-directors. Even after he had resigned his post as Technical Managing Director, and was devoting himself exclusively to the air, he found time to tell *The Autocar* that he was using a 'Silver Ghost' tourer to tow his aeroplane, and that this combination had surmounted Polhill, near Sevenoaks, on top gear. But already the writing had been on the wall. In January 1909 he resigned from the Committee of the Royal Automobile Club, and that month Percy Northey, his erstwhile team-mate in the Isle of Man, joined the staff at Conduit Street to help with the demonstration work.

Up to 1909 he found time to pursue motoring interests outside Rolls-Royce Ltd. In 1907 regional motor shows were still part of the calendar, and it was therefore fitting that as a Mancunian manufacturer he should open that city's exhibition. We find him, incidentally, suggesting the adoption of standardized signs at Olympia: but he was before his time, and the designers and purveyors of ornamental ironwork and timberware were to have a long reign. Only when the Society of Motor Manufacturers and Traders moved their exhibition to Earls Court in 1937 was his proposal implemented. He was also present at the opening of the Brooklands Motor Course in June 1907 taking part in a parade of unusual and historic machinery in the T.T. 20-h.p. car, along with J. S. Napier on its rival, the Arrol-Johnston, and one of the curious straight-eight Weigels built for that year's French Grand Prix. In his flying days, of course, Rolls was to favour the Isle of Sheppey rather than Weybridge, but T. O. Smith tells me that he made occasional visits to the Track, and was in the habit of discovering imaginary faults in his engine when he spotted one of the numerous traps laid by the over-zealous Surrey police. He was less lucky with the constabulary when he ventured into Hyde Park in an elderly Panhard retained as hack at Conduit Street. This had a truck body and was rather a favourite of Rolls's. When stopped by a policeman in Hyde Park, and asked for his name and address, he pointed out to the constable that these were painted on the side of the body. He was rather nettled to find that his offence on this occasion was driving a trade vehicle in a Royal Park.

He would still turn out for important motoring occasions, and even gave up his place in the 1908 Gordon Bennett balloon team to Griffith Brewer in order to take part in the International Roads Congress held in Paris that September. He had already provided the transport for an investigation *The Autocar* was making into the dustless roads of Kent, the work of another delegate to the Congress, Mr H. P. Maybury. On this occasion the Rolls-Royces personally conducted by the old firm of Rolls and Johnson came in for almost as much praise as Mr Maybury's smooth tarmac. 'To speak of the comfort and sweet running of the 40–50-h.p. Rolls-controlled Rolls-Royce in which the writer travelled', ran a panegyric of truly Edwardian prolixity, 'would be but to gilt refined gold, paint the lily, and commend where commendation is unnecessary.'

The Paris Congress, in the manner of its kind, achieved little, and Rolls would have done no harm to the motor movement had he opted for ballooning in Berlin. My father, who contributed a paper on 'The Value of Good Roads', was disappointed, and ascribed the conference's shortcomings to the fact that 'the French language at 180 to 200 words a minute is not easy to understand, even though one be a fair French speaker'—not, incidentally, an attribute of either Rolls or John Scott-Montagu. Rolls chose as his theme 'The Effect of Road Surface on Vehicles'. He advocated the proper balancing of engines (Royce had, of course, solved the problem of crankshaft vibration on 'sixes'), the use of longer springs and wheelbases, and the provision of shock absorbers, which were still uncommon. If he displayed less understanding when it came to suspension, it is not surprising, since as yet the Lanchester brothers were the only people who understood such things. A modern student will, however, be puzzled by Rolls's suggestion for the use of diagonal joins by road repairers, while the reasons adduced are distinctly odd. 'By this means', he explains, 'the bump will be encountered by each wheel successfully and separately, instead of by the two front wheels simultaneously, and then by the two back wheels together.' Clearly independent suspension, already available on the Sizaire-Naudin *voiturette*, had passed him by—not that the little French car was a particularly good example, and those who have driven it tell me that physical appearance, rather than road behaviour, betrays the presence of this advanced feature.

Paris, however, marked his last major public appearance in the world of motoring. Though he was elected to a committee formed by the R.A.C. to organize a party commemorating the tenth anniversary of the Thousand Miles' Trial, he attended neither the preliminary meeting nor the ceremony itself. The daemon that had driven him for so long was at last in full possession. Rolls's 'controlled impatience' was communicating itself to his friends. His bright, almost glaring eyes commanded attention, and his manner was excitable—'he talked a lot with his hands', Lady Brabazon told me. His appearance ranged from the formal on business occasions to the downright untidy: he had been nicknamed 'Dirty Rolls' in his undergraduate days, and his idea of weekend luggage was a razor and a spare pair of socks stuffed into his pockets. In his office at Conduit Street, however, he affected a high starched celluloid collar, and Miss Horner recollects his turning up at Princes' Skating Rink, straight from business and still wearing a frock-coat. Under Mrs Assheton-Harbord's influence his turn-out off duty became generally sprucer, while she also helped to introduce a friendlier *décor* into the cold and 'technical' apartments he occupied in South Lodge. His sense of humour remained unsubtle and closely wedded to his interests. He delighted in the story of a visit to a friend who had lately acquired a De Dion. Accosting the butler in the hall, he asked if Mr J—— was at home. 'No, sir,' came the unexpected reply, 'he has just gone out in his Te Deum.'

As he confessed to Miss Caswell, he had no small talk, and

his outside interests were fitful, apart of course from music. He and Mrs Assheton-Harbord went regularly to concerts at the Queen's Hall. If the gossip columnists reported his presence at an international wrestling tournament, we need not take this as indicative of a serious concern for the sport: after all, the movements of a peer's son were news to this section of the press. His concern with food reform was, however, a more serious affair, for Charles Rolls had always been inclined towards faddism, while his humanitarian views had made him a staunch supporter of the National Anti-Vivisection Society.

Keeping fit was almost an obsession with him. 'I have never had 'flu', he proclaimed proudly in an article written for *Pearson's Weekly* in 1908. 'The method is to stop all unnecessary internal work and waste by cutting off all the food that is not actually required for the proper repair and sustenance of the body: all surplus food beyond this means the infliction of unnecessary labour on the digestive and other organs, at the expense of the system. By confining oneself to two light meals a day—well masticated—the human machine, being no longer handicapped in this manner, is thus able to confine its whole energy to driving out the disease'—and, we may add, to save the drain on its pocket.

He was neither vegetarian nor militant teetotaller, though he seldom drank, taking only an occasional glass of wine in later life. He was a patron of Eustace Miles, the fashionable vegetarian restaurant, and in 1908 undertook the treasurership of the National Food Reform Association, a body which had as its avowed objectives, 'the enlightenment of the public opinion on matters of diet, the exposure of the dangers of the present system of fuel supply, including the adulteration of food and milk', and the association of questions of diet with physical well-being, social reform, and the national and domestic economies. The Association also concerned itself with dietary reform in institutions (there were no professional dieticians then), and sought to 'recommend more hygienic, humane, and scientific methods of selection and preparation of food'. A speech Rolls made to members of the N.F.R.A. suggests, however, that his dietetic principles were adopted because they suited him personally, rather than through any deep-rooted convictions. Unlike many food faddists, he ate sweets and chocolates liberally.

With children he was at his best, as his goddaughter, Mrs Brenda Dakers, recalls. His adventures as motorist, aeronaut and aviator appealed to youthful minds where adult society might dismiss them as the tedious commentaries of a single-minded Philistine. His gift of mimicry must also have been an asset. Massac Buist says:

> He was very clever at adapting imitations of music-hall favourites to serve all purposes of criticism of car developments, instance his idea of conveying complete satisfaction of a new brake scheme. Pulling up the car in front of Mr Royce, in answer to the anxious engineer's enquiry for his opinion, Charles Rolls began a recitative in the voice and action of the late Dan Leno, starting with the words: 'Call that a brake?'

Knowing my own dislike for the intrusion of the facetious into business discussions, I cannot help wondering if this trick of manner may not have given Rolls's critics the pretext they needed to dismiss him as a mere dilettante.

If the development of the balloon was slow, sedate, and aptly geared to its own stately progress through the air, the aeroplane at first showed an equal reluctance to escape from the drawing-board. For every Rolls who recognized that the solution lay in a lightweight engine, there were ten other people who shrugged off heavier-than-air flight as a will o'the wisp. France had her first aerodrome—at Issy-les-Moulineaux—as early as 1905, and in 1907 the British Aero Club was announcing a programme of 'important practical experiments into propellers, aeroplanes, and engines', under the direction of its Honorary Technical Adviser, Professor Waynforth; but although this portentous statement has found its way into several works of history, the less learned sections of the press were drawing attention to a state of affairs in which too many prizes were being chased by too few aviators. No less than £23,025, an astronomic sum in those days of the Gold Standard and negligible income-tax, was there for the winning. The

Daily Mail was offering £10,000 for a flight between London and Manchester, and this was to lie unclaimed till 1910. In France, *Le Matin* had put up £4,000, to go to the first man to fly from Paris to London. The newly-formed Brooklands Automobile Racing Club had only half that sum at its disposal, but then their requirements were far more modest—a single circuit of the Motor Course without touching the ground. A mere half-mile in the air separated aspiring aviators from the Deutsch–Archdeacon Prize, while *The Autocar*, anxious to promote national industry in the face of a prevailing slump, instituted a £500 award for the first successful aeroplane with a British-built engine. Not to be outdone, my father presented two trophies—one in his own name, and the other in the name of the *Car Illustrated*—these were to go to the first aviator to fly twenty-five miles, with a bonus of £5 thrown in for each mile covered after the twenty-fifth. Half of this was to go to the maker of the airframe, as opposed to the engine. Lord Llangattock, now relieved of any responsibility for the affairs of Rolls-Royce, weighed in with a trophy for the first flight from London to the Hendre 'by balloon, airship, or aeroplane'.

In fact, not even these glittering prizes could provoke any action. The Aero Club organized some indoor trials for model aeroplanes at the Alexandra Palace in April 1907 and these attracted three thousand spectators and twenty-nine entries. A. V. Roe's model managed a flight of 108 ft. 6 ins., but the *Automotor Journal* laughed the whole affair off. 'The majority of the machines', its reporter sneered, 'were almost, and in some cases absolutely, incapable of flight.'

There was no aeronautical press, of course. *Flight* first appeared in January 1909, followed shortly by the *Aero* (later the *Aeroplane*) under the direction of the irrepressible C. G. Grey. Before this the *Automotor Journal* shared with my father's *Car Illustrated* the task of presenting the development of flight in an intelligent and intelligible form. The lay press regarded their subject-matter as a joke, and reported it accordingly, as witness the story of Rolls's balloon ascent from a yacht's tender off Cowes! A glance at some of the 'aeronautical notes' which Charles was then contributing to the *Car Illustrated* reveals how thin was the material from which he

182

had to work, even as late as the spring of 1908. His column in the issue of 18 March is given over almost in its entirety to the Aero Club's ballooning plans for Hurlingham, only a passing mention being accorded to the gliding experiments being conducted by Wels and Etrich in Germany. Things were a little better by 8 April, when Rolls was able to give details of the new Farman biplane, a Clément aeroplane said to be under construction for Ernest Archdeacon, and a whole assortment of fresh trophies to attract those elusive aviators.

There was, of course, the airship. Mentally, Rolls by-passed this mare's nest as he had by-passed the motor-tricycle, but his need for flying experience had to be satisfied, and to this end he contrived to fit in a trip in the French airship *Ville de Paris* in November 1907, along with Mrs Assheton-Harbord, Butler, and Lieutenant Frank Lahm, winner of the 1906 Gordon Bennett balloon race. For Rolls and Butler alike this was their hundredth ascent. Rolls (though not Butler, who was notorious among the ballooning fraternity for his hard landings) commented that the descent was rougher than in a balloon. He was diverted by the sight of his burly companion 'seated on a camp stool in the stern of the ship', and excited enough to compare the adventure with something out of Jules Verne or H. G. Wells. Writing in the *London Magazine*, however, he voiced some reservations which indicate that he was tempering the spirit of experiment with caution. If a propeller-shaft broke —and when one contemplates the flimsy assortment of shafting that adorned early dirigibles, one recognizes this as a likely contingency—the propeller would be carried away. Not only would this deprive the airship of control, it would also deprive it of precious weight, and the craft would rise sharply, while the gas expanded and leaked out through the valves. 'As it re-entered the clouds, the gas would contract, the envelope would grow heavy with moisture, and the structure would fall with terrible swiftness.' The weight of the structure was too great to allow the crew to check the descent with a normal load of ballast. The frame of the car would break on impact, with the ground, and the lightened ship would rise again, only to descend still more violently. A minor engine disorder would reduce the airship to the uneasy status of a balloon, and the control car was too light to protect the occupants from the consequences of a really hard landing. Rolls suggested that the only hope for the aeronauts in such a hypothetical case would be 'to land on a wood', a comment which is ironical in the light of the tragic loss of H.M. Airship R.101 at Beauvais in 1930.

This did not, however, deter Rolls from undertaking the manufacture of the drive-shaft and casing for Colonel Capper's Army airship *Nulli Secundus* at Lillie Hall. Let Harry Fleck tell the story:

> Charlie got all the blueprints and dimensions, and shafting and drives were made and the aluminium casing. This was a T-shaped tube suitably flanged with bolts etc. It had to be inspected by C.S.R. It was laid out in the centre of the hall, and bolted up so that Charlie could make his inspection. Everything was O.K., and Charlie duly informed. Some time afterwards one of the lads got a piece of brown paper, pushed it into the tube, and lit it with a match. It put up some good smoke, and looked very much like a ship stoking up, and all hands were laughing their heads off when Charlie drove in and saw the whole thing. He flew off the handle and sacked eight of us whom he could remember as being on the spot, myself included. We had the Saturday, and came in on Monday as though nothing had happened, and we never heard another word about it.

If Fleck and his friends were in trouble, Charles had to face the wrath of his co-directors. What was permitted in the free-and-easy days of C.S. Rolls and Co. was *verboten* in the London Service Station of Rolls-Royce Ltd. Claremont, understandably, raised the strongest objections to the acceptance of outside contracts without the permission of the board, and Charles never tried anything of this sort again. One suspects that the well-known *canard* published in the *Motor* in January 1909—reporting Rolls-Royce's contract 'to make the framework of the new Army aeroplane in weldless steel tubing' stems from confusion with this episode. The resistance of Royce and Johnson to matters aeronautical during Rolls's lifetime is well known, and while Derby never bothered to deny this story, it is hard to conceive of Royce's consenting to manufacture anything that neither he nor his team had designed. Even where Rolls-Royce have availed themselves of other people's ideas—for instance, the Hispano-Suiza mechanical servo, and General Motors' Hydramatic transmission—these have always been adapted and refined to their own standards. The incident of the airship, however, illustrates the attitude of independence that still characterized the London end of the business even after the fusion with Rolls-Royce Ltd.

But by the beginning of 1908, flying had at last started to move out of the region of theory and speculation. The Wrights' first visit to Europe in 1907 had attracted little attention—nor had they flown. But in January 1908, as the motoring press announced the award of the Dewar Trophy to Rolls-Royce Ltd., Henry Farman took to the air, and the handful of spectators who had assembled to watch him cheered loudly. Moore-Brabazon was experimenting at Brooklands: he was shortly to transfer his activities to Leysdown in the Isle of Sheppey, but as yet he was dogged, not so much by weight as by another weakness of the water-cooled engine—frost-cracked cylinder blocks.

In April, Léon Delagrange claimed the Archdeacon Trophy with a flight of four kilometres, while by May the taciturn Wrights, still at Fort Meyer, had beaten this resoundingly by remaining aloft over a distance of seven miles. Farman promptly issued a challenge for £1,000, which they declined. But by the beginning of August Wilbur (his brother Orville was still recovering from the after-effects of a crash) had landed in France and established himself at Le Mans.

Thereafter the tempo quickened. The Wright design might be a dead-end, and as yet it was still dependent on the use of a 'catapult' start from a launching-rail, but Wilbur's cautious approach now justified itself. Blériot, Farman and Voisin were to show themselves his superior in matters of design, but the Wrights were men after Rolls's heart: they had familiarized themselves with the air before exposing themselves to an incredulous public. Their experimental programme had included much work with gliders, a precedent which Rolls was to follow. Oswald Short says of their early exploits in Europe:

'When they came to France, they performed such evolutions as amazed the French'; and W. F. Bradley remembers that it was, above all, their confidence in their creation that impressed beholders. Well may Léon Delagrange have confessed: 'Eh, bien, nous n'existons pas. Nous sommes battus.'

Not that the French were to be out of the running for long, but before August was out Wilbur Wright had stayed aloft for 6 min. 56 sec., and was performing curves and figures-of-eight. The crowds at Le Mans became an embarrassment, and Wright moved to the military manœuvring grounds at Auvours, which gave him more room, as well as being a prohibited area to be entered only on presentation of the correct passes. By early September, he had achieved a duration of 10 min. 40 sec., but a wingtip hit the ground, and the flights were brought to a temporary halt.

Now at last, the records came thick and fast, so much so that the reporters found themselves unable to keep up to date. Delagrange avenged his self-confessed defeat with a flight of 29 min. 53 sec., only to be beaten by Orville Wright in America. Orville stayed up for over an hour, and flew for 6 min. 26 sec., with a passenger—no other than Frank Lahm again. He later made a longer solo flight of 70 min., while we find a manufacturer of acetylene lamps by the name of Louis Blériot entering the lists for the first time. On this occasion, however, he crashed his monoplane. By mid-September Wilbur Wright had effected the necessary repairs, and though as yet he failed to match his brother's best performance, he established a duration record for Europe (39 min. 18 sec.), as well as taking up his first passenger. A few days later he won the Michelin Prize with a flight of 41·6 miles, lasting over one and a half hours, a quarter of an hour longer than Orville's best effort to date. By the beginning of October the *Car Illustrated* was recording not only Moore-Brabazon's purchase of a Voisin biplane, but was describing Wilbur's latest exploit, a flight of nearly an hour's duration with a passenger aboard.

By good fortune, Rolls was already in France, the long sessions of the Roads Congress safely behind him. At Auvours, he watched with interest as Wilbur Wright took up various members of the Bollée family, a privilege Léon Bollée had earned by his acquisition of the manufacturing rights of the brothers' air-cooled vertical-four engine.

Wilbur was in business. During the second week in October, he took up eleven passengers, pausing only to observe the Sabbath. Among these were Butler, Griffith Brewer, and a M. Katznatoff, Chamberlain to the Czar of All The Russias. Among the seven initiated on 8 October was Rolls. He summarized his experiences as follows in *The Times*:

> Once clear of the ground, the feeling of security was perfect, and I was able to watch with great interest the movement of the operating levers. We tore along at a speed of 40 m.p.h., and soon came to the first corner. Here a point of interest to motorists was demonstrated, namely that, no matter at what speeds a curve is taken, the machine 'adjusts its own banking', so to speak. At the will of the operator, it tilted up gracefully when taking a turn, demonstrating that taking a curve on a flying machine will, instead of being more dangerous, be actually safer than on an automobile. On this occasion our flight was more than usually interesting by reason of some strong side gusts that attacked the flyer on certain parts of the course. The prevalence of these and other undulations of the atmosphere rendered very close attention necessary to the two levers controlling the equilibrium and altitude: I noticed that both these were kept constantly on the 'joggle' with slight movement. One has been accustomed to consider the atmosphere as a mass of air, increasing in density with its altitude, but otherwise uniform. Experience on a power-driven flier, however, shows that, far from being the case, the atmosphere near the earth's surface—even in what we call calm weather—is made up of spiral movements of varying diameter, sometimes vertical and sometimes horizontal, undulations of all sorts, little hills and valleys, and 'streams' of air: in fact one might call it a new world conquered by man—a world with scenery of great variation which, though invisible to the eye, is none the less felt by the operator of a flying machine. To maintain equilibrium and steering control while battling with these complex movements of the air has been the great problem

which for centuries has baffled human ingenuity and which is now solved by the Wright brothers after years of systematic study and experiment.

Wilbur's control over his machine impressed Rolls as it had impressed Farman and Delagrange before him: 'Sometimes we flew above the trees, sometimes we flew three feet off the ground, entirely at the will of the operator, who thus showed the most perfect control over his machine that anyone could imagine.'

Though the language at times verged on the lyrical, Rolls was no D'Annunzio, and wasted no time on quoting poetry to himself. One might expect the use of motoring idiom, as the best means of explaining an entirely new concept to his readers, but already he had grasped the principles of the aeroplane, and found it to his liking. He approached it with none of the gloomy forebodings that had tempered his enjoyment of flight in the *Ville de Paris*. One gains the impression, from his careful study of the Wright's controls, that he could have taken it up solo there and then. But that was not Rolls's way.

Over a year was to elapse before he was to become a pilot in his own right. In the meanwhile the Wrights had started a flying-school in France; the first announcement of this was made only a month after Rolls's memorable experience. Charles Rolls, however, took no lessons. He taught himself.

The Daring Young Man in His Flying Machine

Almost any old shingle can fly, but the trouble is getting it up, keeping it up, and bringing it down.
Wilbur Wright, quoted in the *Car Illustrated*,
January 1909

My first experience in flying was to go up with a wallop, and down with a thud.
Hon. C. S. Rolls, speech at the Authors' Club,
November 1909

Thus Charles Rolls was to summarize his first solo flight from the dreary meadows of Leysdown, hitherto the preserve of sheep. One senses again that cunningly-worded hyperbole that enlivened *Some Roadside Experiences*, for Rolls, though he could carry dedication to its extreme while on the job, was not one to miss one ounce of retrospective fun once the first hurdles had been surmounted. As this remark was freely quoted in the contemporary press, it may well be that it inspired the lyrics of the liberally-plugged theme song of a recent film based on those heroic days of aviation.

We may be puzzled that a man of the stamp of Rolls, who had been preaching the gospel of powered flight since 1901, and had assured the *Car Illustrated*, after his initiation with Wilbur Wright in October 1908, that he had 'never had the slightest doubt as to the genuineness of his accomplishments or the correctness of his statements' from the moment of their first meeting in America, did not make his first powered flight for nearly a year. But Charles was always cautious. We must remember that even in the case of the motor-car, he waited two years before taking the plunge—though this gradual approach was to be expected of one who was at the time still a minor and *in statu pupillari*.

Further, there was no comparing the motor-car, crude as it was in 1896, with the aeroplane or the balloon. The latter, be it said, had already reached almost the limit of its development when he ascended with Spencer and the Butlers in 1901; existing balloon-makers were capable of producing a serviceable craft without the tedium of many months of experimentation in the dark. It cannot be questioned that Wilbur Wright was entirely at home with his crude biplane in 1908, and knew exactly what it could or could not do. For him, it was simply the skill that comes of long practice. But already the theorists were reaching the conclusion that the Wright was a 'pilot's aeroplane', and in no wise an indication of the shape of things to come. The later successes of the breed in competition were as much triumphs of man over machine as were such improbable victories as that of Tazio Nuvolari in the German Grand Prix in 1935, when he defeated the finest that the state-subsidized industry of Nazi Germany could produce with an outmoded Type-B Alfa-Romeo.

The experts might know better, but they were still working in the dark. The empirical approach of the Wrights displayed gaps which would horrify any modern designer. Though they had built more than one successful aeroplane before their descent upon Europe, no detailed drawings of the type existed until Horace Short acquired a licence to build Wrights in England. Short, a professional engineer, travelled out to Auvours and prepared a set of exact plans on the spot. He must have been shocked when Wilbur Wright visited Leysdown in May 1909, and told him that these were the first of their kind to be produced for machines which he had been developing since the turn of the century!

The evolution of engines continued to lag behind air-frames. When Rolls first flew, he had a paltry 20 b.h.p. at his disposal, and as yet the car manufacturers continued to turn out adaptations of power units intended for road-going vehicles. Later on, of course, the situation was to be reversed, and we can trace marked similarities between Rolls-Royce's 'Phantom III' of 1935 and the 'Kestrels' and 'Buzzards' that preceded it in the later 1920s. But power for flight was as experimental as the aeroplanes themselves, as witness the variety to be seen at the *Salon de l'Aeronautique* in October 1909. Grégoire and Aster marketed in-line water-cooled 'fours', as did Panhard, though the latter firm offered the option of air-cooling. Darracq paired a conventional 'four' with a flat-twin for ultra-light aircraft such as the Santos-Dumont, and both Renault and Mors followed Wright with vee-fours. Bigger and more complex were Buchet's water-cooled vertical 'six', and the vee-eights of F.I.A.T. and Brouhot, while MM. Gobron *et* Brillié did things in style with an enormous opposed-piston X-8. Even when these engines worked, they were expensive; a Short-Wright airframe cost a mere £200, but Mr E. Keith-Davies, a pioneer pilot who later became the first man to fly in India, has estimated the price of an aeroplane of 1910 complete and ready to fly, at about £1,000. Such power units were also unreliable, and T. O. Smith was wont to strip down Rolls's engines after an hour's flying.

The clubs were, of course, already there, and the ballooning organizations were quick to assume the mantle of the aeroplane, as representing a craft with a future, as opposed to a rather negative present, rapidly fading into the past tense. Britain, in fact, suffered from a surfeit of clubs, and *The Autocar* found it necessary in April 1909 to issue a glossary of these. In addition to the Aero Club (to be accorded Royal patronage in 1910) and the Aeronautical Society, both of which we have already encountered, there was an obscure and ephemeral Flying Club; a body known as the Aeronautical Institute and Club, which had been in existence since 1901, but had little to show for these eight years bar sponsorship of a few balloon ascents; and the Aerial League, a propagandist body which aimed at instilling air-consciousness into Britons, and the forerunner of the later Air League of The British Empire. Since the general public was as yet incapable of distinguishing the exploits of Wright, Farman and Moore-Brabazon from the flying-sauceritis that even then was manifesting itself in the provincial newspapers, its significance was minimal. Rolls, it is true, showed some interest in its activities, and it did sponsor a joint exercise with the Boy Scouts in April 1910, the object of this being an essay on the delivery of despatches; but the principal importance of this episode lies in the fact that it was the occasion of his last balloon ascent.

Then there was Walter Windham's Aeroplane Club. This

was a counter-move against the closed-shop social atmosphere of the Aero Club, which, it was held, was little more than an aerial annexe to the R.A.C. The new venture achieved nothing beyond a brief outburst of bickering conducted through the correspondence columns of the motoring and aeronautical press, and we need express no surprise when we hear that in 1910 the Aeroplane Club amalgamated with that other ineffectual 'anti-body', the Motor Union. There was even a Women's Aerial League: Lady Shelley-Rolls sat on its Executive Council.

Nor was there any dearth of recruits for the new movement: these, of course, came from the ranks of the racing drivers. The infant aeroplane, though it might be spurned by equestrian-minded governments, and derided by a sceptical and ignorant press, was fortunate in that its impact coincided with a lull in serious motoring competition. The French, disgruntled by Lautenschlager's victory on a Mercédès in the 1908 Grand Prix, dropped this event from the calendar for several years; and in any case the prevailing depression in the motor industry was sufficient deterrent to the continuance of costly competition departments. After the 'Four Inch' Race of 1908, the T.T. was suffered to lapse until 1914. There remained in Europe only the Prince Henry Tours, which appealed to enthusiastic non-sporting motorists of the calibre of my father, and to designers such as Ferdinand Porsche and Laurence Pomeroy, Senior, who saw in them a chance to improve the breed without disrupting the production line; and *voiturette* racing, which tended to breed a new generation of drivers. The tough individualists nurtured on chain-driven saurians did not take readily to lightweights of the stamp of Sizaire-Naudin or Delage. Though some of the creations of a too liberal formula, such as the towering Lion-Peugeots with their nine-inch piston strokes, were just as tricky to drive, they were still relatively deficient in performance. It was not until 1911–12 that the 3-litre *voiturettes* of Delage and Sunbeam started to show the monsters the way round the circuits. Thus the ranks of the aviators were joined, not only by the Lathams and Paulhans, who had little or no connection with motoring, but by retired racing drivers like Rougier and the Anglo-French Farman brothers. By the end of 1908, Louis Wagner of Darracq fame was taking flying lessons, and 1909 was to see Cagno airborne in a Voisin biplane.

Flying fields were opening up. In January 1909 *The Autocar* visited Juvisy in France, and found a sea of mud, with tree-felling operations in process. Plans were in hand for a 'long starting-track of wood with a sand dressing', which sounds like an anticipation of World War II practice. The amenities included a grandstand, a small restaurant, and subsidiary buffets in the area reserved for spectators. The journal's reporter lamented that the 'American bar' was not yet open. Even conservative Britain was following suit, and the next twelve months were to see the rise to prominence both of Brooklands and of the various flying-grounds in the Isle of Sheppey. At Weybridge, of course, proper social facilities had been part of the scheme from the start, but in the deserted lands of Eastchurch and Shellbeach, pilots lived the simple life, and there was no provision for casual visitors. No tea was provided even at a sort of 'open day' held at Easter, 1910. This is perhaps one of the reasons why the site was favoured by the early experimenters. True, the Aero Club had a Club House, Mussel Manor, for the use of members, but Short Bros. installed a petrol engine to generate the power for their welding plant, and cattle fences had to be put up—Oswald Short says that the sheep gave no trouble. The approach roads were uniformly bad. By November 1909, when C. G. Grey of the *Aero* visited Eastchurch, the field boasted ten large hangars, housing two Short-Wright biplanes, Professor Huntington's big experimental craft with Wolseley engine, a Voisin-Delagrange, Cecil Grace's Wright, and J. W. Dunne's 'machine of original design', but the aviators were hardly living in the lap of luxury. Grace and Moore-Brabazon had rented bungalows, and F. K. McClean had erected his own, 'but the practice of the Hon. C. S. Rolls of dwelling with the villagers and living on a diet of eggs and milk puddings is nearer the average standard of living indulged in by those who are serious aeroplanists'. Money was short: according to Mr Keith-Davies few of these pioneer aviators held down regular jobs. Car makers might be forming full-scale aviation departments, but they were not going to back private experimenters; while a single hard landing might involve a write-off after months of toil. That such a write-off represented only £5,000-odd of today's monetary values as against the millions sunk in supersonic projects made the loss no easier for the young men of Sheppey to bear.

Other centres followed. McArdle and Drexel opened an aerodrome and flying-school at Beaulieu—this, incidentally, lay to the south of the Lymington road, and not on the site of the later Airborne Forces Experimental Establishment. It failed to make the grade, though the R.F.C. used the ground again in the First World War; the only reminder of those days still visible is the Village Hall of East Boldre, once the officers' mess. That controversial personality, Mr Noel Pemberton-Billing, launched his 'Colony of British Aircraft' at Fambridge in Essex; this was said to boast two enormous hangars, twenty four-roomed bungalows, a general stores, a post-office, and an hotel. It was plastered with 'Keep Out' notices. This security-minded approach was peculiar to Britain at this time. The Short brothers launched out into aeroplane manufacture in such secrecy that the press located their factory vaguely and erroneously in 'West London'; Rolls made many of the preliminary arrangements for his cross-Channel flight in the name of Smith, his mechanic; but in France, spectators were welcomed, and officialdom was co-operative. The French navy lent torpedo-boats to pick up those who came down 'in the drink' during the Nice meeting of 1910, but the 'torpedo-boats' reported at Dover during Rolls's cross-Channel flight were in fact tugs lent by a firm of contractors working on Dover Harbour at the time.

The early aviators were not only distrustful of publicity—they were also clannish. 'Flying was very parochial in 1910', says Mr Keith-Davies, and the free coming and going characteristic of flying clubs in the inter-war period was unknown. Eastchurch-based pilots would only visit Brooklands for a specific event, and though Rolls occasionally appeared at the Motor Course, he never took his aeroplane there. Such information as aviators required on the progress of their rivals they obtained from the pages of the *Aero* and *Flight*.

Outside interest was limited and sceptical. Aero shows were held; the first of these opened in Paris in December 1908 and featured aircraft by Voisin, Santos-Dumont, R. E. P. (Esnault-Pelterie), Wright, Blériot, Antoinette, and Bréguet. London's first full-scale exhibition since 1868, at Olympia, followed in the spring of 1909, and revealed some engaging improbabilities, including a Weiss 'bird-form' monoplane by the still unknown Frederick Handley Page, a curious R.E.P. monoplane with enclosed fuselage and 'shark's fin' tail, a Bréguet biplane intended to have the Gobron-Brillié X-8 engine, a Howard Wright pusher biplane with cycle wheels mounted at its wing-tips, and two astonishing craft that were lost causes even then—de la Hault's ornithopter with eight-cylinder Miesse power unit, and the Lamplough multiplane, which resembled more than anything else the 'mobiles' of modern *avant-garde* sculptors. Even Rolls's balloon *Imp* was on show as a remembrance of things but recently past. It is not until the following year that we find such exhibitions enjoying Royal patronage, and encounter Rolls conducting the Prince and Princess of Wales (King George V and Queen Mary) round the stands.

Progress in flying was, however, rapid. In November 1908 Wilbur Wright won the *Prix de la Hauteur* by reaching the modest height of eighty-four feet above the ground: only a year later Hubert Latham's Antoinette monoplane had attained an altitude of 1,804 feet: while at the end of 1910 the World's altitude record for single-seaters stood to the credit of the Frenchman Legagneux, at 3,100 metres, or over 9,000 feet. Again, in January 1909 Wilbur Wright flew over seventy-five miles to win the Michelin prize, but the Rheims meeting that August was to see records fly in all directions. First of all, Roger Sommer took the prize with a flight lasting 2 hrs. 27 min. 15 sec., on his Vivinus-engined Farman. Then Latham flew a distance of 96½ miles to take the distance record, and before the competitors had dispersed Henry Farman had flown more than a hundred miles non-stop. 1909, of course, also saw the conquest of the English Channel by Louis Blériot, an event which was recognized by more intelligent observers as the death-knell of English insularism.

Flying meetings took their place in the international

calendar. There were five major events in 1909—in the Principality of Monaco, at Rheims in France, at Brescia in Italy, and at Blackpool and Doncaster in our own islands. The first of these, staged at Monaco in March, was an aeronautical echo of Paris–Rouen in 1894. The 'baricycles' and multiple-lever systems of that first motoring contest had their echo in the 'gyroplanes' and 'aeroscaphes' of 1909, while there was even a helicopter, representative of a breed destined to remain chimerical for another thirty years. No wonder the meeting was a farce; of the twenty-three entrants, the *Motor* complained, only seven had flown at all, and 'none of the pilots have achieved anything worthwhile'.

But if Monaco was a damp squib, the display at Rheims in August was not. It must be admitted, however, that the good burghers of that city had never intended anything so advanced as a *semaine aéronautique*. Confronted with a slump in the champagne industry, Rheims had sought to recoup some of its losses by staging an automobile week, complete with a Grand Prix and competitions for touring cars. Unfortunately they chose the wrong moment, and neither the A.C.F. nor the manufacturers showed the least interest. So the city turned to aviation, and to good purpose. Certain it is that a lot of champagne was sold, at half-a-crown a bottle for the lesser sorts, and five shillings for the vintages. It was, however, impossible to buy anything else in the way of alcoholic refreshment, and Henry Knox tells me he had to drive to Châlons in quest of whisky. An added attraction was the first race for the newly instituted Gordon Bennett Aeroplane Cup; this aroused so much enthusiasm amongst the flying fraternity in France that the national Aero Club had to stage an eliminating trial. Only seven of the seventeen entrants put in an appearance, and even the favoured three were unfortunate. France had the humiliation of seeing the Cup cross the Atlantic, and not in the hands of Wilbur Wright, either. The victor was his compatriot Glenn Curtiss, who also won the prize for speed over a 30-kilometre course in the meeting proper. The French, however, shared the remaining honours among themselves, Blériot recording the fastest lap, Farman taking the passenger-carrying prize, and Latham the prize for altitude—though his best performance of

508 feet illustrates the meteoric progress of the aeroplane when we consider that he was to treble this figure—and more— before the year was out. The 'gate' averaged 100,000 a day, though it is not clear whether these came to sample the flying or the champagne! At one memorable stage in the proceedings, seven aviators had been airborne simultaneously. Charles Rolls was present, though not in an active capacity—the *Manchester Guardian* hinted mysteriously that he was maintaining a watching brief on developments in French aviation for the British Government.

Britain's first two flying meetings, at Doncaster and Blackpool, were inauspicious. With so few aviators available, it was hardly wise to allow the dates to clash. October is not a good month, even by the standards of our inequable climate, and the weather was horrible, especially at Doncaster, where the organizers also suffered from the Aero Club's refusal to lend their support. They claimed as the governing body of aviation that their official meeting took precedence and suspended pilots who attended the unofficial one. The *Car Illustrated* found the flights at the officially-sponsored Blackpool week 'hardly inspiring', and wind and rain took command during the last two days, with the consequence that spectators saw only one brief hop by the intrepid Hubert Latham. Farman, however, collected £2,000 for a 47-mile flight, accomplished with the aid of long-range tanks, while Rougier took second place and an impressive £720. Farman also won a speed prize for flying at 36·38 m.p.h., which was creditable in the worst that Lancashire could provide, and Latham's Antoinette won the award for the slowest flight. He and Paulhan were also given 'general merit' prizes for flying in winds of 20 m.p.h. and over. It was decided not to present the trophy offered for the best all-British aeroplane, since the only competitor in this class to get off the ground was A. V. Roe, and he only just managed it.

Britain, in fact, seemed in no hurry to espouse aviation. Moore-Brabazon might have flown three miles at Châlons in January 1909, but the best that the new British Army aeroplanes could manage was a hop of fifty yards—no better than Santos-Dumont's prentice effort in 1906! By the summer, Cody was experimenting at Laffan's Plain, the Army airfield at Farnborough, while Lieutenant Dunne's tailless biplane was being tried in conditions of the utmost secrecy at Blair Atholl; the War Office was proudly announcing that its annual budget for aviation in 1909 would be £78,000, as against £5,270 grudgingly spent in 1908. Cody had in fact flown for over a mile on 14 April, but unfortunately the Prince of Wales, who was present, had requested a repeat performance: this ended in a crash. It is of interest to note that the house of Krupp had already produced an anti-aircraft gun!

If Rolls was slow off the mark, he can hardly be blamed. He had placed an order for one of the batch of six Wright-type biplanes that Horace Short had in hand at Leysdown as far back as February 1909 but, as we have seen, Short had had to start from scratch. In any case, Rolls had been so impressed by Wilbur Wright's mastery of his aeroplane that he determined to follow in his footsteps and learn the controls by practising on a glider. He therefore commissioned such a craft from the Shorts, and this was ready for him by the end of July.

In the meanwhile, his energy was unleashed on such public-relations activities as were possible. While Brabazon and Roe struggled on, the latter hampered first by the civil authorities, who banned him from Hackney Marshes in the early mornings, and then by the military, who forbade him the use of Laffan's Plain, Rolls spent the early spring of 1909 in touring the flying fields of France, with the faithful Massac Buist, in a 'Silver Ghost' Rolls-Royce. They visited the Wrights (Wilbur had now been joined by his brother Orville and his sister Katherine) in their new quarters at Pau, toured Spain and Italy, and inspected a factory where French Wright biplanes were being turned out in series. Buist wrote in the *Morning Post*: 'I should imagine that there will be keen competition presently to get work on machines of this sort, for it is exceedingly clean, quite healthy, and offers any amount of scope for the intelligent man with a real love for his craft.' Later in the year, his prophecy was to be realized with the growth of a substantial aircraft industry in France; in November, the *Motor* was reporting that Blériot had orders for 200 machines, there were a hundred French-Wrights on the stocks, Voisin had already made sixty of his biplanes, Farman were credited with forty made and in process, and Clément-Bayard were talking in terms of a very large batch of the ultra-light 'Demoiselle'-type Santos-Dumonts. With the exception of the last-mentioned, W. F. Bradley considers this a true bill for the period—the 'Demoiselle' was so tiny that it could be fitted into the back of its creator's big Renault when dismantled, and so fragile that it could only support lightweights like Santos-Dumont himself.

Rolls's tour also helped to promote the sales of Rolls-Royce in France, and he was photographed taking the hairpin on the Hermitage hill at Cannes without reversing. He also found time to attend the Biarritz and Bayonne Hunt Ball (though he was no dancer), and spend a night with his family on board the S.Y. *Santa Maria*. His companion had to submit to a regimen of two modest and near-vegetarian meals a day, while Rolls's dissatisfaction at the standard of hotel accommodation at Fréjus led him to drive on eastwards without a meal, although the party had not eaten since dinner the previous night.

When the Wrights came to England in May, he acted as their host, took them down to Sheppey in his Rolls-Royce, and introduced them to Horace Short and his brothers. It was during this visit that Oswald Short recalls a jibe from a hansom-cabby, who yelled 'Old Iron!' at Rolls as he passed by. 'Take it home and eat it', retorted Rolls.

He also spoke at a dinner given in the Wrights' honour by Frank Hedges Butler, and told his audience that 'the absence of dust, police traps, and taxes will make flying popular'. This was an optimistic claim, even from Rolls, but it must be admitted that there were no certificates of airworthiness (no conscientious civil servant could ever have granted one for those clumsy stick-and-string contraptions), no prohibited areas, and no complex radio procedure to keep the airways clear. More truly prophetic—though it is doubtful whether many of the diners realized it—was his warning that the dropping of bombs from airships was already practical, and would be resorted to in the next war: the onslaught of the Zeppelins was only five years away. He also greeted Blériot on his arrival at Dover, and entertained him at South Lodge on his triumphal visit to London. One can sense propagandist over-tones in the visit of the two aviators to the House of Commons, but it is curious that their host on this occasion was Sir Benjamin Stone, an elderly Member from the Midlands whose main preoccupation was the voluminous chronicling of obscure rural customs. It was not until Blériot's visit that Rolls told Smith of his intention to take up powered flight seriously, and asked him to come as mechanic to Sheppey.

Meanwhile Miss Caswell had been asked to 'advertise for a hill' off which he could test the new Short glider, but in the end a small eminence near Eastchurch was found to be suitable, and on 1 August the trials started. His notes on this series of experiments have survived, and give us an insight into the thoroughness of his preparations for the serious business of powered flight.

The glider, like the powered Wrights, used a starting rail, and on the very first day Rolls had to contend, not only with an insufficiency of wind, but also with a series of derailments that finally broke the pulley flange. The following morning he was up at four o'clock. 'Four attempts with rail way down hill', he records, 'but would not rise. Then put rail to top, at first attempt machine lifted nose for first time to 5 or 6 ft., remaining in air about 2 secs. It veered to right owing to rail not facing wind, and cracked right skid and broke a wire.' Experiments were held up, first for the necessary repairs, and then by wind conditions—too little, then too much. It was not until six o'clock that he succeeded in making a straight glide of eighty-five feet. His summary of the day's labours was terse and self-critical: 'I am making landings still too much on back end of skids—tho' much better.'

There were other tribulations; one of his assistants held on longer than his mate during a launch, so that the glider slewed round in a half-circle, but by the end of this first day he had flown 165 feet (not all of it free) and made a free flight of 66 feet in 35 seconds. ('Landed on back end of skids', he notes, disapprovingly, 'but nearly horizontal.') These trials continued on and off until 10 October, which time he felt that he was familiar enough with the basic controls to attempt powered flight on his freshly completed Short-Wright biplane.

The first attempt was unsuccessful, and nearly ended in disaster. Let Mr Smith tell the story:

We had to arrange a monorail 100 feet in length, facing the wind, which often changed before the job was completed —then we mounted the machine on a cross bar straddled across the rail; at the rear end of the rail was a pylon, and we had to haul weights of about half a ton to the top of this. A rope was made fast to the weights over some pulleys; then the rope was taken about half way down the rail over a pulley wheel, and from there to the front of the aeroplane. When all was ready for a start, Mr Rolls would release a catch, and the weights began to drop, which, with the rope attached to the machine naturally assisted it along the rails. One can imagine what happened the first time he attempted to make a flight.

Having got everything ready, the engine was started, and at the final let-go the machine careered along the rail, with what seemed at the moment a terrific speed. When it reached the end of the rail, it suddenly shot straight up into the air, and a second afterwards crashed down on its tail with a tremendous bang.

We found Mr Rolls calmly getting out of the mess, fortunately unhurt. He said: 'This is my first lesson.' I asked what happened, and he replied: 'I am afraid I gave the elevator too much lift, but better luck next time.'

Even at the beginning of his experiments, Rolls knew where the mistake lay. The Wrights' dependence on its starting rail and pylon was one of its worst weaknesses, for it could not take off again after a forced landing without this apparatus. By the summer of 1910, wheeled undercarriages had been applied to these machines, and Rolls was to use such an arrangement at Wolverhampton and Bournemouth, but it must have been a relief to Smith when he received a minute from his employer shortly before the Nice meeting in 1910, telling him that there was no need to ship 'the rails and tower' to France.

The risk of fire was also considerable, thanks to the open exhausts, and to the position of the fuel tank, which was slung loosely over the engine. Those early days at Leysdown—and then at Eastchurch, which Rolls preferred because it had fewer ditches—were often frustrating. In addition to the constant engine overhauls, there were other mechanical troubles occasioned by vibration. Once a magneto came adrift, and Rolls had to force-land. While he and Smith were running an engine test in their hangar at night, the blast of the propellers shook the acetylene lamp from the ceiling on to the aircraft, and Rolls had a small fire on his hands. On another occasion the biplane tried to take off from the rail on its own. Rolls jumped on to the edge of the wing, but the unhappy Smith was dragged underneath, where he managed to cling on to a wire. He could see the twin screws churning away above his head—since the Short-Wright had no undercarriage, they were perilously close to the ground. Even after Rolls had cut the switch, the machine carried on for a good forty yards, and would surely have become airborne had the elevator not been depressed at the time. Occasionally they would seek relaxation in a public-house, only to be chaffed by the 'regulars' who could not understand why they wasted so much time and money on dangerous and useless pursuits. After one particularly good flight, Mr Smith remembers being told patronizingly that 'one day these contraptions may be of some use'. Mr John Adams, Cecil Grace's mechanic in those early days, recalls the way in which the little band of aviators were airily dismissed as 'those mad blokes'. It would be interesting to know how many of these sceptics survived to see Kent turned into an aerial battleground in 1940.

To the world, the aeroplane was the useless plaything of the wealthy and the lunatic fringe of the engineering world. But Rolls was not playing: he was working as he never had before. Partial withdrawal from Rolls-Royce Ltd. might give him more freedom, but it did not help his pocket: though he was to obtain some outside backing for his Channel flight, this lay in the future. 'If this goes on', he observed, half-jokingly to Smith after a particularly bad series of setbacks, 'I shall have to break stones in the road.' And always there was a sense of urgency. Sometimes this rebounded against the two experimenters. Though Rolls still motored a good deal—photographs of the glider experiments show a battered-looking 'Silver Ghost' serving as a tender—he shuttled between London and Sheppey by train, and it was his practice to make use of the boat express to Queenborough which left Victoria Station at 10 a.m. On one occasion Smith, arriving late at the terminus, flung himself in the first train he saw, only to find it was the 'slow' which took two and a half hours to the express's sixty minutes dead. When he eventually turned up at Eastchurch, Rolls was sarcastic: 'I thought you had taken the boat to Flushing', was his comment. A few weeks later Rolls himself fell into the same error, and arrived late. Before Smith could say anything, Charles forestalled him with the words: 'No, I did not go to Flushing, either!'

With his mechanics, Charles Rolls showed a consideration that he seldom manifested with others. Those who shared his interests were amply rewarded. 'I hope you have had a proper rest', one of his notes to Smith begins. Adams likewise remembers Rolls as one of the friendliest and most considerate of the pilots.

Rolls's efforts bore fruit. On 9 October 1909, *Flight* reported that he had flown, and before the year was out he had made his mark in no uncertain manner. Moore-Brabazon, however, beat him in making the first flight of over 250 yards in an all-British aeroplane, thus winning the Aero Club's prize. On this occasion Rolls was one of the official observers. Meanwhile a further prize had still to be won; this had been donated by Sir David Salomons and would go to the first British aviator to fly more than half a mile. Such a performance was, of course, well within Brabazon's grasp, but he sportingly agreed to suspend his attempts for a week to give Rolls a chance. On 2 November, Rolls successfully stayed aloft over one and a half miles to win the Salomons Trophy. There is an engaging sequel to this, for many years after Charles's death Lady Shelley-Rolls gave the cup her brother had won back to Lord Brabazon of Tara.

There was great rivalry among the aviators themselves, as Adams recalls. 'There weren't any union rules,' he comments; 'we were up at four o'clock every morning, waiting for the weather. I was lucky—Mr Grace had a cottage, and my wife house-kept for the Grace brothers, myself, and our rigger, so there was always something to eat before we went out to work'. The first days were, of course, the hardest. Until the aviators had progressed to circuits, every short hop was a straight-line affair, and after each landing the crew had to go out and haul the aeroplane back to the sheds.

The two friends, in fact, derived considerable pleasure from conquering what Rolls termed 'the recognized standard of impossibility'. Brabazon took matters a step further by taking up 'a young porker' to prove that pigs could, on occasion, fly, though this accomplishment was overshadowed by Farman's latest performance in the contest for the *Coupe Michelin*—a flight lasting 4 hrs. 17 min. 5 sec. Ogilvie and Searight were experimenting at Camber, and managed to cram seven short flights into two working days; their engine, alas!, did not take kindly to this treatment, and they were rewarded with run big-ends and the inevitable forced-landing. During December, *Flight* reported enthusiastically on the prowess of both Rolls and McClean at Sheppey. When Rolls decided to move from Leysdown to Eastchurch, he did so by air, without telling anyone of his intentions. We may doubt whether 'automobilists' did in fact 'scour the country', as one press report suggests, but Smith remembers being shown an empty hangar at Shorts' aerodrome by the groundsman, to the accompaniment of the dramatic words: 'Empty is the cage; the bird has flown.' He chased a train for some distance between Eastchurch and Harty, before being forced down with engine trouble, and also made a short flight with Cecil Grace as passenger. His best duration flight in 1909 lasted only forty-eight minutes, but this was indeed creditable for one who was self-taught and had less than two months' solo experience behind him.

1910 promised to be an auspicious year for the new movement. Already the calendar was filling up with a whole series of important meetings. In France alone, Biarritz, Cannes, Nice, Bordeaux, Lyons, Vichy and Deauville were said to be planning aviation weeks; the Aero Club de France had given its blessing to another event at Heliopolis in Egypt; while Berlin, Budapest, Milan and St. Petersburg had announced their intention of getting into the act. The second race for the Gordon Bennett

International Cup was to be held at Belmont, N.Y., in the late summer, and was to be contested between teams from the U.S.A., Great Britain, and France. Louis Blériot had spread the gospel to Turkey-in-Europe, and had been rescued, most improbably, from a crash at Constantinople in a sedan-chair. Already two British municipalities—Wolverhampton and Bournemouth—were advertising aviation weeks, the latter's to form the centrepiece of the town's centenary celebrations. Under the aegis of Mr W. Ballin Hinde, Humber's had opened a full-scale aviation department, while Holland and Holland, the London coachbuilders, were inserting display advertisements for 'aeroplanes built to order'. Among the latest recruits to the movement were a German poet, Dr Karl Vollmoller, and an English clergyman, the Rev. S. Swann. Mr Swann entrusted the erection of his aeroplane to the Austin Motor Co., and was gratified to find that they handled the job in seven days from start to finish. In Belfast, Harry Ferguson, later to win fame with his tractors and his experiments with four-wheel drive, had flown in an aircraft of his own construction. If Britain lagged behind France, she could still claim that an imitation Blériot monoplane had featured in a West-End pantomime (*Aladdin*, at the Lyceum). In a more serious vein, there were said to be seven active British pilots—Rolls, Claude Grahame-White, Neale, Moore-Brabazon, A. V. Roe, Claud Cockburn, and Colin Defries, who was experimenting in Australia. Three of France's pioneers—the Farman brothers and Latham—were of British extraction. Five British manufacturers showed complete aircraft at the second Aero Show to be staged at Olympia, though of these the Humber was a direct copy of the Blériot. Alas! the first meeting of the new season, at Heliopolis, came and went without any competitors from England; Mortimer Singer, Rolls's conqueror in the 1909 Hare and Hounds Race, had been eliminated by a crash in practice.

Also in 1910 came the Royal Aero Club's first pilots' certificates. The first of these, of course, went to Moore-Brabazon, which was only fitting; in later life he was to commemorate this distinction by wearing the number-plate FLY 1 on his car. Rolls was the second recipient—his certificate is dated 8 March, the same day as Brabazon's. Others in the first ten went to Cecil Grace, Claude Grahame-White and Cockburn. Charles Rolls talked of staging a Hare and Hounds Race for aircraft at Eastchurch, while a car-versus-aeroplane match was run off in April between Grahame-White's Farman biplane and F. A. Coleman's 40-h.p. White Steamer. That hardy perennial, the *Daily Mail*'s £10,000 prize for a flight from London to Manchester, at last fell to Louis Paulhan on 28 April. The journey took him 24½ hours, this including an overnight halt at Lichfield. Even Rolls would not have contemplated a serious night flight as early as this, though on more than one occasion he stayed up at dusk over Eastchurch.

During 1910, Rolls had three different aeroplanes. He also retained the glider, though this was put up for sale in April, having served its purpose. The Short-Wright was passed on in April to his former ballooning companion, Colonel Capper. Rolls and Smith delivered it by road to Laffan's Plain, and arrangements were made whereby the former should instruct Army pilots. Rolls, unfortunately, did not live to take up this appointment. He also acquired a Sommer biplane; according to the *Globe* this was successfully flown at Eastchurch 'in a stronger wind than any machine that has yet been out', but somehow the Sommer was not to his liking, and he disposed of it to Lieutenant Gibbs, holder of Aero Club pilot's certificate No. 10. Gibbs was to enter both this machine and his Farman at Dunstall Park and Bournemouth. Rolls's final acquisition was a French-built Wright biplane. On this he made his name as an exhibition pilot, flying it at Nice and Dunstall Park, earning the status of a national hero with his double crossing of the English Channel on 2 June, and dying in the final crash at Bournemouth. A Farman was also among the assets sold up after his death, but I cannot trace that he ever flew this.

The 1909 edition of *Jane's All The World's Airships* also mentioned a Rolls biplane, of which it said: 'This is not the Wright Bros' machine owned by Mr Rolls, but a species of Voisin type embodying a number of his own ideas.' Mr Smith tells me that this aircraft was given the designation R.P.G. (Rolls Power Glider), and was still under construction when its creator was killed. It may well have formed the basis of his plan to set up as an aircraft manufacturer, a project which he discussed with Keith-Davies during those last few days at Bournemouth.

Easter, 1910, saw a new departure in Rolls's movements. Hitherto he had been at the Hendre with his ballooning friends; now he repaired to Eastchurch, where he was still flying the original Short-Wright biplane, now with a stabilizing tail behind the rudders. High winds prevented any spectacular flights over the weekend, though Grace managed to cover thirty miles. According to the *Aero*, Rolls was reduced to 15 m.p.h. on the face of a prevailing wind of the same speed, though this unintentional hovering had its compensations—the Wright, which was probably flat-out at 40–45-m.p.h. in still air, was now recording 60 m.p.h. downwind. There were quite a few visitors, and T. O. Smith remembers one old lady who hung around the aircraft, asking interminable questions. He was reduced to speechlessness when she pointed to the flimsy main planes, and asked him: 'Can you walk along the wings?' She could not know, of course, that only recently he and Rolls had tied a 6 lb. iron bar to a strut near one of the wingtips, to ensure proper balance! Rolls was as yet reluctant to carry casual passengers, though he did consent, after a great deal of persuasion, to take Hilda Moore-Brabazon up from Eastchurch. He was careful, however, to choose a time when Horace Short was absent—but as Lady Brabazon recalls, the designer returned unexpectedly, and she was removed from the aircraft almost by force.

In April, Rolls entered his first flying competition, the international meeting at Nice. This was an impressive gathering by contrast with the premature and half-hearted affair at Monaco in 1909. The authorities had invested £36,000 in the event, and prizes worth £8,000 were offered. On the debit side, the starting arrangements were considered too haphazard, 'there was no real racing', and, in the words of W. F. Bradley, 'whenever an accident or other sensational incident happened, of such a nature that pressmen should be on the spot, troops would be sent to drive them back, and in more than one moment of excitement, bayonets were fixed, and the butt ends of the rifles were used'. Pilots of Wright-type biplanes suffered a peculiar handicap: to avoid 'incommoding other pilots', the starting-rail was set up facing in the direction of the sea.

The worst incident of the meeting was what one can only term a 'bump', scored by the Russian aviator Efimoff against the Briton Rawlinson on his Farman. The two machines did not collide, but Efimoff caught Rawlinson in his slipstream, and forced the latter down into the sea. The organizers fined Efimoff 100 francs for carelessness, but this did not, it was considered, go far towards compensating his victim for the loss of one Farman biplane beneath the Mediterranean wave.

Rolls was unlucky, since the French railway system contrived to lose his aeroplane somewhere between Boulogne and the Riviera; thus he was forced to spend the first two days of the meeting as a spectator. This spell of idleness renders his sixth place in general classification all the more creditable. He finished fifth in the cross-sea contest flown over a 15-mile course from Nice to Antibes and back, and fourth in the distance prize event with a longest flight of forty miles. His unspectacular style met with Bradley's approval: 'There was nothing dashing about the flight, yet on every occasion Mr Rolls handled his biplane in the most business-like manner, and by his three out and home trips to Antibes showed that he was the equal of any foreign aviator.'—high praise indeed, for a self-taught pilot coming up against the *élite* of France for the first time.

Once back from Nice, he set to work preparing for his cross-Channel flight, establishing himself, Smith and the French-Wright in a field near the Duke of York's military school at Dover. Smith's telegraphic address, to judge from surviving communications, was simply 'tent near aeroplane'! Rolls was to avoid publicity as far as possible, a step which seems to have been warranted, as in the event a great deal of the 'first-hand material' and many alleged 'interviews' turn out to be a blend of nonsense and imagination. Disgruntled reporters, who made the long climb to the cliffs above the town time and time again, only to find that the flight had been postponed, invented plausible reasons for the delays; first, they said that Rolls had put off his attempt out of respect to King Edward VII, who had died on 6 May: they then told their readers that one of his mechanics had been spirited off to serve on a jury at the Old Bailey, just as the mechanical problems had been surmounted. Mr Smith, however, tells me that the governing factor was the weather—day after day, the little team was confronted with thick cloud or drifting fog.

Assisting Rolls and Smith was an old friend from the Lillie Hall days, Louis de Silva. De Silva had not followed Rolls into Rolls-Royce Ltd., but flying appealed to him, and he was later to make unsuccessful attempts to qualify as a pilot in France. By 24 May, the position looked promising, and Rolls made a short test flight from Dover. Two days later he was again circling the field at the modest altitude of ten feet, but lubricator trouble forced him down. This fault was rectified, and that afternoon it seemed to the watchers that the moment of departure was at hand. At 3.30 p.m. the Wright was hoisted on to its starting-rail, and Rolls took his seat. He donned his cork lifejacket, but the mist closed in again, and the attempt was called off. A recalcitrant engine wasted a great deal of time on the 27th, but eventually the aeroplane 'jerked into the air', and Rolls made a short flight some 120 feet up. He did not seem happy, though, and came down sharply. A crash was narrowly averted when an elderly lady panicked and ran straight into the path of the machine, but the resultant hard landing fractured a stay, and the machine returned to its shed for repairs once more. On 30 May, it was the water pump that gave trouble.

By this time, the press had given up the unequal struggle. Neither Rolls nor Smith was communicative, and hardly anyone was about when he eventually set course for France at 6.30 p.m. on 2 June. The flight to Sangatte and back was uneventful, but Rolls rightly took exception to certain statements made over his signature, and we may accept the corrected version as published in the *Daily Telegraph*. The mist which still hung over the English shore cleared by the time he was over the Channel; though on the way home it blanketed his vision of the Kent coast, and he was obliged to steer for a while by the sun. Some reporters claimed that he had been forced off course 'by a deviation of wind' but in fact he had always intended to make landfall at Sangatte, and fly over France for a short while before setting course homeward. As for the suggestion that the circuit of Dover Castle with which he finished his double crossing was a last-minute interpolation, due to his discovery that he had some petrol still in hand—this was an insult to so meticulous a planner as Charles Stewart Rolls. He took a message of greeting to the Aero Club de France, which he dropped over Sangatte, but noted that few people appeared to be watching his progress from the French shore. On his return, the field at Dover was thronged by crowds from the town, and Smith had to enlist the help of a sergeant from the military school to hold them back.

In terms of hard fact he had been in the air for ninety minutes which was no record; the crossing had taken forty minutes each way, which was five minutes slower than Blériot's original Channel flight in 1909, and six minutes slower than Jacques de Lesseps, who had crossed in May 1910. His average speed was not much more than 30 m.p.h., if we accept the distance covered as fifty miles; Rolls, incidentally, did not, maintaining that 'I have no means of gauging the distance with accuracy.'

For the first time in his life, he found himself a national hero. He was not, of course, mobbed by hysterical teenagers, as a more enlightened educational system did not breed such creatures, but the degree of adulation to which he was subjected can only be compared with the treatment now reserved by this country for pop-singers. Messages and awards poured in. The Royal Aero Club presented him with a gold medal, a distinction so far accorded only to Wilbur and Orville Wright, Louis Blériot, Henry Farman, and Hubert Latham—he thus became the first Englishman domiciled in England to be so honoured. King George V sent a telegram of congratulation. Lord Brassey wired Lord Llangattock: 'Your son is a hero.' The champagne firm of Ruinart *père et fils* gave him a cup worth £80. In Marylebone, Madame Tussaud's took steps to have the young aviator commemorated in wax—the statue was in fact completed a few days before his death. According to Mr John Tussaud, Rolls was the last subject he modelled for the celebration exhibition. Rolls took the artist to Ranelagh on two occasions during the period of the sittings.

The press forgot their long-standing vendetta with the noble 'scorcher', and went to town. Said the *Daily Mail*: 'This double crossing of the Channel is an encouraging indication that this country is waking up to the real importance of airmanship.' The *Daily Chronicle*, acclaiming 'a daring feat brilliantly performed', rammed the message home even more forcefully. 'Mr Rolls', its leading article continued, 'has wiped out a reproach which attached to us as a nation for our backwardness in the new art of aviation.' The *Pall Mall Gazette* expressed its gratitude in a cartoon in which a jubilant John Bull offered his felicitations: 'Well done, my boy, and thanks. You've given me a lift which I rather badly needed.' The *Motor* suggested waggishly that now 'Britannia Rolls the Waves', and the secretary of the London Vegetarian Association rejoiced that the man of the hour was a vegetarian. This was not strictly true, though the National Food Reform Association enjoyed close relations with the vegetarian movement. A statue was erected to Rolls at the seafront at Dover looking out towards France.

Action, as ever, suited Charles Rolls better than words. The time was not yet ripe for an anthology of 'aerodrome experiences', and no sooner was he safely back at Dover than he and Smith were off to Hounslow to overhaul the Wright in time for its next appearance at Dunstall Park. He did, however, permit himself one off-the-cuff comment. Speaking at a dinner given in his honour by the London Chamber of Commerce, he summarized the flight as 'the first time I have succeeded in taking ten gallons of petrol in and out of France, without paying duty'.

Perhaps the over-zealous attentions of the *octroi* officials at Nice in 1906 still rankled.

CHAPTER TEN

Nemesis over Bournemouth

An aeroplane is just like a ship with a big hole in the bottom. You have got to keep the pumps going all the time, or you sink at once.

The Hon. C. S. Rolls, 1910

In June 1910 Charles Rolls was a national hero; not that such a static rôle would appeal to so restless a personality for any length of time. No sooner was he safely back at Dover than he resumed his programme of testing.

Needless to say, his aeroplane required a complete overhaul after a non-stop flight of ninety minutes, and he had already furnished himself with a base more convenient for South Lodge than Sheppey had been. He had erected a shed on Hounslow Heath, and it was thither that Smith transported the Wright after its conquest of the English Channel. The journey was made overnight—Rolls might be the man of the moment, but the police adopted a jaundiced attitude towards the towing of flying-machines behind cars, and as Smith puts it, such an operation was 'probably illegal'. In any case, Hounslow was also conveniently close to Hurlingham, where the machine was to be put on show. The authorities, though they had raised no objection to balloons, were certainly not going to permit any flying from the metropolis itself. Some test flights were made from Hounslow, but most of the time was spent in setting the engine to rights. Smith remembers a great deal of trouble with distorted valves, while the only means of ascertaining whether the unit was developing its appointed brake-horsepower was by tests with a revolution counter.

Despite the ban on flying in London, Rolls could not resist trying his luck at Hurlingham. He narrowly missed hitting a tree, and Smith dissuaded him from any further attempts. In the meanwhile work went ahead on preparing the French-Wright for its next appearance at Wolverhampton's aviation week, to be held at Dunstall Park.

No longer was there any conflict of interests. The balloon

was dead, and the 'Silver Ghost' had receded from the forefront of Rolls's affections. For some time his appearances at Conduit Street had become less and less regular, until it was clear to Royce and Johnson alike that he would have to decide one way or the other; whether to remain as Technical Managing Director of Rolls-Royce Ltd., and pursue flying solely as a hobby, or to relinquish his post and become a full-time aviator. Rolls-Royce were loath to lose one of their founders, as Johnson told Miss Caswell, and there is no question whatsoever of Rolls's having wished to dissociate himself from the company. Any opposition he may have felt towards the policy decision of 1907 had long since vanished, and a man of his shrewdness would in any case have recognized that the Rolls-Royce *mystique* was best safeguarded by the unchanging image of the product. Even after Charles's death, Napiers were still challenging strongly, and the cars from Acton could put up a good fight in the top-gear-only stakes. But the country magnate arriving at Euston or Paddington might well find himself riding to Clubland in a taxicab bearing the famous 'water-tower' filler cap, whereas it was to be a good decade before aged 'Heavy Twenties' and 'Thirties' found their way into the hands of provincial hire-car operators. To put it simply, Rolls was incapable of pursuing more than one interest at a time, and he could never have contented himself with the status of a 'week-end flyer'. Both Smith and Keith-Davies have testified that flying dominated his life in 1910, and Rolls-Royce remained firmly opposed to any aeronautical ventures, which would lie outside their terms of reference.

The final step was, however, taken by Rolls rather than by Johnson. The minutes of a board meeting held at Derby in January, 1910, reveal that he asked his co-directors if he might be relieved of some of his routine work, which was weighing heavily on him, and thenceforward he no longer demonstrated Rolls-Royces or expatiated on their technical merits in the motoring press. He retained his seat on the board, and Claude Johnson was to recall, after the tragedy at Bournemouth, that the two men last met at a gathering of directors at Derby. Company records confirm that this took place on 8 July, only four days before he was killed. No announcement heralded the change, and the secret was so well-kept that it was found necessary to state, after his death, that the affairs of Rolls-Royce Ltd. would be unaffected. But after January, he transferred his office to South Lodge, Miss Caswell remaining as his secretary.

Meanwhile work went ahead on the French-Wright, which was entered for Dunstall Park, and subsequently for Bournemouth. On paper, Wolverhampton's aviation week sounded a better proposition than the new sport's preliminary canters at Doncaster and Blackpool the previous autumn, and there were no fewer than fifteen entrants. Of these the Hon. Alan Boyle had an Avis monoplane, Colonel S. F. Cody his own design of biplane, Holder a Humber, and Lane his Lane monoplane. Claude Grahame-White, Claud Cockburn, and Rawlinson (of Weir-Darracq fame) were down to fly Farmans. Richard Lisle of Star's had a new monoplane with which this old-established concern was toying, while Grace, Ogilvie, and Rolls featured in the programme as entrants of Short-Wright biplanes. Rolls, of course, had already passed his machine of this type on to Colonel Capper, and was in fact flying the French-Wright. Some aviators were hedging their bets. James Radley, later to win renown at the wheel of a Rolls-Royce in the Austrian Alpine Trials, had a Macfie biplane as well as his Blériot, while Lieutenant Gibbs brought along, not only his Farman, but also the Sommer he had lately acquired from Rolls.

The weather, alas! excelled even Blackpool. Rolls, certainly, did not enjoy himself. As he told Johnson, the Channel trip was 'nothing compared with this aerodrome business, where the corners are sharp, the air uncertain, and at any moment one may find a sea of human heads, instead of a sea of blue water under one's feet'. One feels he would have agreed with *Flight's* assessment of the 1911 Gordon Bennett aeroplane race at Eastchurch; the journal considered that 'the mere circling of an aerodrome' was unlikely to advance the cause of aviation in any respect other than sheer speed. At Wolverhampton, the pilots were frustrated by gusts of wind which at times reached 30 m.p.h. At the inaugural luncheon, Lord Plymouth expressed the view that it was 'criminal folly to urge those who had by their experience the only knowledge of what they could do, to fly when the conditions were unfavourable'. Grounded pilots are often querulous, and those at Dunstall Park proved no exception. Some of them had failed to sign agreements with the sponsors, and found themselves confronted with hotel bills which they had not expected to pay. They retaliated by refusing to take their aeroplanes out of the hangars. Richard Lisle, whose Star monoplane was proving but a poor advertisement for local industry, smoothed matters over as best he could; and though there was precious little flying during the first three days, this was occasioned by ill winds rather than ill-will.

Rolls had fitted his Wright with a small wheeled undercarriage; this dispensed once and for all with the starting rail and weights, but he told the *Aero* that it was 'only suitable for landing on tennis-lawns', and Dunstall Park was quickly reduced to a quagmire by rain and the influx of 20,000 spectators on the last day of the programme. Smith cannot remember his flying at all, and Rolls himself told Johnson that he flew but little, since 'the weather was bad and I have no intention of risking my neck'. None the less, his skilful cornering won him the speed prize; it was not for nothing that he had imitated the painstaking glider trials pioneered by the Wrights. Others were less fortunate. Grace overshot the aerodrome, and ended up in a field, to the detriment of a skid and his propeller, while both Ogilvie's Short-Wright and Radley's Blériot succumbed to gusts of wind.

And so the fanfare and trumpets of Bournemouth's Centenary Celebrations, billed as 'the first International Meeting in Great Britain', with a whole host of illustrious Patrons headed by Royalty, H.R.H. Prince Arthur of Connaught and H.S.H. Prince Francis of Teck. Others lending their support included the Secretary of State for War, Lord Haldane, his under-Secretary, Lord Lucas, the Lord Mayor of London, and my father. A motoring flavour was lent by some familiar Brooklands figures among the officials; Major Lindsay Lloyd was one of the three Clerks of the Course, and timekeeping arrangements were entrusted to A. V. Ebblewhite and T. D. Dutton. The prize list was, of course, formidable, the plums being £1,000 for the respective winners in the speed and altitude contests.

Rolls would have agreed that oversea flight was easier, and therefore worth only the £800 awarded. 'General merit', that stand-by of harassed judges, rated £500, while passenger flights were included under the heading of 'weight-carrying' (first prize £350). There was £300 to be won for the longest flight, assessed in terms of distance rather than duration, and £250 each for alighting and 'starting'; the latter, be it said, was not based on a competitor's ability to coax a recalcitrant engine into action, but for the more practical attribute of a short take-off run. As yet slow flying was not highly regarded; the days of three-figure landing speeds were to come only when 100 m.p.h. could comfortably be exceeded in level flight, and thus the pilot making the slowest circuit would win only £100. 'Competitor's assistants' were not forgotten, but the best a member of the ground staff could hope to pick up was £60. In addition, the *Car Illustrated* put up another £150 in special awards for all-British machines in certain events, and even the Motor Union bestirred itself to offer a £200 prize for the British pilot attaining the greatest altitude during the meeting.

British aviation, hitherto rather amateurish, was fast finding its feet, and a complicated code of signals was devised, eight different emblems being flown on the aerodrome at Southbourne to indicate which of the eight events was in process at any given time. In addition, a black flag signified that no flights were being made, a white flag was a warning to spectators that flying would shortly start, and a red flag was hoisted when flying was under way.

While previous flying meetings had been isolated events, Bournemouth had really gone to town, with a motorized battle of flowers, 'two grotesque carnivals and confetti battles, under the personal superintendence of M. Spagnol, of Nice', five fancy-dress balls, and a splendidly Ruritanian 'special pink *redouté* masked ball, everyone attending being dressed in fancy or domino costume one particular shade of pink'. For the musically-minded the programme ran the whole gamut from the Band of H.M. Coldstream Guards, or the Bohemian Orchestra (which suggests the very essence of Palm Courtery), to the town's own admirable Municipal Orchestra, conducted by such pillars of the British school as Sir Edward Elgar and

Sir Edward German. There was a 'Young England Day' with a march-past of two thousand members of the Boy Scouts, and cadets of the Royal Navy, Royal Marines and Merchant Navy. There was no such thing as a parade of historic cars, if only because the Veteran and Vintage cult as such did not exist, but my father had his 1899 Paris–Ostend Daimler on show. Motorists were well catered for generally; colossal 'auxiliary garages' were erected, where cars could be cleaned and serviced. Chauffeurs were billeted in a camp with sleeping accommodation and mess-rooms. The R.A.C., the A.A., and the Motor Union collaborated in a drive to discourage profiteering at the expense of the motorist.

All this was, of course, necessary, since as yet the flying fraternity drew its recruits from the ranks of the more sporting motorists, yet *The Autocar* remained cynical. The journal complained that the police of the neighbourhood were uncomfortably zealous, that five shillings per night was an excessive rent for a garage, and that in any case Bournemouth was too warm in summer. Some people are hard to please! But even if these strictures were unduly harsh, they had a salutary effect, for by the end of May the magazine was able to announce a substantial reduction in the garage charges, while the Mayor of Bournemouth convened a special meeting of five hundred hoteliers with the specific object of keeping prices within reasonable limits.

Nobody, in any case, could have blamed Bournemouth for doing everything in its power to make its Centenary Celebrations a fortnight to remember, and the *Daily Telegraph* went into raptures over this demonstration of municipal zeal. 'For the better part of a fortnight tomorrow', ran its preview published on 6 July', Bournemouth will positively be rioting in revelries and festivities. Where it has been possible to improvise a temple of gaiety and mirth, wherever greensward or sheltered glade seemed likely to serve the purpose of the celebrations, there have the sleepless organizers staked out their claims.' Not even the recent death of King Edward VII could damp their ardour.

Nor could any complaints be levelled at the new aerodrome which had been created in the suburb of Southbourne, within easy access from the town by train. Bournemouth was taking no chances with the weather, and wanted no quagmires such as had greeted the unhappy aviators at Blackpool and Wolverhampton. The site was cleared, drained and levelled, these operations necessitating the removal of some three miles of hedges and earth banks, not to mention forty small 'vegetable allotments', though it is pleasant to record that the owners of these were 'reasonably compensated'.

In a resort renowned for its equable and health-giving climate, the more orthodox junketings could be assured, as was Brooklands, of 'the right crowd', even if Weybridge's claim of 'no crowding' might not apply. The masked balls, the parades of decorated automobiles, and the Viennese twitter of strings in a palm court were a diet admirably suited to the tempo of life in 1910. Even had there been no Aviation Week, the town must surely have gained, in the optimistic words of the *Bournemouth Guardian*, 'a lasting and powerful impetus to that popularity of the "Evergreen Valley" which already stands, and justly stands, at so high a level'. In fact, the well-planned programme of events at Southbourne attracted no fewer than nineteen entrants, almost the entire *dramatis personae* of contemporary British aviation. Best-known among these were Rolls, Moore-Brabazon, Cecil Grace, S. F. Cody, Claude Grahame-White and Alec Ogilvie. Nor was the epithet 'international' an empty one, for from France came Morane, later to be famous as a builder of high-speed military aircraft, the racing driver Wagner, and Edmond Audemars. Jean Christiaens, another racing motorist, represented Belgium. The pseudonym 'Jones' masked the identity of actor Robert Loraine. Biplanes still predominated, thirteen pilots favouring them as against four who preferred the monoplane. As at Wolverhampton, some entrants gave themselves a choice of machines, both Barnes and Grahame-White bringing a monoplane and a biplane apiece. Airframe makers whose products were represented at the meeting were Avis, Blériot, Cody, Santos-Dumont (Demoiselle), Farman, French-Wright, Hanriot, Humber, Short and Sommer. Ominously the publishers of the programme rounded off their text with a list of 'martyrs of the aeroplane': statistical morbidity is no prerogative of our own times.

The Short glider at Eastchurch.
Photos by courtesy of the Royal Aero Club.

Trouble at Eastchurch. Early flying, said Rolls, was a case of 'going up with a wallop, and down with a thump'. The latter seems to be more relevant here. *Photo by courtesy of Monmouth Museum.*

Ancestor of the 'Queen Mary' transporter? In 1910, Rolls was using this 'Silver Ghost' Rolls-Royce tourer to tow his aeroplane from one field to another. *Photo by courtesy of* THE AUTOCAR.

Difficulties with the launching rail. *Photos by courtesy of the Royal Aero Club.*

Trying the Short glider at Eastchurch, August 1909. *Photo by courtesy of Monmouth Museum.*

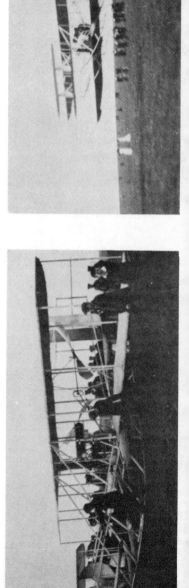

Across the Channel. Rolls and his Wright at Dover before his unsuccessful flight on 1 June 1910. *Photo by courtesy of Miss Florence Caswell.*

THE GREAT CHANNEL FLIGHT
2 JUNE 1910.
Photos by courtesy of the Royal Aero Club.

Over Dover Castle.

Rolls starting his first unsuccessful Channel flight.
Photo by courtesy of the Royal Aero Club.

Rolls flying at Eastchurch on 20 January 1910.
Photo by courtesy of the Royal Aero Club.

'In the most business-like manner' Rolls puts the Wright through its paces at Nice in 1910.
Photo by courtesy of Rolls-Royce Ltd.

Rolls at the controls of his machine. *Photo by courtesy of the Royal Aero Club.*

Rolls at Bournemouth in the aeroplane in which he met his accident. *Photo by courtesy of the Royal Aero Club.*

Aftermath. Rolls's wrecked machine at Bournemouth, July 1910.
Photo by courtesy of H. A. Rand.

Rolls was certainly preoccupied when he arrived at Bournemouth, though the reporter who credited him with 'a look of doom, some strange prognostication of a sudden and fearful end that turned his cheeks grey', was clearly padding his copy in the light of later knowledge. None of those who saw him in the days preceding the tragedy—Smith, Keith-Davies, Miss Caswell and Lady Brabazon—can recall any premonition of disaster. Quite the contrary—for Rolls had told Smith of his future plans, which were to include a spell as an instructor for Army pilots at Laffan's Plain, followed by a visit to America, where he intended to compete in the Garden City meeting, and renew his acquaintance with his old mentors, the Wright brothers. He discussed with Keith-Davies his plans for forming an aircraft company, possibly with the object of producing the R.P.G. biplane, and offered the young aviator an opportunity of 'getting in on the ground floor'. There was, of course, the hurdle of finance to be surmounted. Rolls was not a poor man—he left over £30,000—but the resignation of his post as Technical Managing Director of Rolls-Royce Ltd., had involved a major cut in his income and he told the *Daily Graphic* that he had sunk over £4,600 into flying during the first six months of 1910.

There were other more immediate worries. For the Bournemouth meeting he had equipped his aeroplane with (in the words of C. H. Gibbs-Smith), 'an additional rear outrigger built to surround the existing rudder outrigger and to carry—at first—a fixed tailplane to give a measure of inherent longitudinal stability, and act as a damper to the over-sensitive longitudinal control inevitable with the front elevator'. This was found to give insufficient control, so a second elevator was made to replace the fixed tailplane. The new elevator did not arrive until 7 July, and was not fitted to the aircraft until three days later, giving him no time to conduct any flight tests before the meeting opened. Rolls travelled down by train; Miss Caswell recalls that on the eve of his departure from London he collected a 'ticket' for speeding in Hyde Park.

First to arrive at Bournemouth was W. E. McArdle, who flew over from Beaulieu in the Blériot entered by his partner Armstrong Drexel, complete with a Gladstone bag which took the fancy of the reporters, especially as he was well-known in the local motor trade under the name of 'Motor Mac'. The flight had occupied thirty-five minutes for twenty-eight miles. Less publicity-minded was S. F. Cody, who threw a coat over his head when beset by trippers armed with cameras. The official programme started at 9 a.m. on Monday, 11 July, and Rolls was the first out, notwithstanding the hurriedly-completed modifications to the Wright. 'His start', said the *Bournemouth Daily Echo*, 'appeared as easy and as simple as the "push-off" with an ordinary bicycle.' By the end of the day Drexel had broken the British altitude record with a height of 1,950 feet, though this was to be beaten resoundingly before the week was out by Morane, who attained 4,107 feet. Rolls also tried for the altitude contest, but his effort was something of a preliminary canter, and he failed to reach the 1,000-foot level. He further distinguished himself with a slow circuit in 4 min. 13 sec., a record that was not bettered at Bournemouth. Christiaens made a flight lasting over two hours, but Grace crashed his Short-Wright.

Highlights of the second day's programme were to be the quick-starting and alighting contests, and Keith-Davies recalls that Rolls had set his heart on winning the latter, as befitted one who took such pride in the mastery of man over machine. In this competition, a circle one hundred yards in diameter had been marked out on the ground, with a large white patch in the centre at which aviators had to aim. This circle's location was about as inconvenient as it could be, since it lay only sixty yards from the grandstand, and about the same distance from the judges' box. A pilot's problems were accentuated by the prevailing wind, officially estimated at 17–20 m.p.h., which was blowing across the circle in the direction of the judges' box. According to the *Motor*'s representative, occasional gusts were reaching the velocity of a good 25 m.p.h. Rolls told Smith that the markings on the landing circle were none too distinct, and asked him to stand near the area to help him get his bearings.

Others, too, had misgivings on the subject of flying conditions. Edmond Audemars had already crashed his Demoiselle —he was unhurt, and seeing Rolls making ready to take-off, he walked over to him, and begged him to defer any further attempts till the afternoon, when the wind might have died down. Rolls was, however, not to be put off. Audemars noted the time—eleven a.m.

Shortly before twelve-thirty Rolls shook hands with Sir Thomas Lipton from the seat of the Wright, and taxied out for his second attempt in the alighting competition. Wind conditions being what they were, pilots had the choice of three alternatives; an approach down-wind, which involved the risk of overshooting and possible collision with the judges' box: a cross-wind approach: or meeting the wind head on and touching down with the nose of the aircraft pointing in the direction of the grandstand. Rolls had tried the second method without notable success, and now it was clear that he proposed to try his hand at the third. In the words of the *Motor*:

In little more than two minutes, he had curved over nearly half the aerodrome inside the far pylons, and was making the necessary turn behind the line of the grandstands. This was the only way open to him, since he had decided to face the wind in the completion of his pre-alighting manœuvre. He turned gracefully and well, apparently under perfect control, at a height of some one hundred feet, and brought his aeroplane round over the R.A.C. end of the stand, and above the heads of those in the enclosure until it was making directly towards the point at which he aimed. Standing vertically below him, as he passed above the barriers which separated the enclosure from the flying-ground proper, I instinctively realized that he was keeping too high for a comfortable finishing angle. His altitude above the barrier may have been seventy feet. I believe that Rolls had refrained from making an earlier considerable alteration in his angle of descent while he still was over the enclosure, and between the lines of the grandstand and the barrier, wholly out of splendid consideration for the spectators beneath him.

As soon as he was over the aerodrome proper, he started to descend sharply. Continues the *Motor*'s account:

There was a sickening snap. Some part of parts of the tail-plane had given way just inside the line of the barrier—witnesses who had profile views say that a failure of some kind had already occurred when the biplane was over the enclosure, but there was no evidence of it in the flight when viewed from below. An involuntary spasm of the nerves went through one's system, and then there was a thud. Rolls was down, under our very eyes, it seemed but a few paces away.

The Wright nosed over, and its pilot was thrown clear of the machinery. When the rescue party reached him, there seemed a hope that he might not be badly hurt. Apart from a hook caught in his clothing, he was free of all debris, and there were no signs of disfigurement. But he died within a few seconds from concussion of the brain. A photographer who tried to take pictures of the tragedy was manhandled and his camera smashed.

There have been countless explanations of the crash, and ever since that July day in 1910 writers have been telling us 'what really happened'. Both Keith-Davies and Smith agree that Rolls realized he was flying too high; instead of making a second circuit he lowered his elevator and went into a dive that was too steep to be safe. The sharp pull-out was the finish. The longerons were distorted into a position where they either broke or were sliced by the propellers.

Mr C. H. Gibbs-Smith, who has made intensive researches into Rolls's fatal accident, has come to a different conclusion. Nobody can be certain whether Rolls intended a trial landing, or was merely trying a new type of approach. There are conflicting reports as to whether he switched off or not, though Smith is of the opinion that Rolls had the engine running at the moment of impact. Certain it is that the run-up was undertaken at a very steep angle, and that he was relying on the two elevators to bring his nose up again. At an altitude of seventy feet above the ground, he applied full elevator, with a sudden movement of the lever. At this juncture, spectators heard the 'loud crack', and the Wright dived straight into the ground with the elevator canted over. The main impact was taken by the forward elevator, which broke. The upper wing then made contact with the ground, and the aeroplane turned over. Though all four cylinders were wrenched off the crankcase by the crash, the engine itself did not shift, while one of Keith-Davies's theories is disproved by the fact that the propellers were found to be intact on inspection.

Gibbs-Smith maintains that the cause of the disaster was the attachment of the second rear elevator to the same type of outrigger that had carried the original tailplane—an understandable error in view of the limited time at Rolls's disposal. The standard outrigger was incapable of coping with the stresses demanded of it by a sudden application of full elevator. Further, the elevator's hinges were set very close together, and there was thus a large unsupported surface. Given torsional instability in the rear elevator, violent application of the lever would rotate it, twist the outrigger structure, and break the booms. Had Rolls been higher off the ground, he might have saved himself by using his forward elevator to compensate. It is interesting to note that Smith agrees with this diagnosis of an outrigger failure.

Flying was suspended for the rest of the day. A human fence was formed round the wreck to ward off the morbid and the souvenir hunters, and the body was removed, first to a tent near the judges' box, and then to Boscombe mortuary. Lord and Lady Llangattock, on their way down from London to board the *Santa Maria* at Poole, were taken off the train, and the news broken to them. Elsewhere, the festivities continued. 'While the doctors were feeling for any little sign of life', reported the *Daily Chronicle*, 'the band in an adjoining field was still playing *The Dollar Princess*, and as I drove away from the field of death many motors passed me, gaily decorated with flowers and carrying men and girls in fancy dress, whose laughter rang out clear and loud as they sped on their way to the battle of flowers.'

On the following day flying was resumed, but all zest had vanished from the proceedings. Grahame-White made some noteworthy passenger flights: Robert Loraine disappeared in a blanket of fog over the sea, only to land safely in the Isle of Wight: Christiaens, Rawlinson, and Boyle all crashed, the latter sustaining serious injuries, while the now traditional dispute was sparked off on this occasion by the French contingent, who considered that Morane should have won the starting competition, and protested that the British aviators Dickson and Grahame-White had been allowed to make their attempts after closing-time. They closed their hangars and hauled down the *tricolore*, but their protest was overruled. In any case, Morane did not do so badly out of Bournemouth, since he collected £800 for the best oversea flight, and £1,000 for the best speed of the meeting—55·70 m.p.h., with a fastest lap of 56·64 m.p.h. But the *Motor* noted that a number of Rolls's friends found the atmosphere of Southbourne unendurable after the tragedy.

Those who had acclaimed his cross-Channel flight a bare month before now united to mourn him. 'Earnest, persistent, courageous, and modest', *The Autocar* summarized his character, 'Charles Rolls was of the stuff of which the best Englishmen are formed, and his country can ill afford to lose such in the prime of their lives.' Said the *Motor*: 'That so careful, so unassuming, and so quiet an experimenter as Rolls should have been called upon to pay this price seems very hard.' The *Daily Mail* paid tribute to him as one who 'assisted in removing the fetters on mechanical invention. Rolls died a martyr to knowledge: his memory and example will be an incentive to continued effort in an art that crowned him with victory, and claimed him as her sacrifice'. A spokesman from the Society of Motor Manufacturers and Traders remembered his early work as one of the protagonists of the motor-car in Great Britain: 'The whole industry will always stand indebted to him as one who rendered the very greatest assistance to the movement at a period when so many difficulties and so much prejudice had to be overcome.' In the House of Lords, my father asked that a message of sympathy be sent to Lord Llangattock, and Lord Denman, speaking for the Government said that they wished to be associated with such a message.

A memorial service was held at St. James's, Piccadilly, and during this period Rolls-Royce Ltd. closed their Conduit Street showrooms. Charles was buried in the remote little churchyard of Llangattock, the Monmouthshire hamlet from which his father took his title. A member of the Royal Household represented King George V at the service.

So Charles Stewart Rolls, pioneer and prophet, went to his grave, while a thunderstorm raged overhead. Perhaps the best epitaph of all came, not from any of his companions on land or air, or from the sonorous prose of the press that had alternately lambasted and eulogized him, but from that fellow-advocate of food reform, Mr Eustace Miles: 'I never heard anyone say anything against him except that he had too much to do.'

Epilogue

He was, in the highest degree, a practical scientific worker, and his place cannot be adequately filled by anyone else.

The *Aero*, July 1910

Charles Rolls's family was not destined to outlive him by long. His father died in 1913, and he was succeeded by his eldest son, who in his turn was to succumb to wounds received in action with the Royal Field Artillery in 1916. As Henry had died shortly before John, the title became extinct. Lady Llangattock died in 1923, leaving only one surviving child, Charles's sister Eleanor (Lady Shelley-Rolls), who lived on at South Lodge until September 1961.

Eleanor Shelley-Rolls, of whom the *Daily Express* said that 'she knew more about turbines and bridge-building than about knitting', had no children, though she left an estate estimated at £3,500,000, including a great deal of property in Southwark. The family had long since ceased to occupy the Hendre, which passed through a number of hands before ending up as a home for mentally-handicapped children run by the Glamorganshire County Council. Extensive alterations have effaced most traces of the house's former inhabitants, though the great organ, now silent, still stands in the hall. The family saloons of the school's staff now park where Rolls-Royces once rested.

A brief note in the Rolls family papers (now in the care of the Monmouthshire County Archives at Newport) reports the dispersal of Charles Rolls's aeronautical effects. Short Brothers took back the Short-Wright biplane which he had lent to Colonel Capper, and allowed his executors £200 for it. Frank McClean paid £275 for the hangars at Eastchurch, and the shed at Hounslow went to the War Office for £150. The military also took over the little balloon *Imp*, but there was no longer any demand for such things, and the price paid was a derisory £25. His 'Short biplane'—presumably the unfinished Rolls

Power Glider—found no takers. £172 8s. 5d. was realized on assorted aircraft spares and equipment.

The ultimate fate of most of his cars is unknown. The so-called 70-h.p. 'balloon tender' Rolls-Royce, has vanished without trace, as have the 96-h.p. Gordon Bennett Wolseley, the two T.T. 'Light Twenties' from Manchester, and the three Mors racers. Only his Paris–Ostend Panhard is preserved in the City of Norwich Museum.

On 19 October, 1911, Lord Raglan unveiled a monument erected to Charles Rolls's memory in Agincourt Square, Monmouth, in the presence of Lord and Lady Llangattock, the Hon. John Rolls, and Sir John and Lady Shelley-Rolls. Frank Hedges Butler was among others who came to pay their last tribute to the pioneer motorist and aviator. There were speeches by the Mayor of Monmouth and by Lord Llangattock, who was visibly moved. His son's death had affected him far more than it had his wife, who even twenty-four hours after the tragedy at Bournemouth was seen unconcernedly discussing Charles's career with a bevy of reporters. The memorial, executed by Sir Goscombe John, R.A., depicts Rolls in the garb in which he flew the Channel, holding in his hands a model aeroplane, which, in the words of the author of *Two Brave Brothers*, he is 'examining, admiring, and criticizing'. It stands to this day in the shadow of the Rolls Hall, surrounded by parked cars.

Charles Rolls lies in Llangattock Churchyard, and his grave can be reached only by an ill-surfaced lane which I found tricky to negotiate when I visited the spot during the great blizzard of February 1965. It epitomized for me the oblivion that has descended upon him.

The house of Rolls-Royce went from strength to strength. Within two years of Charles's death, the 'Silver Ghost' was firmly set upon that pinnacle towards which Claude Johnson had always striven, and when war came in 1914 Henry Royce turned his efforts in the direction which he had hitherto repudiated, despite all Rolls's attempts at persuasion. The initial 75-h.p. six-cylinder 'Hawk' aero-engine was speedily followed by the 275-h.p. 'Falcon' and 360-h.p. 'Eagle', both vee-twelves, while the 40–50-h.p. car won new laurels, not only as staff transport, but also as an armoured fighting vehicle. Colonel T. E. Lawrence was to assert that in desert conditions only two automobiles were of any use—the Rolls-Royce and the Model-T Ford, and, ironically enough, another enthusiastic user was the Soviet leader Vladimir Ilyitch Lenin. After the Armistice, private-car production was resumed, and the inter-War period saw not only a series of 40–50-h.p. 'Phantoms' descended from the 'Ghost', but also a line of smaller cars designed to meet the needs of a new era of financial stringency. In 1931 the name of Bentley, renowned for its purposeful sporting machinery and a then unparalleled record in the Le Mans 24-Hour Race—an event that in its original form would have appealed to Rolls—was acquired by Rolls-Royce Ltd., and once again sporting machinery issued from their factory. Though the company remained adamant in their renunciation of racing, works assistance was granted to E. R. Hall, a private owner of $3\frac{1}{2}$-litre (and subsequently $4\frac{1}{4}$-litre) Bentley cars, with the result that he took second place in three consecutive races for the Tourist Trophy—1934, 1935 and 1936. In these Bentleys of the 1934–39 era, in fact, Rolls-Royce had reverted to very much the sort of car that Rolls had advocated in 1906. The motor car division has now moved from Derby to Crewe, and plays only a small part in the technical and industrial complex that is Rolls-Royce today, but the 'Silver Shadow', the 'Phantom V', and the T-series and 'Continental' Bentleys continue to uphold the traditions set in train by Rolls, Royce and Johnson in 1907.

Throughout the lean years between 1919 and 1939, aero-engine development forged steadily ahead, and it is to Royce's foresight that we owe the Royal Air Force's survival against the might of the Luftwaffe in 1940. The Hawker 'Hurricanes' and Supermarine 'Spitfires', with which the Battle of Britain was won, were powered by Rolls-Royce engines, as were the 'Lancaster' and 'Halifax' bombers which pounded the Third Reich night after night, and the 'Seafires' and 'Fireflies' of the carrier-borne Fleet Air Arm, while many of the United States Army's Curtiss and North American pursuit aircraft had 'Merlin' engines built by Packard, the *marque* which Rolls had trounced with his 'Light Twenty' at the Empire City Track in

1906. Rolls-Royce was the first British aero-engine manufacturer to put gas turbines into series production: before the War was over, Gloster 'Meteor' fighters—like the 'Hurricane' and the 'Lancaster', productions of the giant Hawker-Siddeley combine under the direction of Rolls's old friend Sir Thomas Sopwith—were in operational service, while within a few months of VJ-day a similar machine was to raise the world's aeroplane speed record to 606 m.p.h., to the accompaniment of as much excitement as had greeted Charles Rolls's first sallies in his Peugeot in 1896. The old lady living in the village of Tangmere—headquarters of the High Speed Flight in 1946—who claimed to have been knocked off her feet by 'one o' they jets', was surely first cousin to the dames who fled indoors when horseless carriages chugged along the road from London to Cambridge.

Further, the reign of Queen Elizabeth II was to see Rolls-Royce enjoying Royal patronage. All Charles's surviving friends testify to his desire to see his own make take its place in the Royal Mews, and he would have rejoiced when the 'Phantom IV' succeeded where the 'Ghost' had not.

Of his friends, Moore-Brabazon gave up flying after Charles's crash, but had a long and distinguished career in politics and public affairs. He was raised to the peerage as Lord Brabazon of Tara in 1942, and died at the age of seventy-nine in 1964. Shortly before his death he drove a Mercedes-Benz 300SL across Salisbury Plain at well over 100 m.p.h., and in 1963 he handled a 1904 Thornycroft—a product of the A.C.V. Group of which he was Chairman—in the London–Brighton Run, to gratify a long-standing ambition. Late in life he agreed to become Patron of my Museum at Beaulieu, a role in which he took great pride. His speech at the Official Opening in May 1959, though chiefly dedicated to my father's work as a protagonist of the motor-car, also paid generous tribute to the other godparents of British motoring, among them Charles Rolls. Royce survived a dangerous illness in 1911, and thereafter never returned to Derby, dividing his time between the Sussex coast and his villa on the French Riviera: to the end he was busy on new designs. Johnson died in 1926, worn out by a lifetime devoted to the cause of automobilism.

Rolls's foresight in signing up an agency for Royce's cars was justified, for of the other *marques* he sold or attempted to sell, only Panhard has survived, and the Avenue d'Ivry kept going thanks only to a complete *volte face* in 1945, when their previous programme of expensive sleeve-valve machinery was jettisoned in favour of a small and cheap air-cooled 'twin' with front-wheel drive. The company is now wholly owned by Citroën, a firm which took over some of the factories of the old Mors concern. Orleans were moribund by 1908. The brothers Dufaux played with private cars for a few more years, before devoting their energies to a series of very successful motor-cycles and proprietary power units which they marketed under the name of Motosacoche. By contrast, Minerva abandoned motorcycle manufacture after 1914, and throughout the 1920s and early 1930s their big sleeve-valves 'sixes' and 'eights', sold under the slogan 'The Goddess of Automobiles', competed with a fair degree of success in the carriage trade which Rolls-Royce had made their own. Yet in the decline of Minerva, as much as in that of Napier, lies the moral of the decision reached at Derby in 1907. When the depression struck in 1929, Rolls-Royce were making the 'Twenty' and the 'Phantom I', plus a range of aero-engines: Minerva's range ran the whole gamut from an uninspiring small 'six' rated at 12–18-h.p. up to the lordly 6-litre Type AK, not to mention a diversity of trucks and buses. As the economic situation worsened, they joined forces with Imperia and Excelsior, and the group's final private-car products to reach the public were a series of small front-wheel-driven machines based on the German Adler. The last of these was made in 1949, and there has been no revival of the great Belgian *marque*, though Standard 'Vanguards' were made for a while under licence, and so was a cross-country vehicle based on the Land-Rover.

Britain's aircraft industry remained very small beer until a world war forced the Government to take energetic action, and by 1918 Britannia certainly ruled the air, a state of affairs largely due to Henry Royce's admirable engines, to the fighting scouts of Thomas Sopwith, and the torpedo-carrying seaplanes of the brothers Short. Though Sopwith's company was to succumb in the post-war recession, he was soon back in business and by the outbreak of the Second World War his Hawker-Siddeley Group embraced four major aircraft manufacturers—Armstrong-Whitworth, Avro, Gloster and Hawker—plus the aero-engine and motor-car business of Armstrong-Siddeley Motors. With the fusion of these interests with the Bristol group in the 1950s, his empire was to grow even bigger, though the regrettable actions of subsequent Governments have brought recession once again to this great industry. Shorts concentrated on large marine aircraft until their nationalization during World War II, but the name survives in Short Brothers and Harland, still a major force in aviation, with works at Belfast. It is perhaps significant that the majority of British aircraft that flew with the R.A.F. and Fleet Air Arm between 1939 and 1945 can trace their ancestry back to Rolls: either through Rolls-Royce, which he helped to found, through Sopwith, whom he introduced to ballooning, or through the Shorts, whom he set on the road to success—while Rolls's great friend Moore-Brabazon was to hold the post of Minister of Aircraft Production for a while.

How does Rolls stand up to analysis? As a man, he emerges with diminished stature, for he seems to have been incapable of those warm human relationships by which men are judged. Sir Thomas Sopwith has described him as a 'natural solitary', and such friendships as he enjoyed stemmed from a community of professional interest rather than personal understanding. It was possible to share an interest with Charles Rolls, but never, in the idiom of a later era, 'to get on to his wavelength'. How much of this was due to his home life, we shall never know. But to a naturally lonely child, that curious detached assortment of relatives, living their own lives in a contented disinterest under the same roof, must have been frustrating. There is no evidence to suggest that Charles was unhappy: he had never known anything else and, since he never married, he was not destined to experience any kind of home apart from the Hendre and South Lodge. The constant intrusion of technicalities into his surviving letters may not be typical—there is reason to believe that only correspondence relevant to his career has been preserved—but most of us have childhood memories which we retail in later life, and Charles apparently had none.

What we know of the first ten years of his life comes from his own lectures, and was only recorded to underscore his subsequent devotion to engineering and allied subjects.

Overall, he emerges as a curiously unlovable person. Take away his professional interests—the motor car, the balloon and the aeroplane—and a void is left. People remember his quick temper, his 'banana-skin' sense of humour, and his extraordinary meanness—in a spacious age any man would indeed be memorable in the wrong sense if he quibbled over the cost of a slice of bread on a ten-shilling lunch, or split twopence change with a waiter. They recall his undignified conduct after the débâcle of the 1905 Tourist Trophy, and his lack of consideration for others. What they forget are the generous gestures—his request for replica medals for the crew of his Panhard in the Thousand Miles' Trial, his spontaneous tribute to Henry Royce after his victory in the second T.T., and the unfailing way in which, however weary he might be in those early days of flying, he always considered the well-being of Smith, the mechanic who shared his every tribulation. Perhaps the truth is that Rolls only unbent with those who were as single-minded as he was; and few measured up to this exacting standard. Even those who could throw themselves so whole-heartedly into motoring or aviation would eventually find distractions—sport, social life, or marriage. Rolls played no games—if we except *Hare and Hounds*—social interludes were merely incidental to the main task of selling locomotion —on land or in the air—to Britain, and he was in too great a hurry to concern himself unduly with the opposite sex.

Rolls the man may remain elusive: we may conclude that he would be an uncomfortable companion at somebody else's press party, the sort of person we would avoid as being almost a monomaniac. But of Rolls the pioneer we must form an entirely different conclusion. As a journalist myself, I have a feeling that Rolls would be a heaven-sent P.R.O. at one of those functions that I attend all too frequently, where a new model is launched. I feel that I would be spared all the double-Dutch, all the dog-Greek, the Orwellian statistics, and the peculiar brand of double-think that is employed to explain away the excesses of styling departments. Rolls would come straight to the point, and tell his audience why a car was designed the way it was, and precisely what it would do.

Charles Rolls was a visionary—it is significant that his prophecies for the future of the aeroplane were *published* in 1901 and 1906, and his reservations on the subject of the airship in 1907; not brought to light in retrospect after he had been proved right. He knew what he wanted; in 1904 he was not just content to find a car to replace the Panhard in the Brook Street showrooms. He made it clear that the vehicle he would sponsor must be a great name in its own right, and not just a great name whose currency was limited to the *cognoscenti*, such as Isotta-Fraschini or Bugatti at a later date —these were virtually unknown to the man in the street until the Veteran and Vintage movement swept the world in the 1950s. Nowadays even the professional bore in the Lounge Bar can reel off the names of the classic *marques*: but Rolls-Royce has been a household word from pre-1914 days.

Further, he was more than a mere visionary. Not for him the chimerical world of the death-ray: he put his dreams into practice. While Queen Victoria was on the throne he was forecasting the universal acceptance of the motor-car; though he did not live to see this, it is significant that it was during his lifetime that the first of more than fifteen million Model-T Fords rolled off the assembly lines in Detroit. He was a consistent advocate of the small, cheap runabout, to sell for a little over one hundred pounds: such vehicles might not interest him personally, but he would have rejoiced to see, in the immediate pre-war period, the emergence of the Morris Oxford, Singer Ten, and Calthorpe 'Minor' from amid a welter of motorcycle-based cyclecars—the shape of things to come. He foresaw the possibilities of the aeroplane in 1901, and nine years later he was to set the seal on what had already been proved by Louis Blériot—that Britain was no longer a 'tight little island'.

We may perhaps dismiss the balloon as a light-hearted interlude in a life that was as serious as it was impersonal, but nobody can question the services he rendered to aviation. Scoffers may assert that it was his title that singled him out from Brabazon, Grace, Gibbs, or Dickson. This may be true: but above all things the new movement needed a central figure, and Rolls fulfilled that need. He was no designer; he was not the greatest pilot of his era, and he did not live long enough to accumulate a whole catalogue of record flights as did the Mollisons or Lindbergh in the inter-war years. Nor, for that matter, did Alcock and Brown, the conquerors of the Atlantic in 1919, yet they are remembered. Rolls's career as a pilot started in October 1909, and ended over Southbourne in July 1910; he flew at only three meetings—Nice, Wolverhampton, and Bournemouth—yet in that time he had achieved a great deal. Unlike many other well-to-do young men, he followed a strict plan. His eight years of ballooning had taught him his way about the air: his gliding experiments at Leysdown had familiarized him with the controls of an aeroplane; and thenceforward he was the cautious, systematic experimenter, for all his sense of urgency. At the unveiling of the memorial at Monmouth in 1911, the mayor summarized him as 'one who has done much to raise England, and to rouse her from a dangerous indifference and apathy in a field where human genius would yet prevail'. Not only was Charles Rolls one of the godfathers of the British aircraft industry by virtue of his encouragement of the Short brothers, he undoubtedly served as one of the corner-stones of British aviation.

It is fashionable, of course, to decry his importance in the history of Rolls-Royce. Most of the crowning splendours of that firm's career—the Austrian Alpine Trials, the exploits of the armoured cars in the Middle East, the Schneider Trophy contests of 1929 and 1931, the Battle of Britain, and the renowned jet and propeller-turbine engines—came to pass after his death. The father-figure of Henry Royce, Mechanic, towers over the whole saga. Royce fashioned the cars, and Johnson not only stood watch over the *maestro*, but sold his products; thus what fame remains to Rolls is owed to his partners, and to his convenient association with them. It is easy to gloss over the pride with which the late Lord Hives, Royce's right-hand man at Derby and subsequently Chairman of Rolls-Royce Ltd., recalled his apprenticeship with C. S. Rolls and Co. In the world of the motor-car, one may argue, where would Rolls have been without Royce?

Few, however, would contemplate the mirror-image, and

ask where Royce would have been without Rolls. The engineering of those first cars—from the 10-h.p. 'twin' to the 'Silver Ghost'—owed little or nothing to the young engineering graduate from Cambridge, but those who would assign all the credit to Royce forget that in 1904 he was unknown, and that his name would have cut no ice with the landed proprietors who formed the main clientele for the better class of car. There were many contenders, and few potential sales. Only a dedicated reader of the weekly motoring press—and of the advertisements as well as the editorial matter—could have named every *marque* to be found in the motor-showrooms of Mayfair, Long Acre and the Euston Road. Merit alone would not sell a vehicle; a make had to have a sponsor. It is surely not an impertinence to suggest that Royce, had he failed to find a Rolls to promote his twin-cylinder car, might have stayed in the business for two or three years. He would perhaps have exhibited a chassis amid the potted palms of Islington or Olympia, and earned the acclaim of technical journalists such as Swindley of *The Autocar* or Foster Pedley of the *Car Illustrated*: but in all probability he would have abandoned the experiment as uneconomic, and gone back to his electric cranes at Cooke Street. We may question whether the absence of Rolls would have had any effect on the quality of Royce's cars, and admit that his main contribution to this was the conscientious testing that culminated in his victory in the 1906 T.T. We may go further, and claim that the particular model Rolls helped to evolve was merely one of Royce's prentice efforts, and not at all the sort of machine that instilled the magic into the name —but the name and established reputation of Rolls persuaded motorists to investigate the Rolls-Royce. By the time Henry Royce had perfected his idea of what a car should be, his potential customers were familiar with his earlier work, thanks to the energetic selling methods of his partner.

It may be difficult to single Rolls out from other members of the small band of pioneers who worked tirelessly to sell the motor-car to Britain, but it must not be forgotten that while others talked, he drove. Certain it is that he was one of the first of the few, and one who played his part in the introduction of the new locomotion to Britain; and unlike many of his companions, he made it his business to understand the machinery he was promoting. Rolls employed mechanics and made liberal use of them; but he did so for his own convenience, and not because he was incapable of carrying out their work himself. Not only was he prepared to work on the vehicles he sponsored, he also enjoyed driving them. Thus his influence was directed towards the evolution of what one can term a 'Driver's car'. It is a matter of personal opinion whether the Rolls-Royce of today merits this epithet, but there can be no doubt that the cars of Charles's day did—and still do. Rolls's attitude was always that of the keen driver, even if a goodly proportion of his clientele employed chauffeurs; having experienced his 'sprinting gear' at first hand, I can see the reasons both for his initial advocacy, and for its ultimate abandonment in 1909. It was probably Johnson rather than Rolls who brought about its demise, but Rolls the 'driver's driver' must have recognized that the device's jarring, high-pitched whine, especially on a car as silent as the 'Silver Ghost', diminished appreciably the satisfaction of effortless cruising speeds in the region of a mile a minute.

Often have I heard Rolls dismissed as 'a celebrity, yes, but a great man, no'. How many of us achieve greatness—whatever this may mean—at the age of thirty-two? Rolls went to his death in his prime, and we can only conjecture, and conjecture uselessly, what course his career would have pursued had he survived. Perhaps his fame was due to his arrival on the scene at a time when his talents could best be applied. In 1870, he would have been dismissed as an aristocratic dabbler, a by-product of the eccentric squirearchy; lack of funds would have frustrated him in 1930: while in our present times his birth and education alone would invoke cries of 'privilege' from what Mr Constantine FitzGibbon has termed 'the dotty Left'.

The age of the internal-combustion engine needed a central figure, and in Britain this central figure was Rolls. As we have seen, he was always a man of action; yet even had he failed to match words with deeds, he would still have personified a generation's conversion to a new mode of transport.

Index

237